JAMIE PARKER is a Strategy Consı  advises both public and private sector cli across economics, politics and current history. He holds a First-Class Honoı Cambridge and was winner of the Pv his essay on tax reform. *Painting Britain Blue* is his first published book.

PAINTING BRITAIN BLUE

Jamie Parker

SilverWood

Published in 2021 by SilverWood Books

SilverWood Books Ltd
14 Small Street, Bristol, BS1 1DE, United Kingdom
www.silverwoodbooks.co.uk

ISBN 978-1-80042-088-5 (paperback)
ISBN 978-1-80042-089-2 (ebook)

British Library Cataloguing in Publication Data
A CIP catalogue record for this book is
available from the British Library

Page design and typesetting by SilverWood Books

Contents

Preface

After a decade of Conservative-led government, the Labour Party should once again have been preparing for office by the end of 2019. Instead, having been buried beneath Boris Johnson's landslide victory – a fourth consecutive Conservative electoral victory – Labour entered the 2020s as far from power as ever before, representing an increasingly narrow voter base and faced with a hostile electoral system. Such was the severity of the circumstances in the immediate aftermath of the 2019 election and the daunting scale of the task ahead that some commentators began asking if the British Labour Party was dying, destined to suffer the same fate as other European socialist parties, such as those in France and the Netherlands. The Conservatives have long been seen as the natural party of government, but structural shifts in voting behaviour over recent years indicate that we might be living through a more fundamental re-alignment in our political system, the consequences of which are still yet to be fully realised or understood.

How can we explain Labour's relatively poor electoral performance and the continued success of the Conservatives in spite of their long years in government? Much ink has been spilt trying to answer this question in recent years. Since the 2019 General Election, in which Labour's so-called 'Red Wall' was smashed to pieces, attention has intensified, and a proliferation of articles and books have appeared offering explanations for Boris Johnson's victory. Specifically, there has been a focus on why so many life-long Labour voters switched to the Conservatives for the first time, a dramatic phenomenon that surprised and continues to fascinate many political commentators. Working-class, 'small-town' voters in provincial England and Wales, having been overlooked and even deliberately ignored for decades suddenly now find themselves in the political spotlight. The veteran Labour pollster Deborah Mattinson confesses in a recent *Times* column that in the two decades prior to the 2019 election she had 'never run a poll or focus group in a so-called Red Wall seat...assum[ing] these seats were in the bag'.[1] Such historic neglect of these areas is hardly exceptional; it typifies a New Labour-era view that within a first-past-the-post electoral system, swing seats in Middle England determine the outcomes of major electoral events in British politics.

The overwhelming tendency so far has been to view electoral politics in recent years through the prism of Labour's political difficulties and failure to mount effective opposition to Conservative governments that looked at times as though they were close to collapsing. In many ways, a Labour-centric approach seems unsurprising. Intensive polling of Red Wall voters in the aftermath of Johnson's landslide, together with focus groups and in-depth interviews, gives an impression of Labour's gradual, long-term decline in 'left behind' towns that had been struggling for decades. By 2019, these voters were left feeling that their views were no longer respected by a party they had voted for their entire adult life. As such, an accepted wisdom is forming about Labour's loss of its industrial and post-industrial political heartlands: beginning in the early 21st century under Tony Blair's leadership, the party became increasingly metropolitan, urbanised and middle class. This process contributed to electoral defeats in 2010 and 2015, and then accelerated after Jeremy Corbyn assumed the party leadership and following the shock Leave vote in the EU referendum. By the end of the decade, according to this narrative, issues of leadership, coupled with the party's handling of Brexit (notably the eventual migration to a second referendum position), proved to be the tipping points that pushed sufficient numbers of voters across Labour's Northern heartlands into the arms of the Conservatives, thereby handing Johnson a landslide majority.

Existing accounts offer a useful insight into why millions of voters abandoned (or felt abandoned by) the Labour Party through the early 21st century. However, they often fall short of fully explaining why many of these voters turned in growing numbers to the Conservative Party over the course of the decade after c.2010. It would be wrong to simply assume that Labour's difficulties necessarily equate to Conservative success: in the 2010 General Election, for instance, discontent with the Labour government provided Nick Clegg and the Liberal Democrats with an uplift in popularity and electoral support, as well as benefiting David Cameron's Conservative Party. Similarly, there was for a long time a belief that while millions of traditional Labour voters in Northern England might express dissatisfaction with their party by abstaining or voting for a protest party like UKIP, for one reason or another they would not vote in sufficient numbers for the Conservative Party to make a meaningful impact in general elections.

Through the 2010s, the Labour Party retreated into representing a socially and geographically more confined subset of voters: increasingly younger, more affluent, and metropolitan in outlook, and largely residing in university towns and big cities like London. As they did so, the Conservatives advanced into the politically unoccupied space left behind by Labour in Northern England, the Midlands and Wales to reach millions of new voters and bring them into their broad, national electoral coalition. Importantly, the Tories achieved this while maintaining their share of more affluent voters, as well as considerably widening their lead over Labour among older sections of the electorate (who have a high propensity to vote). Although in many respects two sides of the same coin, it is important to explain both the reasons for Labour's political retreat and for the Conservative's advance.

In an increasingly crowded field of political commentary and academic research, this book sets out to offer a new perspective on the contrasting performance of the two main political parties in the 'long decade' between 2007 and 2020.

Part I

Part I begins by considering the reasons for the Conservative Party's long-term electoral success from 1900 to 2007. How is it that the Conservatives, supposedly the party of the rich, have proved so much better than Labour, the purported party of ordinary working people, at winning general elections? As I show, Conservative victories at the ballot box have long rested on an ability to bring a large section of the upwardly mobile working classes into the party's voter coalition. Sustained periods of Tory rule in the 20th century, most notably during the 1930s, 1950s and 1980s, were supported by the conversion of a large proportion of working-class voters into the Conservative electoral column.

As such, to completely understand Labour's fraught relationship with working-class voters, it is necessary to reach further into the past than to the modernisation and metropolitanism of the Blair era. Since its inception in 1900, the Labour Party has always had a complicated and contingent political relationship with working-class voters. At various points over the past 120 years, this relationship has been liable to come apart as Labour leaders have struggled to connect with a substantial section of the upwardly mobile working class who have abandoned the Labour Party for the Conservatives. Strikingly, the British working classes are not, and in many respects never have been, natural Labour voters.

I also re-evaluate the medium-term impact of the New Labour years on British electoral politics in Part I. It is increasingly argued that the metropolitanism and modernisation of Blair's political project, especially the relaxed immigration policy in government, sowed the seeds of Labour's present crisis with small-town, working-class voters. Although a 'cultural gap' began to emerge in Labour's voter coalition from the early 2000s, it should not be forgotten that this was the most electorally successful Labour government in history and many of Blair's policies, for instance on national security and issues of law and order, appealed directly to working-class voters.

Part II

In Part II, I turn to the focus of the book and consider reasons for the recovery and then continued electoral success of the Conservative Party after c.2007, as well as Labour's difficulties in mounting effective opposition and re-gaining power after 2010. It is tempting to assume the Conservatives were kept in power over this period by forces beyond their control, such as Labour's incompetence in opposition, Jeremy Corbyn's limitations as leader or strategic electoral advantages brought about by the Leave vote in 2016. Although these factors were clearly relevant and are considered at length in this book, it is important also to recognise the immense flexibility and pragmatism demonstrated by the Conservative Party in the face of changing circumstances.

In line with their historic mission, the Conservatives have demonstrated a characteristic willingness to do whatever is necessary to win and hold onto the levers of power. Beginning after 2005 with David Cameron's leadership, consecutive Tory leaders contributed in different and important ways to help their party increase its national vote share at general elections. In the 2010 and 2015 elections, Cameron won back and consolidated the support of voters in Middle England and wiped out the Liberal Democrats in South-West England. Under Cameron and Osborne, the Conservatives also began picking up seats across the North, the Midlands and Wales by appealing to ordinary working-class voters with policies such as a new National Living Wage, freezes on fuel duty and constrained welfare spending. Then, after the EU referendum, under Theresa May's leadership, the Conservatives continued to make significant inroads into Labour's post-industrial heartlands in provincial England and Wales in the 2017 election. May also won a slew of seats in Scotland and cemented hers as the party of the Union north of the border. By 2019, Johnson's landslide victory gave his party not just its biggest parliamentary majority in a generation, but also strong representation across all parts of the United Kingdom. Twenty years of rising vote share culminated in the Conservatives winning a commanding 44% of the national vote while the Labour vote collapsed.

I re-evaluate the challenges facing Labour as a party of opposition in Part II and argue, for instance, that the 2016 Leave vote did not make an electoral annihilation inevitable for Labour. On the contrary, Brexit presented an opportunity for the Labour Party to demonstrate that it was still capable of representing its Northern heartlands by respecting the referendum result and then setting out and uniting behind a credible future relationship with the EU based on close alignment. Equally, it should not be forgotten that the EU question seemed to be doing as much damage to the Conservative Party as it was to Labour in the years after the referendum result. The fact that the 2019 election was ultimately fought with Brexit not 'done' was a contingency that significantly advantaged Boris Johnson and the Conservatives, but the result was by no means inevitable.

I also re-consider the combined impact of Corbyn's leadership and Brexit on the Labour Party, as well as the dynamic of British politics more widely. Corbyn's preference for a Brexit policy that both respected the 2016 referendum result and aimed at softening the impact of Britain's exit by advocating a permanent customs union was both tactically and strategically rational. Such a moderate, compromise position was the correct policy for a party whose voter coalition was desperately divided by Brexit. However, Corbyn was the wrong man to articulate this compromise because he was unable to command sufficient authority within the Parliamentary Labour Party and because he was personally repellent to swathes of the electorate, especially thousands of voters in Labour Leave seats.

Finally, while it is important to understand the reasons for the dramatic migration of Labour voters to the Conservative column in the decade after 2010, one must not overlook the role smaller political parties have played both in influencing the two main parties and in determining the outcome of important electoral events. Conservative electoral hegemony has been to a large extent supported by the correspondingly poor performance of the Liberal Democrats after the 2015 election, as well as being tied in important ways to the performance of the SNP, UKIP and the Brexit Party. In Part II, I consider the influence and contribution of these smaller parties to electoral politics in the recent past.

Part III

Part III examines the key themes addressed in Parts I and II with the aim of understanding why it is that the Conservative Party has proved so successful at winning and holding power from 1900 to the present day. I then conclude by considering what Labour can do to stop them in the future. Before the Labour Party can embark on a meaningful electoral recovery and restore itself as a serious electoral competitor, let alone a party of government, it must first fully understand not just why it has been shedding support across the United Kingdom, but also why the Conservatives have been gaining millions of votes over a period of many years. Serious and considered self-reflection is necessary, not least because, as George Santayana observed, 'Those who do not learn history are doomed to repeat it.'

Jamie Parker
London, March 2021

Introduction

It would normally be expected that opposition parties will advance in electoral terms over long periods of single-party rule. There are many reasons for this. Governments in the later part of their second or third terms tend to find it difficult to continue fighting elections successfully as they struggle to defend their record in office – it is often said that 'oppositions don't win elections, governments lose them', as the latter become characterised by a degree of entropy. A long spell in government tends to have the effect of damaging a party's brand – after 18 years in office, the Conservative brand appeared tired and demoralised going into the 1997 election, and by 2010 there was nothing 'New' about New Labour. It is also the case that one-off events can sometimes destabilise a governing party's electoral foundations, such as Black Wednesday in 1992, which undermined the Conservative Party's reputation for governing competence, or the financial crisis in 2008, which dispelled the myth that Gordon Brown had ended 'Tory boom and bust'.

Opposition parties, meanwhile, can usually reap certain benefits from being out of government. Being on the opposition benches affords the leadership time and space to rigorously challenge the government of the day, often resulting in an uplift in popularity. Particularly strong oppositions, such as those led by Tony Blair in the late 1990s or David Cameron in the second half of the 2000s, use this time to develop coherent strategies for government and articulate the direction in which they wish to take the country should they win. Reflecting on his period in opposition, Blair recalls the importance of using it as an opportunity for 'thinking time'. Crucially, the strategies developed often acknowledge the appeal and achievements of their political opponents: Blair deliberately did not berate voters for giving Thatcher three terms in office, and in turn Cameron referred to Blair as the 'master', recognising his obvious political skills.

Since 2010, the historical pattern of opposition parties gaining support and momentum at the expense of the governing party has clearly not been followed. Despite their fair share of difficulties in office over the preceding decade, the governing Conservatives under Boris Johnson emerged from the 2019 election politically in the ascendant as they entered a fourth consecutive term in office. Between May 2010 and December 2019, the Conservatives only actually governed independently with a working majority for a total of two years (between June 2015 and 2017); the remaining years were spent either in coalition with the Liberal Democrats or reliant on the DUP through a supply and confidence arrangement. Nonetheless, the Tories have maintained a tight grip on the levers of power and, unusually for a governing party, have increased their vote share in every one of the past six general elections (since 2001), expanding their voter base across not just England, where the party has traditionally been strong, but Wales and Scotland too.

Labour meanwhile has spent the decade after 2010 electorally in retreat, shedding votes across all parts of the United Kingdom (with the exception of London) under consecutive leaders. It is the Labour Party whose brand, despite its long years in opposition, has been wrecked by savage infighting and credible accusations of widespread and institutional anti-Semitism. By the time of the 2019 election, far from establishing a coherent and compelling narrative of the kind of country Britain could be under a Labour government, the party's entire *raison d'être* was thrown into question. Life-long voters were forced into asking themselves who the modern Labour Party stands for. The verdict was devastating: Labour's representation in the House of Commons fell to its lowest level in 85 years.

Strikingly, Conservative electoral hegemony has been established against a background of difficult decisions in government, such as over public spending during the Cameron-Osborne years, and civil war over Britain's withdrawal from the European Union during May's premiership.

These circumstances have arguably given voters ample reason to punish the governing party at the ballot box and replace them with someone else. In 2015, pundits seemed convinced the country was on course for a Miliband-Sturgeon government, as voters balked at the prospect of more austerity under the Conservatives. Similarly, there was a widespread perception that had the May government collapsed in autumn 2017, Corbyn would have been swept to power by an electorate tired of Tory infighting on Europe. In many respects, the challenges of the decade after 2010 – especially difficulties the May government faced after the Referendum gaining parliamentary support for a negotiated withdrawal agreement – ought to have done more damage to the Conservative brand than they ultimately did because the party's reputation has long been predicated on perceived governing competence and pragmatism.

The search for explanations

How then can we explain the contrasting political fortunes of the two main parties after c.2007?

In the aftermath of the 2019 election, a conventional wisdom began to emerge about the reasons for the Labour Party's difficulties and the corresponding success of the Conservatives. Beginning during its time in government in the early 2000s, Labour began a gradual retreat across its Northern heartlands and became a more metropolitan, liberal and middle-class party under Blair's leadership. Initially, small-town, working-class voters abstained as they felt overlooked and ignored by the Labour government of the day. Then the rise of UKIP, propelled by Nigel Farage's leadership, provided these voters with an avenue through which to channel certain grievances and concerns, notably over the vexed issue of immigration. Through the 2010s, working-class voters increasingly turned to the Conservatives, complaining that under Corbyn's leadership and following the EU referendum, the Labour Party 'no longer represents people like us'.

Although it is accepted that the roots of Labour's present crisis can be traced back over a period of decades, debates over the short-term triggers that led the party to its worst electoral defeat in 85 years continue to rage. What was the tipping point that pushed sufficient numbers of former Labour voters to support the Conservatives and thus hand Boris Johnson a landslide electoral victory in 2019? In conventional accounts, Corbyn's victory in the leadership contest in September 2015 and the Brexit vote nine months later are seen as key turning points that deeply divided the Labour Party at a time when it should have been uniting to oppose the government of the day. In particular, it is common to blame the hollowing out of Labour's representation in its traditional heartlands across the North and Wales on a combination of Corbyn's style of leadership and the divisive EU question. Paula Surridge's view that 'Labour had been moving away from working-class voters for some time, but when Corbyn took over this became turbo-charged' captures this line of argument clearly.[1] Michael Ashcroft's polling in the aftermath of the 2019 election also confirms that Labour-Conservative switchers were motivated to do so overwhelmingly out of a desire to prevent Corbyn from becoming Prime Minister and in order to 'get Brexit done'.[2] With the benefit of hindsight, Corbyn's stint as leader and the Brexit vote appear to have been electoral gifts to the Conservatives, acting as double hammer-blows that drove the Labour Party *further from*, not *closer to*, power.

Isolating culpability for Labour's problems with either the party's leadership after 2015 or the divisive Brexit vote in 2016 suits the agenda of competing ideological groups within the Labour movement itself. It is convenient for allies of Corbyn to emphasise the difficulties thrown up by Brexit so as to distract from their leader's personal failings. Radicals in the party argue that the divisive EU question split Labour irreparably and derailed Corbyn's otherwise popular policy programme, which appealed to 'the many not the few'. Removing Brexit from the equation would have led to a significantly different electoral outcome for Labour because Corbyn and the policies he espoused, such as pledging to reverse damaging Tory austerity; committing to the revitalisation of public services; and an ambitious Green New Deal programme, were inherently popular. The 2017 general election, in which the Brexit issue was marginalised, and Labour won a commanding 40% of the popular vote, is taken as evidence of the widespread popularity of the Corbynite political offer.

Conversely, moderates in the Labour movement tend to associate the party's electoral difficulties with Corbyn himself and deficiencies in leadership, side-stepping the role played by Brexit. His radical left-wing agenda, vulnerabilities on questions of national and economic security, and perceived unsuitability for the office of Prime Minister made a Labour victory in a general election inconceivable under Corbyn's watch. Internally, he divided the Labour Party at a time when it should have been coming together and uniting in opposition to the Tory government. Externally, his leadership actively repelled large swathes of the electorate, including swing voters in Middle England that Labour would need to win back to form a majority in the House of Commons. His radicalism and lack of patriotism also cost the support of many traditional voters in Labour heartlands. Focusing attention on Corbyn's deficiencies has an added benefit for Labour moderates as it gets them 'off the hook' for their electorally fraught stance on Brexit; it was figures from the New Labour era, such as Tony Blair and Andrew Adonis on the right of the party, who, more than anyone else, made the argument for a second referendum as a means of reversing Brexit.

Challenging the conventional wisdom

While existing accounts offer useful insights into Labour's electoral difficulties, they suffer from several important limitations.

First, the chronology established in the conventional narrative, which locates the origins of Labour's decay in its Northern heartlands in the early 2000s, risks giving a misleading impression of the party's historical relationship with working-class voters. It implies that the 20th century was a kind of 'golden age' for Labour and the British working classes, characterised by harmony and a common political purpose, only to be ruptured by Blair's New Labour project. As I will show in this book, the reality is more complicated. The British Labour Party was repeatedly liable throughout its 120-year history to loosen its grip over a section of aspirational working-class voters, who frequently abandoned them for the Conservatives. Although the scale and extent of the realignment of low-income voters in recent history (especially during the 2019 election) has been unprecedented, there has been a strong propensity for a section of working-class voters to support the Conservatives stretching back into the early 20th century and beyond. Strikingly, the Conservative Party has a long tradition of producing leaders, from Baldwin and Macmillan through to Thatcher and Johnson, capable of transcending their party's association with the interests of a wealthy privileged few and speaking directly to the aspirations of millions of ordinary voters.

Furthermore, although claims that Labour's present crisis of confidence among working-class voters can be traced back to the metropolitanism of the Blair years are not without merit, they ought to come with a health warning. It is true that certain cultural questions, not least over rising immigration levels under Blair's watch, did indeed drive a wedge between the institutional Labour Party and its heartlands, resulting in higher levels of non-voting and abstention in the early 21st century in these areas. Equally though, this was the most electorally successful Labour government in British history and Blair, the party's most electorally successful leader, was hardly ignorant of the aspirations and motivations of the upwardly socially mobile working-classes. He understood better than most Labour politicians why thousands of these voters had supported Thatcher in the 1980s, and in many respects the Blair government spoke directly to this constituency of working-class voters by taking a robust stance on issues of law and order (including introducing tough counter-terrorism measures), vigorously defending a pro-American, pro-NATO foreign policy, and making significant public investment in health and education. No doubt there will be those in the modern Labour movement comfortable with the notion that the origins of the party's current predicament can be located in the Blair years, the reality seems more complicated.

Second, existing approaches have tended to focus heavily on Labour failure rather than the successes of the Conservatives both as a governing party and a political opponent. We have become accustomed to framing contemporary politics in negative terms: referring to Labour's *loss* of the working-class vote, rather than the Tories ability to *gain* these voters' support or Labour *retreating* across their Welsh and Scottish heartlands, instead of the Conservatives and SNP *advancing*. Following this logic, it is easy to imagine the past ten years in relatively simplistic terms, essentially being a story of a complacent Conservative Party being kept in power by hapless Labour oppositions, implying that voters were somehow 'forced' to vote for Labour's political opponents.

As a result, it is common to overlook the impressive performance of the Conservative Party as a political operation after c.2007. Although they have struggled with their fair share of problems in office since 2010, the Conservatives have responded swiftly to changing circumstances, demonstrating characteristic flexibility and pragmatism. More fundamentally, as I will show throughout this book, the Conservative Party has on many occasions throughout history shown itself better able to speak to the aspirations and values of the British electorate including, crucially, a large section of the upwardly socially mobile working class. In this respect, the long decade after 2007 was no different.

Beginning under David Cameron, consecutive Tory leaders have reached beyond the party's traditional social and geographical voter base. On becoming leader, Cameron de-toxified the Conservative Party brand to win back the millions of voters that had been lost to Blair in the late 1990s and early 2000s. In the 2010 election, he increased the Conservative seat count by 96 and restored his party to an electorally competitive position and one in which it was capable of winning power once again. Running parallel to efforts to soften the Conservative Party's image, Cameron also sought to restore the Conservatives as the party of law and order, pledged to reduce immigration to the tens of thousands and argued for constrained welfare spending after the purported profligacy of the Blair–Brown years. In 2015, the Tories were rewarded for their stewardship of the economy and returned to government with the first Conservative majority in over two decades as well as an increased national vote share. Apart from wiping out the Liberal Democrats in the South-West and suburban London, Cameron also picked up seats across Northern England and Wales, including the Shadow Chancellor's Morley and Outwood constituency.

Then, after the EU referendum, Theresa May recognised early on the strategic opportunity presented to her party by the Leave vote. In her first speech as Prime Minister on the steps of Downing Street, she made a bold appeal to those who were 'just about managing', identifying the underlying causes that had contributed to Brexit. Although her government ultimately failed in its core purpose of delivering on the result of the referendum, history might eventually be kinder to May's premiership. In the 2017 election, the Conservatives achieved a significant swing against Labour in Leave voting parts of Northern England, the Midlands and Wales; an important prelude to the dramatic gains the Tories would go on to make across these areas two years later. In Scotland, the Conservatives enjoyed their best election results in a generation in 2017, and as Prime Minister, May took extremely seriously her party's role in preserving the integrity of the Union of the United Kingdom. This was reflected above all in the withdrawal agreement her team negotiated with the European Union, which was designed to deliver the referendum and at the same time hold together the four constituent parts of the United Kingdom.

By the early summer of 2019, Boris Johnson was able to capitalise on a national climate of Brexit-induced exhaustion ('Brex-austion'). His promise to decisively end three years of bitter parliamentary stalemate and thus allow the country to move forward resonated with an electorate that had long before grown tired of the seemingly unending Brexit psychodrama. So too did Johnson's commitment to turn a page on the fiscal austerity of the preceding years by committing his government to a bold and ambitious levelling-up agenda. In December 2019, the Conservatives won a large parliamentary majority by sewing together a broad national electoral coalition of traditional, affluent Conservative voters in Southern England and thousands of small-town Leave voters, thus demolishing Labour's Red Wall.

The third limitation of conventional approaches lies in the temptation to read the history of the past decade backwards and suggest that the 2019 election was an inevitable product of Labour's failure to produce a leader with suitable qualities for the office of Prime Minister in 2015, or of the shock Leave vote in 2016. Focusing heavily on these turning points implies that a silver bullet might have existed to neutralise the party's troubles, pull lifelong Labour voters back from the brink of voting Tory, and clear the path to power. This in turn has encouraged an *if only* approach to the recent past: If *only* there had been a more competent opposition in place, led by someone different, then Labour could have replaced the Tory government at various junctures; *if only* someone else had led the Labour Party during the EU referendum campaign, then Britain would have voted to Remain and Labour's working-class heartlands would never have abandoned them for the Tories.

Important and fractious as they were, Corbyn's leadership and the Brexit vote did not make the Labour Party's eventual electoral annihilation in December 2019 inevitable. There were any number of contingencies and complexities, which I explore in this book, that could have made many different outcomes possible. Had, for instance, some Labour MPs responded differently to May's efforts in early 2019 to gain parliamentary consent for her withdrawal agreement and a general election was fought with Phase I of Brexit 'done', the political dynamic would surely have shifted decisively in a different and potentially more favourable direction for the Labour Party. It could be argued that Brexit offered the Labour Party an opportunity to redress the growing institutional bias towards the metropolitan half of its voter coalition by coalescing around a softer, more moderate Leave option.

Finally, we need to better understand and explain the complicated interaction between the impact of Corbyn's position as leader of the Labour Party and the divisive Brexit question. While Corbyn himself overall was an electoral liability for Labour – actively repelling large sections of the British electorate – he used every ounce of his political influence and authority to resist the electorally fraught second referendum position. He did this despite immense pressure from trade unions and party members, to whom he owed his position as leader, to change tack and adopt an unambiguously Remain stance.

As such, I argue in this book that a re-evaluation of Corbyn's response to Brexit is required. His advocacy of a soft, moderate Brexit position – via a permanent customs union position – was strategically rational given Labour's divided voter and internal coalition. It is ironic that allies of Corbyn defend him in all the ways and on all the issues for which he ought not to be defended, such as his radical policy programme, personal suitability for the leadership, and principled stance on issues of foreign policy. Yet on the issue for which he was vindicated (resisting

23

a divisive second EU referendum position), he has not been given the credit he deserves.

In reality, it is Labour moderates who must do some soul-searching on their response to the Brexit question. They must confront the fact that forceful lobbying for the Labour Party to adopt a second referendum position as part of efforts to overturn the 2016 result was electorally damaging – confirming long-held suspicions that the party was uninterested in the views of millions of voters across traditional Northern and Welsh heartlands. As such, it is unclear how a Labour Party led by a moderate such as Owen Smith and adopting an unambiguous Remain position, would have been any more successful in navigating the electoral ramifications of the Brexit question. Heaping culpability on an individual, such as Corbyn, might be politically convenient, but it is not satisfactory in explaining Labour's problems in recent years.

Part I: The party of the people (1900-2007)

This book begins by offering a long-term historical perspective of the contrasting electoral performance of Labour and the Conservatives. Part I reflects on the reasons for the formidable record of the Conservative Party over the 20th century and lays bare Labour's recurring difficulties in winning and holding political power in the UK. It is sobering to think that just three Labour leaders have won parliamentary majorities in the House of Commons at a general election – Clement Attlee, Harold Wilson and Tony Blair – since the party's formation in 1900.

Chapter 1: Winning the working-class vote (1900-1997)
In Chapter 1, we will see that time and time again over the past 120 years, the Conservative Party has shown itself better able to speak to the values and aspirations of the British electorate. Crucially, the Conservative voter coalition has long incorporated a large section of the upwardly socially mobile working classes, underpinning large parliamentary majorities in the House of Commons at various points. The British Labour Party, which was ostensibly founded to provide political

representation for historically overlooked working-class interests, struggled throughout the 20th century to fully engage these voters and secure their support at the ballot box. As such, certain unifying, and timeless, values – especially aspiration, the principle of equality of opportunity and rewarding hard work – have underpinned the Conservative Party's long-standing claim to be the true 'party of the people'.

Chapter 2: New Labour, New Britain (1997-2007)
Chapter 2 considers the medium- and long-term impacts of the Blair government on both the Labour Party itself as well as British politics more widely. This period was in many respects an aberration in British political history because it was the Conservative and not the Labour Party that was electorally unresponsive, backward-looking and riven with infighting. In 1997 and 2001, Blair won historic majorities in the House of Commons by conveying a clear vision for the future direction of the country, as well as demonstrating the political flexibility necessary to a sew together a broad national voter coalition that incorporated a large section of Middle England. As late as the 2005 election, the Tories were still unable to inflict serious damage on the New Labour fortress and their efforts to mobilise cultural issues, such as rising immigration levels, failed to deliver meaningful results at the ballot box.

Against the background of Labour's electoral success in the early 21st century, it is increasingly argued that new wedge issues – notably cultural questions of identity – widened and deepened the gulf between the metropolitan, liberal part of the Labour coalition and small-town, socially conservative Northern voters. In the official Labour Together 2019 election review, the authors acknowledge that 'the roots of our 2019 loss stretch back over the last two decades', which they attribute to weakening ties with traditional communities from the Blair years onwards. In particular, the growing salience of immigration as a live issue in British politics, and New Labour's failure to address voter concerns about the rising numbers of people entering the UK, is regarded as crucial in explaining Labour's present difficulties with working-class voters.

Although New Labour devoted significant energy and considerable resources to appeasing Middle England, it would be wrong to think of Blair's government as being ignorant of the motivations and values of the working classes. The Prime Minister's robust stance on law and order, pro-NATO foreign policy and willingness to talk tough on counter-terror measures appealed directly to this constituency of voters. It just so happens that grievances over rising immigration levels, a key policy issue where Blair took his eye off the ball, rose rapidly up voters' priorities in the mid- to late-2000s. Such was his confidence in his ability to convey a pro-European, socially democratic and cosmopolitan vision for British society in the 21st century, that Blair might have believed the electorate would come to accept immigration as part of the architecture of modern Britain and something to be welcomed, not resisted. If this is the case, then he was proved wrong.

Part II: Painting Britain Blue (2007-2020)

Part II focuses on the reasons for the contrasting political fortunes of the two main parties over the long decade from 2007 to 2020. This section of the book begins in 2007 because, following Blair's departure from Number 10 and a sharp deterioration in the UK economy, the Conservative Party's fortunes began to significantly improve. It ends in 2020 following Johnson's landslide election victory.

During this period, consecutive Conservative leaders contributed in different ways to increasing the party's national vote share, as well as its representation across England, Wales and Scotland. David Cameron inherited a Conservative Party in 2005 that represented just 198 seats, predominantly in affluent parts of Southern England. After four general elections and a decade in government, the Conservatives were completely transformed: emerging in 2020 as a formidable national party of government with 365 MPs and seats across all parts of Great Britain.

The Labour Party, meanwhile, increased its vote share among a socially and geographically confined subset of English voters, stacking up large majorities in urban, metropolitan seats, but at the same time retreating from small towns in provincial England and Wales. After the

2019 election, Labour was left representing just 202 seats nationally, concentrated overwhelmingly in big cities such as London and Birmingham, as well as university towns. In Scotland, Scottish Labour's vote share fell to just 19%, the party's worst performance in over a century, and once again Labour was left holding just a single seat north of the border.

Part II is disaggregated into five chapters. Chapter 3 considers Cameron's time as Conservative leader, focusing on the period between 2007 and 2016. Then in Chapter 4, I assess the impact of the EU referendum on British electoral politics during Theresa May's premiership from June 2016 to July 2019. Chapter 5 examines Johnson's first term as Prime Minister during the 'long election campaign' from July to December 2019. Finally, Chapter 6 draws attention to the trends underpinning Conservative electoral success over the long decade from 2007 to 2020, while in Chapter 7, I analyse the significant role smaller parties have played in influencing electoral events.

Chapter 3: British politics after Blair (2007-2016)
In Chapter 3 I argue that the financial crisis of 2007-08 significantly undermined Labour's economic credibility, a key foundation of Blair's landslide victory in 1997 and continued electoral success in the early 2000s. The crisis itself, as well as Gordon Brown's immediate response to it, gave the Tories an opportunity to present themselves as the fiscally credible alternative to a decade of Labour profligacy. Importantly, Cameron and Osborne successfully located the causes of the crisis in Labour's mishandling of public finances in the preceding decade and convincingly won the argument that spending reductions were an economic necessity rather than a political choice. Such was the economic dislocation caused by the events of 2007/8 that they cast a long shadow over British electoral politics and played an important role in securing Conservative victories both in the 2010 and 2015 elections. Indeed, arguably, Labour still struggles with the effects of the crisis to this day.

The financial crisis also fuelled the growth of smaller right-wing parties, especially UKIP, and gave voters an outlet through which to channel frustrations with Labour policies in government, not least the fact they had allowed high levels of immigration to go in a sense unchecked. For some time, it was thought that Farage's 'purple army' posed a greater electoral threat to the Conservative Party than it did to Labour. However, such thinking was challenged by UKIP's electoral success not just in the South-East and East of England but also the North-East, Midlands and Wales in European elections, by-elections, and local elections. UKIP's impact was felt in general elections too. A surge in support for the party in the 2015 election, for instance, helped the Conservatives win several Labour-held seats in Northern England and Wales.

Chapter 4: Surviving Brexit (2016-2019)

In Chapter 4, I assess the impact of the EU referendum and shock Leave vote in June 2016 on British electoral politics up to July 2019, when Boris Johnson became Prime Minister. With the benefit of hindsight, it is tempting to draw a straight line between Corbyn's surprise success in the 2015 leadership contest, the Leave vote a year later and the 2019 election disaster. However, Labour's electoral catastrophe was not an inevitable consequence of the Brexit vote. Had the Labour leadership engaged constructively in cross-party talks with the government in early 2019, they could have secured concessions on workers' rights or environmental protections and claimed them as Labour achievements. Alternatively, had a relatively small number of respect-the-referendum Labour MP's supported Theresa May's withdrawal agreement in March 2019, the political dynamic would have shifted decisively in a different direction. It was not inevitable that a general election would be fought with Brexit not 'done'; it was a contingency that significantly benefited Johnson and the Conservatives.

I also re-evaluate Theresa May's premiership during this period. May's achievements in office are often overshadowed by her failure to win a majority in the 2017 election and her government's inability to secure the UK's exit from the EU. In practice, May's time as Prime Minister provided much of the groundwork for her successors' later achievements. In 2017, she increased the Conservative vote share by 6% nationally and achieved a significant swing against Labour in Leave-voting areas in the North, the Midlands and Wales. Her withdrawal agreement, which aimed at delivering the result of the referendum and holding the four constituent parts of the United Kingdom together, formed the basis of the agreement Johnson would bring back to the House of Commons in October 2019.

As national political parties with broad voter coalitions, both the Conservative and Labour parties were divided over how best to respond to the shock Leave vote. Ultimately, though, the fact that Conservative splits pertained overwhelmingly to the means by which the Leave vote should be prosecuted, rather than the end of whether the UK should remain in the EU or not, allowed May's government to present a coherent political narrative about the need to deliver Brexit and allow the country to move forward. For Labour, the Brexit vote posed an existential dilemma. The divides running through the Labour Party were more difficult to manage because Labour MPs could not agree whether to accept the referendum result and move on or attempt, via a second referendum, to prevent Brexit from happening.

Chapter 5: End game: 2019 General Election

From the moment he entered Downing Street, Johnson placed his government on an offensive 'war-footing' in preparation for an early general election, as is argued in Chapter 5. Johnson effectively fought a six-month long election campaign running from July 2019, when he became Prime Minister, to December when the ballots were counted. By focusing on the urgent need to deliver the referendum result, as well as shifting the government's domestic priorities on issues of law and order, the National Health Service and regional growth policy, he aligned closely with the priorities of a broad section of the electorate. By the time of the election, having made every effort to secure Britain's exit from the EU, Johnson was well placed to capitalise on a national climate of Brex-austion. His pledge to 'Get Brexit Done' resonated with a public that was deeply weary of the indecision and uncertainty over Britain's EU relationship. In December 2019, the Conservative vote share rose for a sixth consecutive election, to

44%, and unlike his recent predecessors, Johnson could credibly claim to have triumphed on the Europe question.

Chapter 6: Electoral trends (2007-2020)

Chapter 6 examines the underlying trends underpinning the Conservative electoral hegemony over the long decade between c.2007 and 2020. After 2007, Conservative leaders consistently outpolled their Labour opponents on the question of voters' preference for Prime Minister, and the Conservative Party enjoyed a commanding lead on the metric of economic competence from the financial crisis onwards. These crucial advantages over Labour supported Conservative efforts to make election campaigns more presidential and at the same time to present Labour leaders and their Shadow Chancellors as a risk to national and economic security.

The demographic profile of Conservative and Labour voters also changed considerably over this period. Consecutive Conservative leaders contributed in different ways to expanding the party's voter base across England, as well as Wales and Scotland too. As a result, the Conservative Party that emerged from the 2019 election was completely unrecognisable from the one David Cameron had led into the 2010 election a decade earlier: older, more socially and economically diverse, and enjoying considerably better representation across the whole United Kingdom. The Labour Party's support base, meanwhile, became socially and geographically more confined over this period, winning over younger and more middle-class voters in metropolitan seats and university towns but lacking broad national appeal. Given the propensity for the elderly to turn out and vote, and in the continuing absence of an anticipated 'youthquake' to significantly move the dial in Labour's favour, these trends have underpinned the Conservative Party's electoral success since 2010.

Chapter 7: Smaller parties

To gain a complete impression of the electoral dynamic after 2007, I assess the role smaller parties have played in Chapter 7.

Despite failing to gain meaningful parliamentary representation in Westminster, both UKIP and the Brexit Party profoundly impacted both the two main political parties. These parties were also ultimately successful in their primary aim of securing Britain's exit from the EU. As a result, it is simply not possible to fully understand British electoral politics in the 21st century without examining the success of right-wing, Eurosceptic parties in England and Wales.

The Conservatives responded effectively to the threat posed by UKIP and the Brexit Party on their right flank at various points, which helps to explain how they maintained its electoral position. The UKIP threat was first minimised when David Cameron publicly announced in 2013 his intention to hold a national referendum on EU membership in the event of the Conservative Party winning an overall majority at the next election. Then, in June 2016, after the Leave result, Farage's party was once again tamed as Theresa May's government pledged to honour and deliver the referendum result. Finally, Johnson's landslide victory in December 2019 and the swift negotiation of a Free Trade Agreement with the EU the following year, eliminated the resurgent threat of the Brexit Party.

In Scotland, the rise of the SNP since c.2014 has completely transformed the political dynamic north of the border, virtually wiping out the historically dominant Labour Party and providing the political space for the revival of the Conservative Unionists as the official party of opposition. Nationalism in Scotland has also had an impact on the behaviour of English voters: in the 2015 and 2019 elections, Conservative victories were aided by claims that a minority Labour government would require formal SNP support to govern.

The rise and fall of the Liberal Democrat Party in the past decade has also profoundly impacted the two main political parties. Before the 2010 election, the phenomenon of 'Cleggmania' contributed to David Cameron's failure to win an overall parliamentary majority and propelled the Liberal Democrats into the first formal coalition government in generations. However, since the rout in 2015, the failure of the Liberals to stage an electoral recovery and move on from their time in government led to a sustained period of electoral malaise. Overall, the beneficiaries of Liberal Democrat weakness have been the Conservatives, allowing them to entrench support in South-West England after the 2015 election and protecting against a Liberal resurgence in other affluent, middle-class seats across Southern England in the 2017 and 2019 elections.

Part III: Why do the Conservatives keep winning?

The final part of the book situates the long decade after 2007 within a long-term historical perspective (broadly, the past 120 years) by reflecting on the themes and issues raised in Parts I and II. Although we have become accustomed to significant upsets in our political system and 'unprecedented' events in recent years, British politics in the 2010s has been characterised by continuity as well as change. As in many other decades, the Conservative Party has enjoyed a long, unbroken stretch of electoral hegemony and, as in the past, this success has been underpinned by the conversion of a significant number of upwardly socially mobile working-class voters to the Tory column. Once again, the Conservatives have demonstrated the flexibility and pragmatism to sew together a broad electoral coalition, while the Labour Party has languished on the opposition benches, divided about how to respond to Conservative successes at the ballot box and led by individuals lacking widespread political appeal.

In this section, I consider the key themes that have characterised British electoral politics over the past 120 years to account for the contrasting performance of the two main parties at the ballot box from 1900 to the present day. It is not for nothing that the British Conservative Party has been the most electorally successful political operation in Europe over the past century. Conservative leaders have time and again reached for certain popular policies that have cut across class, income, and geography, to forge broad and sustainable voter coalitions.

Conclusion: A new politics

It might be assumed that Johnson's landslide represents the end of the story; with the divisive politics of Brexit and Corbynism consigned to history, the 'liberal' centre-left could bounce back, like a spring recoiling under the weight of populist insurgency. This might well be true.

However, there are also reasons to believe the UK's political architecture has been fundamentally altered by the dramatic events leading to the Conservative landslide in 2019.

Under current electoral trends, the 2019 election could represent merely a continuation of evolving patterns of voting behaviour that have been occurring over a period of years, even decades. For a long time now, the Conservative Party has been reaching deeper into lower income, more socially- and economically-deprived areas; in some cases, such as in the 2017 and 2019 elections, winning seats that had never before been blue. Labour, meanwhile, has become increasingly a sectional, regional party, attracting the passionate support of middle-class metropolitan voters in urban centres and university towns, but offering little to the wider electorate. The roots of the breakdown of the Labour Party's relationship with its heartlands goes deep and ancillary questions, including immigration and the wider cultural wars, will continue to play a role in our politics for years to come. Even after the 2019 election, a majority of Labour-held seats (52%) had voted Leave in the referendum, underlining the electoral risks posed by embracing a strategy that simply accepts a loss of small-town, working-class voters.

More fundamentally, the party must also re-discover its fundamental purpose in British politics. Over the course of the 21st century, the institutional and Parliamentary Labour Party has experienced a major and debilitating disconnect with the very people – living in working-class communities in provincial England and Wales – it was founded to represent. This disconnect was exposed by the Leave vote and Labour's eventual migration in July 2019 to a second referendum position on EU membership. Repairing the relationship with small-town voters outside the big metropolitan cities and university towns will be among the biggest strategic challenge facing the new Labour leader, Keir Starmer.

Worse still, Labour's moral authority has been severely undermined by events following Jeremy Corbyn's leadership after 2015. The tolerance of anti-Semitism during Corbyn's time as leader, which resulted in the humiliation of Labour being investigated by the Equality and Human Rights Commission, has severely compromised the moral authority of a party that exists in large part to advance the cause of equality. As the former Labour Prime Minister Harold Wilson put it in 1962, 'This party is a moral crusade, or it is nothing.'

When Tony Blair was swept to power in 1997, it was frequently remarked upon at the time that many young people had no idea what it was like to live under a Labour government. They might either have been too young to remember the Wilson and Callaghan years, or they might not yet have been born when Labour had last been in power. Viewed from this perspective, the electoral dominance of the Conservative Party since 1979 became even more vivid to contemporaries. A fourth consecutive electoral defeat in 1992 provided the necessary impetus for the Labour Party to embrace serious reform and undergo a process of full-scale modernisation. As Blair told his party on becoming leader in 1994, 'Power without principle is barren, but principle without power is futile. This is a party of government, and I will lead it as a party of government.'

At the beginning of the 2020s, one is reminded of the experience of these young voters. By 2024, the Conservatives will be asking the electorate for an unprecedented fifth electoral term in office. As a result, there will once again be many people who will not remember the end of the Blair– Brown years and their entire life experience will have been formed under Conservative governments. Having been defeated four times at general elections, the Labour Party today finds itself once again at a crossroads. The choice facing the party is not about whether or not to return to the New Labour years, but rather whether Labour is willing to do what is necessary to show the electorate they have changed and have earned the right to govern once more.

Terminology

Social class

This book makes frequent reference to social class, particularly in relation to the two parts of the Labour Party's voter coalition: on the one hand the metropolitan, middle-classes and on the other, traditional working-class voters.

The composition of each of these two groups has changed significantly over the course of Labour's 120-year history. For much of the

20th century, the metropolitan middle-class half of the coalition was composed of well-educated socialists drawn to the Labour movement by a desire to advance the economic interests of the poorest and most vulnerable in society. Labour's traditional working-class voters, whereas, tended to be unionised manual workers largely working in the Britain's booming shipyards, steelworks and coalmines. Geographically, these voters resided in industry-intensive regions of South Wales, North-East England, the Midlands, as well as Scotland.

In the 21st century, the metropolitan part of Labour's coalition has become more important. Degree-educated millennials living in the private rented sector now represent Labour's core support base. Occupationally, these voters are more likely to work in public-sector professions, in particular the NHS and education, as well as the not-for-profit sector. Changes in British society have also meant that black and minority ethnic (BAME) voters in big cities such as London and Birmingham have also become an increasing source of Labour support.

The other part of Labour's coalition, consisting of traditional working-class voters, has also changed significantly. Many of these voters live in small towns in provincial England and Wales, in former coal mining and other industrial communities. Occupationally, they might still work as manual tradesmen or in heavy industry, although as the UK has transitioned to a late capitalist, service-based economy, they increasingly work in the tertiary sector, for instance in call centres or retail roles. These voters could also be retired or employed casually.

Importantly, the relationship between income and social class is more complicated than might at first be assumed. An individual who identifies or is classified as working class does not necessarily have low household earnings; tradesmen, such as plumbers, builders and carpenters make a good living from their work. Likewise, numerous professions frequently classified as middle class, such as the teaching profession, higher education and those working in the not-for-profit sector, command more modest levels of income.

Part I

The party of the people

(1900–2007)

Part I considers the reasons for the long-term electoral success of the Conservative Party and the Labour Party's difficulties in winning and holding power throughout the 20th century, focusing on the divisions running through Labour's voter coalition and the party's failure to maintaining the support of working-class voters. Far from spelling the Conservative Party's demise, the 1918 Representation of the People Act, which significantly widened the British electoral franchise, proved to be the beginning of a century of Conservative electoral hegemony.

In Chapter 2, I reflect on the New Labour years, which were the immediate backdrop to the long stretch of Conservative government after 2010. Under Blair's leadership, Labour managed to remove many of the obstacles that had previously presented a barrier to the party's electoral prospects, most conspicuously voting in 1994 to remove the Clause IV provision – which had envisaged an economic model based on the 'common ownership of the means of production, distribution and exchange' – from the Labour constitution. In return for modernising the Labour Party and making it relevant in the 21st century, Blair was rewarded with large parliamentary majorities in 1997 and 2001, as well as a historic third term in office in 2005.

Among the many criticisms of the New Labour government, it is common for critics to locate the party's present difficulties with working-class voters in the Blair years. Chapter 2 re-examines this period of British politics, recognising both the difficulties mass immigration caused the Labour Party and at the same time acknowledging that in many other respects, for instance on issues of law and order, Blair was actually very close to working-class voters.

1

Winning the working-class vote
(1900-1997)

Much attention has been given in recent years to the difficulties Labour has faced in maintaining the support of 'traditional working-class' and low-income voters. While it is true that the breakdown in political allegiances in the 21st century has been unprecedented and driven by new phenomena, such as the EU referendum in 2016, the Labour Party has never had a monopoly of the working-class vote in Britain. In reality, the relationship between Labour and working-class voters has always been a complicated one characterised not by harmony but complexity and contingency. As such, this relationship has been liable to break down spectacularly at various points in the past 120 years. Periods of British political history in which Labour found itself locked out of power for long stretches of time, such as in the 1930s, 1950s and 1980s, were accompanied by the Labour Party's failure to speak to the concerns and aspirations of ordinary voters.

At the same time, the Conservatives have never hesitated to drive a wedge between Labour and its working-class voter base by appealing to patriotic, aspirational upwardly socially mobile Britons. It is notable that the Conservative Party, despite being historically associated with the political interests of the privileged few, has time and time again proved better able to connect with ordinary voters and has spoken a political language they can relate to and understand. Throughout the 20th century, the Labour Party's failure to win and maintain the support of a large section of upwardly socially mobile, aspirational working-class voters proved to be a significant electoral constraint.

Viewed within this historical perspective, some of the problems Labour has experienced in the 21st century – especially the rupture between the leadership and certain sections of the British working class – have resonance throughout the party's 120-year history. What is perhaps most striking is that working-class voters are not, and in some sense have never been, natural Labour voters.

Labour's early divides

In 1893, the Independent Labour Party (ILP) was founded by Keir Hardie, a trade unionist, to provide a political voice in parliament for working-class people. In collaboration with an increasingly interventionist Liberal Party and aligned with the trade union movement, Hardie's party identified closely with the interests of millions of unionised manual workers across Britain.

Labour sought greater legislative protections for workers, including improved safety standards in manual professions and greater employer liabilities should an employee be involved in an accident while carrying out their work. Progressive legislation, such as the Workmen's Compensation Act (1906), which established the right of working people to claim for personal injury, and the Mines Act (1908), which introduced a statutory 8-hour cap on the number of hours worked per day, resulted in part from the lobbying efforts of the nascent Labour Party on behalf of workers in parliament.

To support the primary objective of advancing their economic interests, Hardie encouraged greater working-class representation in parliament. His MPs came from a wide variety of backgrounds at a time when the dominant Conservative and Liberal parliamentary parties were drawn overwhelmingly from the landed gentry and middle classes. In

1906, among the first Labour MPs ever to be elected to parliament were former cotton-spinners, engineers, and cabinet-makers. George Kelley, for instance, who was elected as Labour MP for Manchester South-West in 1906, had been apprenticed in the printing trade in York before becoming an MP; and the party's second leader, Arthur Henderson, had worked as an iron moulder in Newcastle upon Tyne before embarking on a career in politics. The trade union movement financially supported the candidacy of potential Labour MPs, helping them overcome a significant obstacle to entering parliament in the early 20th century.

The growth of the early ILP coincided with a period of electoral enfranchisement in which millions of adult British males were granted the right to vote. In 1884, the Representation of the People Act extended voting rights to the counties and boroughs (covering in total 60% of adult males). In 1918, out of the ashes of the First World War, universal male suffrage was achieved, although equality was not achieved until 1928 when all adult women were enfranchised. At the time, the Labour Party might have been regarded as a natural ally of many of these new voters, serving as a mouthpiece for the interests of the skilled and unskilled working class; indeed, in the early 1900s, Labour's membership and support base was drawn primarily from unionised manual workers in industries like cotton, coal and steel. In terms of electoral representation, Labour constituencies were heavily concentrated in industry intensive areas of Northern England and South Wales.

However, while its primary purpose was to advance the interests of its working-class voter base, the Labour Party was, even at the time of its inception, a coalition of diverse interest groups. Hardie and his new MPs might have come from modest backgrounds, but many other senior and influential socialist thinkers in the early 20th century Labour movement came from distinctly middle- and upper middle-class backgrounds. Some of the key figures within the Fabian Society, such as George Bernard Shaw, Sidney and Beatrice Webb and Annie Besant, came from families with significant material wealth and status in society. Beatrice Webb's father, for instance, was a businessman and a former Chair of the Great Western Railway, and Webb lived with her husband in the affluent North London borough of Hampstead.

These socialists were well-educated middle-class reformers attracted to progressive Labour politics by a desire to improve the economic and social outcomes of the newly enfranchised population. Socialist academics, including those affiliated with the Fabian Society, provided an intellectual underpinning to the early Labour movement; identifying and analysing perceived injustices brought about by a capitalist economic model. The early Fabian slogan 'Educate, Agitate, Organise' captures the spirit of late-19th century progressive politics; each active verb offers an insight into what the organisation was trying to achieve. First, 'Educate' because the Fabians wished to raise the political awareness of millions of newly enfranchised workers, many of whom would have received very limited formal education. Indeed, in Edwardian Britain, some would probably not have been able to read or write. The need to 'Agitate' was important because of the urgency of the problems facing British society at the time. Urban poverty, unsanitary working and living conditions as well as high levels of deprivation required radical political agitation of various forms – including strikes and direct action – to accomplish the necessary transformation of the British economy and wider society. Finally, it would be necessary to encourage workers to 'Organise' to effectively coordinate and mobilise their political interests.

Each half of the early Labour Party's coalition – on the one hand middle-class, well-educated socialists, and on the other, unionised working classes – had, by virtue of their education and social background, different views of the world. Although they shared common interests, particularly the advancement of working people's economic interests, cultural differences produced an inherent instability and tension within the Labour Party, a tension that manifested in different ways.

At a general level, socialist reformers and agitators frequently over-estimated the extent to which the manual working class would actively seek to participate in a class struggle with their capitalist paymasters. The perennial disappointment for these reformers was how little ordinary working people in Britain seemed to be engaged with or care about day-to-day politics. Without a discernible political ideology codified within a single document or constitution, the Conservative Party was closer to the average British voter who also did not tend to be ideological. Most voters did not spend their precious free time obsessing over day-to-day politics or seeking opportunities to ferment the overthrow of capitalism. In 1920, Philip Snowdon, who went on to become the first Labour Chancellor of the Exchequer, lamented that 'the very people for whom [the socialist] works and sacrifices are often indifferent and seldom show any gratitude.'[1] The appetite for a workers' revolution, if there was any, was not coming from the workers.

The Labour Party's success in appealing to working-class voters was contingent and influenced by a range of factors, such as the part of the country in which they lived or the type of employment they held. As Martin Pugh points out, 'culturally and politically the British working class constituted several distinct communities, some of which were more susceptible to an independent Labour Party than others.'[2] It was simply not possible therefore for the nascent Labour Party to speak to the British working-class, let alone capture its votes, as though it were a monolithic whole. Although unionised workers were more likely to vote Labour due to the party's affiliation with the trade union movement, even in Edwardian Britain, only a modest proportion of the British workforce was unionised. Despite being the first nation on the planet to industrialise, Britain's labour markets, to a greater extent than other advanced European economies like Germany, were fragmented and localised, with thousands of family-run businesses employing fewer than 20 workers. The conditions for a collective Labour movement in Britain were, in many respects, unfavourable.

In east London, for instance, where dock workers were commonly employed on a casual basis and were thus unlikely to be affiliated to a trade union, voters were far less susceptible to an organised Labour movement. Likewise, workers in small-scale industry, such as the textile factories in the West Riding of Yorkshire, were less likely to be attracted to the Labour Party because of the close employee–employer relations in small, family-run cotton mills. The Tory Party was politically well embedded in these areas as a result, especially among the working-class population.

Mobilising the industrial working-class masses to advance their economic interests would require organisation and, by extension, intervention from social reformers. Some of these interventions might have been welcomed – such as the aforementioned legislative protections for workers in high-risk occupations to improve safety or the introduction of a basic state pension to provide their families with some financial security. However, the boundary between social reform, paternalism and interference was fine and there was a section of the British working class that resisted such interventions from often well-meaning middle-class reformers. For instance, many socialist reformers were keen to emphasise the virtues of sobriety and frugality. Some figures in the early Labour Party disapproved of working men gambling and drinking, believing such practices contributed not just to immorality but also high levels of household indebtedness. Such paternalism repelled certain sections of the working-class, who were drawn to a strand of boisterous 'popular Toryism' based on an appeal to enjoy small freedoms – such as gambling or a pint – after a long day's work.

The Conservatives also proved adept at sewing together a political alliance of more affluent, middle-class business owners (such as those working in the brewing industry) and working men who wanted to enjoy a pint after a long day's work. While reformers in the early Labour movement might have regarded the interests of these business owners (capital) and labour (ordinary workers) as being necessarily antagonistic, the Conservative Party has historically been most successful when it has been able to connect the interests of these two groups. By pulling different interest groups together, rather than seeking to divide them on class lines, the Conservatives could present themselves as unifiers while Labour fermented harmful national divisions.

Working-class support for Britain's global empire
Important foreign policy questions, such as contemporary debates over Britain's global empire and the country's role in the world, clearly reflected a disconnect between middle-class socialists and the working classes. In the late-Victorian and Edwardian era, there was widespread support for the British Empire. While the extent and depth of this support among the industrial working class is disputed by historians, as Martin Pugh has argued, it seems clear that many exhibited patriotism

and strong bursts of national pride. Deploying a strategy that Labour leaders in recent history would recognise, Pugh identifies 'this [as] a time when the Conservatives acquired the habit of impugning the patriotism of their political opponents and portraying them as, at best, feeble friends of Britain's enemies or, at worst, traitors'.[3] Imperial expansion and the projection of British power abroad provided a useful wedge issue for the Tories, allowing them to win support from working-class voters.

Outbursts of patriotic support for the Conservative Party manifested at the ballot box. In 1900, a 'Khaki' election was fought against the backdrop of the ongoing Boer War in South Africa. The Conservative and Unionist Party saw an opportunity to capitalise on the climate of national pride following British military victories at Ladysmith and Mafeking and were returned with a landslide majority by rallying voters behind the Union Jack.

As well as being driven by ideology, working-class support for the Empire was also fuelled by economic self-interest. In parts of the country where docks, arsenals and munitions factories loomed large in the local economy, such as was the case in Portsmouth, Woolwich and Sheffield, the working-classes were more likely to vote Conservative. Enthusiasm for imperial expansion was inextricably linked to support for military and naval spending because of the investment in domestic manufacturing these activities stimulated and the high paid jobs they created across the country.

Many socialist academics, meanwhile, viewed Britain's overseas empire disdainfully: a moral stain that created economic exploitation both at home and overseas. Working-class enthusiasm for imperial expansion was something academics struggled to explain: how could working men support a system that so economically disadvantaged them? In *Imperialism: A Study*, the economist J.A. Hobson offered a theory of domestic under-consumption. He argued that imperialism was driven by the pursuit of overseas markets by businesses seeking higher profits and returns on investment. As a result, the domestic market was starved by under-investment. Hobson and others suspected that governments used imperial propaganda to manipulate the masses into supporting the Empire as a means of distracting them from their dire living and working conditions. It was therefore tempting for well-educated socialists to 'explain away' working-class attitudes to the Empire with conspiracy theories such as these.

A broader distaste for British, and particularly a form of English nationalism, among the country's academic community is later remarked upon by George Orwell in 1947 in his classic essay, *The Lion and Unicorn*. Orwell wrote that 'England is perhaps the only great country whose intellectuals are ashamed of their own nationality. In left-wing circles, it is always felt that there is something slightly disgraceful in being an Englishman and that it is a duty to snigger at every English institution, from horse racing to suet puddings. It is a strange fact, but it is unquestionably true that almost any English intellectual would feel more ashamed of standing to attention during "God Save the King" than of stealing from a poor box.'

A Conservative century

It was common for contemporaries to predict that mass enfranchisement in the early 20th century would render the Conservative Party, which ostensibly represented the interests of a small and privileged few, obsolete as a viable electoral force in British politics. The natural beneficiaries, as the guardians of the economic interests of the working classes, would surely be the Labour Party.

The reality turned out to be almost the complete opposite, or at least more complicated. Far from being made irrelevant, the Conservative Party enjoyed a long period of electoral hegemony in the two decades immediately following the universal male suffrage being granted in 1918. Ironically, the Tories were as successful, perhaps even more so, in the 20th century, faced with a broader and more socially inclusive electorate, as they were in the 19th century, when the franchise was limited by property ownership. As such, there is little substance to claims that the Conservative Party is, or ever has been, the party of the propertied elite.

Labour's bifurcated voter coalition, and the inherent tension it produced, proved to be a recurring constraint on the party's ability to gain and hold power for much of the 20th century. Long periods of opposition, such as in the 1950s and 1980s, accompanied a failure on the part of Labour leaders to connect with a significant proportion of upwardly socially mobile, aspirational working-class voters.

In the post-war period, divisions within the Labour Party over how to respond to a sustained period of material affluence contributed to 13 'wasted years' in opposition between 1951-1964. Over the course of the 1950s, ownership of household appliances like washing machines and televisions rose precipitously, ushering in a period of rising national living standards. Keen to further fuel consumer confidence and spending, consecutive Conservative governments pledged to 'set the people free' of post-war state rationing and restrictions. In 1952, the Tory Chancellor R.A. Butler used his budget to set the tone for the coming years by cutting income tax, increasing tax relief (lifting some two million people out of paying income tax altogether) and raising family allowances. As Pugh argues, Butler was 'outflanking Labour by appealing to certain sections of working-class opinion, especially the better paid, calculating that they would appreciate lower direct taxes'.[4] In a direct appeal to ordinary aspirational working households, the Tories presented themselves as the party of higher living standards – to the extent that by 1959 Harold Macmillan felt able to famously proclaim that 'Our country has never had it so good.' The Conservatives were comfortable occupying a political space that was economically interventionist – for instance preserving peaceful industrial relations by bargaining with trade unions – and at the same time offering personal tax cuts to ordinary working households.

Recognising that a certain section of the upwardly socially mobile working-class might have middle-class aspirations to own their own home, the Tories also embarked on a huge post-war programme of house building. After his election victory in 1951, Winston Churchill tasked his Housing Minister at the time, Macmillan, with 'build[ing] the houses for the people' and his government met its ambitious target of constructing 300,000 new units per annum. A booming private sector construction industry had the double benefit of fuelling a sustained period of economic growth and providing the post-war 'baby boomer' generation with new homes.

Labour, meanwhile, struggled to respond to the period of widespread consumer affluence and were associated by voters with the austerity and rationing of Clement Attlee's government immediately following the Second World War. Some aspects of 1950s British society – such as the growing commercial advertising sector and rapid expansion of television to reach the masses – were interpreted by figures in the Labour movement as being symptomatic of damaging American commercial influence. An aversion to the capitalist free market was conflated with anti-American sentiment by a certain section of the British left. A growing mass media and commercial broadcasting network was met with hostility and cynicism by some figures within the Labour Party who feared working people were being manipulated by vested interests such as big business, greedy advertising companies or the media.

In 1960, the Labour MP Richard Crossman warned that his party should 'refuse in any way to come to terms with the affluent society', and Nye Bevan, who had served in Attlee's government as Health Minister, infamously described the affluent society as 'an ugly society... A society in which priorities have gone all wrong'.[5] The Labour Party identified itself as the enemy of post-war affluence, arguing that rising consumption was accompanied by a culture of greed and excessive materialism. In doing so, the party also presented itself an obstacle to millions of aspirational Britons, who understandably welcomed improved living standards after the hardships of the Second World War.

Opposing the material comforts of the post-war economic boom was electorally catastrophic, pushing upwardly socially mobile, aspirational working-class voters into the arms of the Conservatives. David Sassoon remarks that 'the left-wing battles of the 1950s against the consumer society were as hopeless as those of the Luddites...against machines.'[6] The Conservatives steadily increased their share of seats in the House of Commons through the decade, culminating in the 1959 general election, when Macmillan led a one-nation party to a landslide victory, winning seats across all parts of the whole United Kingdom.

Thatcher's Britain
The caricature of the identikit Conservative voter of the 1980s is the male, pin-striped banker living in London or the South-East of England. While voters with this demographic and income profile were likely to vote

for the Conservative Party, fundamental to Margaret Thatcher's electoral successes after 1979 was the conversion of a significant proportion of upwardly socially mobile working-class voters to her vision for Britain's economy and society. To win large parliamentary majorities in the 1983 and 1987 elections, the Tories sewed together a voter coalition of middle classes in Southern England and aspirational working-class voters across provincial England and Wales.

Aimed at giving power 'back to the people', some of the flagship policies of the Thatcher government spoke directly to a constituency of working-class and lower-middle-class voters. The Right to Buy housing scheme, which significantly extended home ownership by allowing council house tenants to purchase their properties at discounted rates, was one such example. Between 1979 and 1995, some 2.1 million properties were bought from the government by their occupants, in the teeth of Labour and trade union opposition. (Seeing the political damage their position was doing to the party, Labour would eventually, in 1985, drop their opposition to the policy). The fact that council properties were sold by the government at one third of full market value, rather than at market rates, illustrates Thatcher's political flexibility and willingness to compromise on ideological beliefs in favour of desirable outcomes. She was not the first Conservative Prime Minister to recognise the political, economic and social opportunities promoting a 'Property Owning Democracy' presented her party, and nor would she be the last.

A young Tony Blair saw at first hand the powerful political impact the government's housing policy was having on the ground. On the campaign trail in the 1987 election, Blair approached a housing estate brandishing his red ribbon only to be warned that because the properties were all privately owned, he need not bother canvassing there because they would all be voting Conservative. The Labour Party once again found itself the enemy of ordinary voters' aspiration for financial security and ambition to own their own home. As such, housing created a divide in working-class communities, with the majority of council house tenants voting Labour (49%) and 47% of working-class homeowners voting Tory.

The Thatcher project had created a new constituency of upwardly socially mobile Conservative voters who owned their own homes, could

51

buy their own cars and were able to share in the benefits of stable macroeconomic conditions. This was a clear and coherent political message: Thatcher's government promised voters to build a strong economy, improve household living standards and restore national pride. This final point is particularly important. Economic revival was about more than creating and expanding opportunities, it was also about reversing a post-war narrative of Britain being a nation in 'decline'.

In general elections, the Conservative Party appealed to the aspirational instincts of the British electorate with a political offer that cut across social class and geography. In one election leaflet ahead of the 1987 election, a large blown-up image of the Prime Minister was captioned with the words 'Don't hope for a better life, vote for it' written beneath it. For millions of voters in the 1980s, the Conservative Party offered a sound basis for future prosperity. While the Labour Party indulged in infighting and wedded itself to outdated industrial practices, the Conservative Party offered disciplined political messaging, a confident leadership team and modern broadcasting campaigns aided by the elite advertising agency, Saatchi and Saatchi.

To build a broad electoral coalition, Thatcher understood the limits of what was politically possible in her quest to transform the structures of the British economy. Over the course of her premiership, spending on the National Health Service rose above inflation, totalling an £8 billion increase over the decade after 1979. When it came to institutional reform, there were limits to what the electorate would tolerate and certain sacred cows, most notably the NHS, could not be slain. Nigel Lawson, who served as Chancellor of the Exchequer, famously observed that the NHS was the closest thing Britain had to 'a national religion', a recognition within the Conservative Party that certain aspects of the post-war architecture would need to be preserved. In this, Thatcher mirrored her post war predecessors, including Churchill and Macmillan, by insisting the NHS is 'safe with us'. Such pragmatism was also reflected in the government's management of public finances after 1979. Although Thatcher and her Chancellors presented themselves as frugal stewards of the national finances, only in two years between 1979 and 1997 did the UK run a budget surplus whereby tax receipts exceeded government spending.

Foreign policy questions once again drove a wedge between the institutional Labour Party and working-class voters over this period. Dubbed the 'longest suicide note in history', the 1983 election manifesto pledged that a Labour government would withdraw Britain from the European Economic Community as well as committing to a policy of unilateral nuclear disarmament at a time when the Cold War remained a live issue in British foreign policy and Soviet Russia an enemy of Western democracies. Thatcher and the Conservatives did not hesitate to capitalise on Labour vulnerabilities on issues of national security and contrasted Michael Foot with an earlier generation of post-war Labour leaders, such as Clement Attlee, who had been far more robust on the question of defence. The result was decisive. The Conservatives won their largest parliamentary majority since the Second World War in 1983 and converted Labour strongholds such as Bridgend in Wales and Darlington in North-East England. In the East Midlands Report into Labour's catastrophic defeat, the authors agreed that 'the party failed to convince the mass of the electorate that we are fully committed to the defence of this country'.[7] Patriotic working-class Labour voters were repelled by their party's equivocation on issues of national defence: would a Labour government do whatever was necessary to protect its citizens? If voters have to hesitate before answering such a seemingly uncontroversial question, a political party is in trouble.

It is striking that as Labour began a slow and gradual electoral recovery in 1987 and 1992, the working-class Conservative vote proved the most difficult to dislodge. Even by the 1987 election, Labour's manual working class vote remained stubbornly low by historical standards at 43%. This was a relatively small increase on the previous two elections and was small in absolute terms for a party that had purportedly been founded to represent the political interests of these voters. Not only was Labour's relationship with working-class voters liable to break down spectacularly, but it also took many years to be repaired and rebuilt.

Throughout the 20th century, the Labour Party's claim to represent and speak for the British working class was frequently thrown into doubt. Consequently, Labour's electoral record was chequered, and the party was frequently consigned to long stretches on the opposition benches. These opposition years were accompanied by a significant proportion of the working class abandoning Labour for the Conservatives, who were able to promote a popular brand of Toryism based on an appeal to the aspirational instincts of the British electorate. Despite historically being associated with the political interests of the rich, propertied classes, the Conservatives might credibly have been able to argue that theirs was the true party of the people.

2

New Labour, New Britain

(1997-2007)

The late 1990s and early 2000s were in many respects an aberration in modern British political history. For most of this period, it was the Conservative Party and not Labour that was internally divided and unresponsive to changing electoral demands, producing a series of leaders who were incapable of mobilising widespread electoral support. After 1997, New Labour consigned the Conservative Party to its longest period of opposition in British history.

After becoming Labour leader in 1994, Tony Blair set out to modernise his party and signal to the electorate that he was serious about doing what was necessary to regain its trust and votes. To overcome the perennial challenge of constructing stable and sustainable voter coalitions, Blair reached deep into previously hostile political terrain across Middle England and told his Director of Communications, Alastair Campbell, in 1995 that his aim was nothing less than to 'put the Tories out of power for a generation'. The progressive politics of the third way was cast as a means by which New Labour could broaden its appeal across the whole United Kingdom, thereby allowing the party to win large and lasting majorities in a first-past-the-post system.

In pure electoral terms, Blair was extremely successful, and he was generously rewarded by the electorate with historic landslide victories in 1997 and 2001. He remains by far the Labour Party's most successful leader electorally, and the only one to secure three consecutive victories. The Conservatives, having governed Britain for eighteen years, were reduced to a derisory 165 seats in the 1997 election, the party's lowest count in almost a century. As late as the 2005 election, Michael Howard was unable to increase the Conservative seat representation in the House of Commons above 200, a reflection of the difficulties Blair's leadership of the Labour Party continued to present, even following the Iraq War.

New Labour's successes at the ballot box have not prevented Blair and his government from being subjected to significant criticism, not least from within the modern Labour movement itself. One charge that is increasingly levelled is that the professionalisation and modernisation of the Labour Party after 1994 came at a long-term political cost to the party's relationship with working-class communities across England and Wales, who felt increasingly overlooked by the leadership. The Labour Together 2019 Election Review typifies this argument and states that 'the seeds of this defeat stretch back over the last two decades, with the link between Labour communities we were founded to represent profoundly broken.'[1]

In this Chapter, I consider the impact of Blair's reforms of the party and the key policy positions his government adopted. On important cultural questions, most starkly over immigration, Blair's government took its eye off the ball. By allowing such a significant increase in the number of people entering the UK after 1997 and relaxing border controls in government, the Labour Party brand became inextricably linked with a policy of mass immigration, as well as its social and economic consequences. Small-town, working-class Labour voters might have felt 'shut out' of the debate over immigration, something right wing parties such as UKIP were able to capitalise on.

At the same time, though, it is also recognised that Blair was hardly ignorant of the motivations and political interests of working-class voters. Many domestic policies, including higher health and education spending, a tough approach to issues of law and order, and Blair's hawkish, pro-NATO foreign policy spoke directly to this constituency of voters.

Appeasing Middle England

Blair's New Labour project was above all else a response to the electoral challenges the party had faced in the preceding decade, especially the 'Southern discomfort' felt in Middle England about a high tax, high spend Labour government. Blair told his advisors in 1994 that the key to winning the next election would be the mantra of 'reassurance, reassurance, reassurance'. Primarily, Blair sought to persuade Middle England after two decades out of office that Labour could be trusted to govern once more and manage the economy competently.

Pledges to leave income tax brackets unchanged and match Conservative spending proposals for the first three years in office represented a concerted effort to reassure voters that Labour could be trusted with the national finances. The decision to give operational independence to the Bank of England also reflected the government's determination to situate itself as the economically competent alternative to the Conservatives, whose reputation had been badly damaged by the Exchange Rate Mechanism fiasco in 1992. Under Blair's premiership and Brown's chancellorship, this Labour government would avoid returning to the steep redistributive taxation policies of the 1970s. On the contrary, New Labour celebrated the contribution of businesses and entrepreneurs to society and Peter Mandelson infamously admitted he was 'relaxed about people getting filthy rich as long as they pay their taxes', reflecting the self-professed 'newness' of New Labour.

Implicit in such a strategy was a privileging of the interests of middle-class voters in swing seats in Southern England where, it was increasingly recognised, general elections were won and lost. Some working-class communities in traditional Labour heartlands might have felt overlooked, even ignored, during New Labour's quest for political hegemony. Reflecting on this period, the veteran Labour pollster Deborah Mattinson confessed after the 2019 election that she had never 'conducted a poll or focus group [in these areas]...assuming they were in the bag'.[2] This was hardly unusual. The former Labour MP for Vauxhall, Kate Hoey, has since described the intransigence of many of her parliamentary colleagues to the views and concerns of working-class voters because politically they had 'nowhere else to go' in the early 2000s. Hoey suggested that unpopular policies, such as 'a derisory increase in the state pension' were possible during the New Labour era only because of the absence of credible political competitors at the time.[3]

As Robert Ford and Maria Sobolewska argue, there has been a 'long divorce' between Labour and its core voter base since the 1990s and 'Blair made ideological moderation a central part of his party reform agenda, weakening Labour's longstanding links to the working class and left-wing ideology in order to boost Labour's appeal to middle-class swing voters.[4] With dwindling party memberships and few willing volunteers to canvass ahead of elections, both the main political parties were increasingly forced to prioritise 'swing votes' in seats that seemed pivotal to winning elections, abandoning 'safe' seats and voter groups.

A sense of complacency about Labour's electoral position in parts of Northern England, the Midlands and Wales might have been justified based purely on electoral arithmetic. Given the size of Labour majorities in these areas, Blair had little to fear. His own Sedgefield seat in County Durham, for instance, was rock solid, with a 25,000 Labour majority in 1997. In an era before UKIP was a serious contender in British elections, and with the Conservative brand toxic in former mining communities, working-class voters had few places to turn to register discontent with the Labour leadership. As a result, with few political competitors to capitalise on the perceived failings of Labour policy, high levels of voter abstention characterised elections in the early 21st century. In the 2001 General Election, for example, turnout nationally fell to just 59%, the lowest level since 1918. By 2005, Blair's large working majority in the House of Commons was secured with just a 35% vote share and working-class support for Labour was haemorrhaged as non-voting rates increased.

Immigration

Immigration became a totemic issue for Labour during their time in government and became a millstone around the party's neck thereafter.

The issue of immigration reflected a growing disconnect between the party's leadership and a core constituency of Labour voters living in provincial England and Wales. It also drove a wedge between the metropolitan part of Labour's voter coalition and traditional, working-class voters.

Under New Labour, immigration rose considerably in a relatively short period and was largely seen as an economic benefit to the UK by the party leadership. Having been relatively stable throughout the 1990s, net migration rose from 48,000 in 1997 when Blair entered Downing Street, to over 268,000 just seven years later. The New Labour leadership, as well as much of the Parliamentary Labour Party, favoured relaxed, rather than restrictive immigration policies. In October 2000, the Home Office Minister, Barbara Roche, suggested the UK ought to loosen immigration controls to attract 'wealth creators' and meet skills shortages. Two months later a seemingly innocuous report by the Performance and Innovation Unit quantifying the potential benefits of immigration to the UK economy passed over the Prime Minister's desk. According to its authors, the foreign-born population in the UK contributed 10% more to government revenue than they received in spending.[5] Given migrants tended to be young and economically active, higher immigration contributed to an expanding national economy and helped address the demographic challenges posed by a rapidly aging population.

The Prime Minister was careful to couch his arguments about the merits of immigration in economic terms and told the Confederation of Business and Industry in April 2004 that, 'There are half a million vacancies in our job market and our strong and growing economy needs migration to fill these vacancies.'[6] Big business was supportive of higher immigration, not least because it provided an abundant source of relatively low-cost labour and relaxed borders helped burnish New Labour's credentials as unashamedly pro-business party.

In 2004, Blair's government took the controversial and often-cited decision of declining to apply transitional immigration controls when several Central and Eastern European states joined the EU. This decision was driven in some part by the Prime Minister's desire to demonstrate British commitment to the European project at a time when the

59

Chancellor had effectively vetoed Eurozone membership. It was also based on a flawed assumption that migration levels would be relatively small and manageable. Believing that the UK had few connections with the new member states such as Poland, the government predicted that net migration would increase by between just 5,000 and 13,000 annually after 2005. This turned out to be a considerable underestimate and as many as 1.5 million people migrated to Britain in the five years following the accession of Eastern European countries. In fact, there *were* historical ties between the UK and Poland. During the Second World War, following the Nazi invasion of Poland, the government formed an exiled administration in London and Polish airmen served in the Battle of Britain to defend the nation from the Luftwaffe. There were other reasons why immigration from the new member states might be higher than the government assumed. With the ubiquitous English language and flexible labour markets, the UK was an attractive destination for economic migrants seeking higher living standards.

It is not clear whether a policy of mass immigration after 1997 was a result of a grand design or a consequence of other factors beyond the government's control, such as EU expansion and greater mobility of labour globally. It might have been some combination. In some ways it is irrelevant whether it was intended or not. Either way, Labour presided over a sustained rise in immigration during their time in office and apparently did little to stop it. As a result, the Labour brand became intimately associated with a policy of relaxed borders and future leaders would have to take responsibility for its consequences long after Labour left office.

Mass immigration divided Labour's bifurcated voter coalition; creating a lasting 'values divide'. Better-educated, middle-class voters living in metropolitan areas tended to be comfortable with relaxed border controls and higher immigration levels. As a result of their formal education, these individuals enjoyed greater financial security, in turn reducing the possibility that migrants might be in competition for their jobs; thus, insulating them from the effects of immigration. By virtue of living in large, metropolitan cities such as London, these voters tended to have a correspondingly internationalist outlook and were more likely to have travelled widely, experiencing other European and non-European cultures. An abundant pool of migrant labour from the EU also provided wealthy, middle-class families in the Capital with hard-working nannies and au pairs for their children, as well as cleaners for their homes.

For a wide range of economic and cultural reasons, 'small-town' working-class Labour voters were far less comfortable with the scale and speed of immigration after 1997. These voters tended to have a different conception of national identity and citizenship, rooted in a person's country of birth. They were more likely to self-identify as English or British rather than European. Working-class voters were also less geographically mobile themselves and their roots with their local community and town were strong.

Working-class voters living in provincial England and Wales tended to be more resistant to mass immigration despite the foreign-born population being comparably low in the areas they lived; indeed, the migrants that came from the EU, the Commonwealth and beyond overwhelmingly settled in big, metropolitan cities where the greatest economic opportunities exist. Although nationally there was a substantial increase in the ethnic minority population in the decade after 2001 from around 4.5 million (7%) to over 8 million (12%) in 2011, much of the increase was concentrated in big cities.[7] It is therefore striking that support for immigration was, and is, lowest in parts of the UK in which the level of immigration is correspondingly low, suggesting that attitudes are driven by a perceived rather than a real threat.

While many immigrants to Britain were able to integrate relatively successfully into domestic labour markets and more successfully than in other European countries, the question of how to absorb the scale of immigration given the diversity of backgrounds and values presented an important challenge and arguably one the Blair government failed to address. Similarly, the aggregate economic benefit of hundreds of thousands of working-age migrants entering the UK had to be weighed against the impact of immigration on public services, housing demand and wages in certain sectors of the economy. The Cambridge economist Robert Rowthorn has argued for instance that, depending on the profile of immigration, the effect on GDP per capita could be 'positive or negative, but either way it is unlikely to be very large'.[8] During the long economic boom of the late 1990s and 2000s, a growing economy and flexible labour markets meant the UK could absorb the additional labour supply, and migrants helped meet skills shortages in a range of sectors, including construction, hospitality and the health service. However, beneath the surface, the UK was becoming an employer-of-last-resort for the EU and the economy could not sustain the momentum indefinitely.

'Left behind' communities
The tension between Labour and working-class voters over this period extended beyond cultural questions and into the sphere of economic policy too. Beneath the long boom between 1997 and 2007, the UK economy was becoming structurally and geographically more unbalanced. As a result, economic growth was concentrated overwhelmingly in big metropolitan cities, such as London and Manchester. Financial services, and the wider service economy ecosystem, boomed, creating high paid jobs and driving up house prices in London and the suburban commuter belt. Other than redistributing the fiscal gains from South-East England to the regions through welfare payments, there was little effort to develop a coherent industrial strategy to revive 'left behind' areas across England and Wales.

New Labour presided over a sharp decline in manufacturing, driven by a strong pound, the conspicuous absence of a credible industrial strategy and perniciously high energy costs. Between 1997 and 2010, manufacturing shrank as a proportion of GDP from 18% to 10%, which disproportionately disadvantaged areas outside of London and the South East, including small, provincial towns in England and Wales. As Kitson and Michie argue, Blair's landslide in 1997 had the potential to be significant for British industry; however, 'any hopes proved unfounded... New Labour avoided any active industrial policy, generally claiming instead that governments could not or should not pick winners'.[9] There was little effort to alter the economic architecture inherited from the Thatcher and Major governments. Blair's enthusiasm for globalisation in turn encouraged a belief that it did not matter where goods or services were made, once again putting him at odds with working-class voters who tended to be more supportive of industrial 'national champions'. In

2005, one of the few remaining British owned car manufacturers, MG Rover, collapsed with the loss of 6,500 jobs, resulting in the closure of the Longbridge production plant in Birmingham. Many more jobs in the supply chain were also lost.

The Prime Minister's political mind was deeply attracted to a belief not only that globalisation was a powerful modernising force, but also one that could not be stopped. In his words, 'You might as well debate whether autumn should follow summer.'

As with immigration, globalisation was creating benefits throughout this period for the UK economy as a whole; however, these benefits were felt unevenly by different groups in society and across different parts of the UK. In general, British citizens enjoyed better living standards as the costs of consumer goods fell, airfares became cheaper and international opportunities expanded. Under closer inspection, though, many of these advantages accumulated with the middle classes, who were able to make use of Erasmus programmes to study abroad; take multiple foreign holidays in a year and employ reliable nannies from Central and Eastern Europe. Working-class communities, whereas, were disproportionately impacted by the erosion of the UK's domestic manufacturing base and since the 2016 Brexit vote, it is increasingly recognised that a section of the British working class was 'left behind' as the UK transitioned hastily to being a service, import-led economy in the 2000s.

Later down the line, the 2008 crisis highlighted the incoherence of New Labour's economic policy. Having spent the preceding decade resisting calls for a more interventionist industrial strategy to advance British manufacturing industry, Gordon Brown's government stepped in to provide a huge package of support for the financial services sector. Recapitalising banks that would otherwise have failed might well have been entirely defensible in the unique circumstances of a global financial crisis; however, it contributed to a feeling that it was one rule for the powerful (the bankers) and one rule for everyone else (including the British manufacturing sector). Given that Labour has historically relied on presenting itself as the party of ordinary people, and the Tories as representing the interests of only the rich and privileged, this did significant damage to Brown's government and the Labour brand.

It is increasingly argued that changes in the profile of the Parliamentary Labour Party during this period created a 'cultural gap' between the institutional party and working-class voters in provincial England and Wales.

Blair's landslide victories ushered in a new generation of Labour MPs, which in turn contributed to a significant change in the composition of the Parliamentary Labour Party. We saw in Chapter 1 how Hardie had encouraged working-class people into parliament in the 1900s. By the end of the century, the profile of Labour MPs had changed beyond recognition, with more members coming from professional, middle-class backgrounds, with private educations and university qualifications. Tom O'Grady's research quantifies this change and illustrates that while in the 1987 parliament, some 64 members (28%) of the Parliamentary Labour Party had a working-class job before entering parliament, by 2001, this figure had fallen to just 49 (12%).[10] This trend would continue through the 21st century and as Ian Lavery and Jon Trickett recently pointed out, 'A new political class came to be dominant in our party to the extent that in 2017 only four Labour MPs came from a background of manual labour while 137 came from a professional political background.'[11] Despite a long tradition of Euroscepticism in the Labour Party, the vast majority of backbenchers were also committed to European integration and Single Market membership by the late 1990s. Given many of these MPs owed their political careers to Blair's electoral successes, there was little incentive to challenge the authority and intellectual hegemony of the New Labour leadership.

Since the 2019 election, greater attention has been paid to the widening 'cultural gap' between a socially liberal Parliamentary Labour Party and more socially conservative voter base during the early 2000s. Reflecting on changes in the Labour Party over this period, the former Labour MP for Stoke-on-Trent, Gareth Snell, lamented how Labour policy in government had been decided overwhelmingly by 'people in cities' who knew little about the views and concerns of voters living in small provincial towns.[12] Over this period, the party apparatus accelerated the process of parachuting centrally approved candidates into safe seats in Labour heartlands, such as Ed and David Miliband, who were sent to represent Doncaster and South Shields (despite themselves being from Primrose Hill and having no connection to the local area). While one could argue that it should not have been a problem that these MPs did not have Northern accents and lacked a local network, it did suggest a certain detachment between more metropolitan Labour MPs in the parliamentary party and the communities they served.

The disconnect between Labour and working-class voters manifested in declining support among working-class voters in the early 2000s. At the high point of the 1997 election, the Labour Party enjoyed a commanding 55% share of C2DE (working-class voters), a lead of 31% over the Conservatives. By 2005, the gap had been eroded to 15%. Some of these voters abstained, while others might have been attracted to smaller protest parties such as UKIP. There was also a recovery in the Conservative vote share among working-class voters from the disastrous performance in 1997 to a more respectable 29% in 2005, and the party's 'are you thinking what we're thinking' slogan made some traction in working-class areas.

New Labour reconsidered

While modern electioneering techniques might have led New Labour to focus energy and resources on winning support in swing seats in Middle England, it cannot be said that the Blair government entirely overlooked the political interests of the working classes. Nor can it be said that Blair himself was personally ignorant of the motivations of Britain's aspirational working-class and lower middle-class voters. In fact, as Martin Pugh has pointed out, as a young MP in the 1980s, Blair identified more closely with his Sedgefield constituents and their politics than with the metropolitan socialism he encountered in north London, which tended to be more ideological and philosophical. As we saw in the previous chapter, his encounters as a young MP with aspirational property-owning Conservative voters in the 1987 election campaign resonated with Blair and he shared many of their values and beliefs.

Blair's pragmatic belief in moderate policies 'that work' and have widespread electoral appeal underpinned broad voter coalitions in consecutive general elections. In many respects, New Labour repaired the relationship between the Labour Party and working-class voters, which had broken down spectacularly in the preceding two decades. In 1997, Blair won 55% of the working-class vote. Unlike plenty of figures in the Labour movement, Blair recognised the reasons why millions of upwardly socially mobile, aspirational working-class voters turned to Margaret Thatcher in the 1980s. He understood, for instance, why Right to Buy was popular with this constituency of voters – who embraced enthusiastically the opportunity to own a home of their own. As a result, private housebuilding rose after 1997, while council house construction remained a very small proportion of total council housing stock.

New Labour remained close to working-class voters on other domestic policy positions, such as issues of law and order. As leader of the opposition, Blair stated clearly that his government would be 'tough on crime, tough on the causes of crime'. Given that many of victims of crime were the most vulnerable people in society, usually from economically disadvantaged communities, he believed there was nothing inherently 'right wing' about taking robust action to tackle criminal activity. In his autobiography, Blair reflects on the way certain antisocial behaviour was making the lives of people in deprived communities 'a misery' and reflects on his determination to stop it in 1997 when he came to power.[13]

Similarly, Blair was prepared to talk and act tough when it came to issues of national security. From 2000, terrorism acts were passed in the House of Commons allowing the police to detain terror suspects by an increasing number of days (doubling from seven days in 2000 to 14 in 2003). Blair's government also made the case passionately for the renewal of Britain's Trident nuclear capability into the middle of the 21st century – what Blair described as the 'ultimate insurance'. In a parliamentary vote in 2007, 95 Labour backbench MPs voted against plans to commence a £20 billion renewal of the nuclear submarine system, thus overturning the government's majority, and Tory votes were required to guarantee the passage of the legislation. The Prime Minister faced down critics within his party to present his government as robust on issues of national defence: pro-NATO, committed to the special relationship with the United States and willing to invest in the UK's independent nuclear deterrent.

Ultimately, New Labour's policy programme in government impacted different voter constituencies in complicated and overlapping ways. For instance, younger, more metropolitan voters might repudiate Blair for aspects of his economic policy, such as the perceived accommodation of Thatcherism, as well as foreign policy failures, most obviously Iraq. However, they would likely have supported New Labour's relaxed immigration policies and investment in public services. Traditional working-class Labour voters, whereas, might have felt overlooked on certain cultural questions, most notably immigration. However, Blair's government did not entirely neglect the working-classes and New Labour made significant investment in the NHS and education system and the Prime Minister was willing to 'talk tough' on anti-terror legislation, defence and national security.

In some respects, the first decade of the 21st century witnessed a clash of two competing traditions within the Labour Party. On the one hand, there was a new generation of Labour MPs swept to power in the landslide of 1997. Many of these MPs owed their new political careers to Tony Blair's modernisation of the party and their world view was shaped in a Blairite mould, based on an enthusiasm for globalisation, cross-border cooperation (especially as members of the EU) and a recognition of the role of markets in a successful, functioning economy supported by the state. On the other hand, there were those MPs who emphasised the party's roots as a champion for working-class communities. They held onto, perhaps even romanticised, the class struggles of the previous century and aligned closely with voters living in Labour's industrial and post-industrial heartlands, especially unionised workers in the manual professions and manufacturing sector of the economy. Many, although not all, were from a tradition of left-wing Euroscepticism, such as Kate Hoey and Dennis Skinner.

The latter group were side-lined and marginalised during the New Labour years. If the Labour Party had traditionally favoured a closed economy and greater state controls in the 20th century, then New Labour reversed this logic by advocating an open economy and greater freedom for the market economy. Some Labour MPs welcomed this philosophical change, seeing the electoral benefits Blair was reaping in the late 1990s and 2000s. Others were more resistant to it.

Overall, Blair's judgement that to be electorally relevant in the 21st century, the party would need to undergo fundamental reform, along with full-scale modernisation, was clearly correct. New Labour was anchored in a position on the electoral spectrum that was economically moderate and socially liberal, as well as being robust on issues of national security and law and order. A moderate policy programme made large parliamentary majorities possible within a first-past-the-post system, and Blair was able to make the 'political weather' for almost a decade in government.

However, New Labour's complacency about its political position across Northern England, the Midlands and Wales had important consequences for the party. As Claire Ainsley argues, 'New Labour were right to suppose that Labour could not build a parliamentary majority based on the traditional working class alone, but they were wrong to assume those voters would have nowhere else to go.'[14] As we shall see in the next section, the rise of challenger parties such as UKIP over the course of the 2000s, coupled with a strong Tory revival after 2007, posed a direct threat to Labour in their industrial and post-industrial heartlands, something that would have important electoral consequences.

Part II

Painting Britain Blue

(2007-2020)

Part II focuses on the reasons for the contrasting electoral performance of the two main political parties over the course of the long decade after c.2007. This section of the book begins in 2007 because, for several reasons, the Conservative Party's political fortunes began to improve considerably in that year. The departure of Tony Blair from frontline British politics and his replacement with Gordon Brown as Prime Minister, coupled with a sharp deterioration in the British economy from the early autumn, provided a reformed Conservative Party under the leadership of David Cameron with the opportunity to seriously challenge an increasingly tired and directionless Labour government. Having returned to power in 2010, the Conservatives went on to win four consecutive general elections, a feat only once before achieved in British history, during the Thatcher–Major years. For a governing party to increase its vote share three general elections in a row, as the Conservatives did in the 2015, 2017 and 2019 elections, is unprecedented in modern times.

Each Conservative leader contributed in different and important ways to expand the party's voter base after c.2007. The Cameron project aimed principally at making the party relevant in modern Britain by adopting a more Europhile posture, detoxifying the Conservative brand and winning back seats in Middle England that had been lost to New Labour in the preceding decade. At the same time, Cameron set his sights on 'small-town' working-class voters and began picking up seats in Northern England and Wales by reducing personal taxation levels, introducing a National Living Wage and pledging to reduce immigration to the 'tens of thousands'. After the EU referendum, May and Johnson expanded the Conservative voter coalition to incorporate a larger proportion of working-class voters. As a result, the Conservative Party that emerged victorious from the 2019 election was almost completely unrecognisable from the one Cameron had led into the 2010 election: representing more older voters, with a considerably broader range of affluence levels (including some of the most deprived parts of the country) and considerably strengthened not just across England but in Scotland and Wales too.

Strikingly, Conservative electoral success has been achieved despite suffering splits over various issues, most notably Britain's external political relationship with the European Union. Between 2010 and 2020, there were just three discernible periods during which the Conservative Party can be said to have been genuinely harmonious. The first of these was in the immediate aftermath of the 2015 election, when Cameron won a surprise majority with the promise of a national referendum on EU membership, which helped silence his critics. The second was immediately after the referendum in June 2016, when the party was united in a belief that the Leave vote ought to be respected, and rallied behind Theresa May, who seemed well suited to unite both the Conservative Party and the country as leader. The final period of harmony was immediately after Boris Johnson's 2019 election victory in which he won an 80-seat majority having pledged to 'Get Brexit Done'. Although the Conservatives have been divided, it can be argued that their leaders have proved more effective than their Labour opponents at managing those divisions.

Over the same period, the Labour Party struggled to capitalise on the difficulties the Conservatives faced in government. After Blair's resignation in the early summer of 2007, the Labour Party was led by a series of individuals who were judged unfavourably by voters compared with their Conservative equivalents. On balance, these leaders were more a liability to be managed rather than assets to be exploited by their party. On the vital metric of economic competence, Labour has been unable to recover from the devastating impact of the 2008 financial crisis and Labour Shadow Chancellors have been less trusted than Conservative Chancellors to manage the economy.

Under consecutive leaders, the Labour Party has retreated into a confined political space, identifying increasingly with the political interests of metropolitan voters in big cities and students in university towns, but lacking widespread national appeal outside these areas. Its success in winning back student voters from the Liberal Democrats and increased support among voters in the private rented housing sector under Miliband and Corbyn's leadership has not been sufficient to compensate for the loss of small-town, working-class voters.

3

Politics after Blair

(2007-2016)

Tony Blair's resignation as Labour leader and Prime Minister in June 2007 had immense consequences not just for his party, but also for British politics more widely. Having spent ten years in office, he was Labour's most electorally successful leader with three consecutive election victories, as well as being the second longest serving Prime Minister of the 20th century. As late as 2005, Cameron and his Shadow Cabinet team acknowledged the challenge Blair continued to present as a political opponent. His obvious gifts as a political communicator earned him considerable respect on the opposition benches and the Shadow Chancellor George Osborne referred to Blair as the 'master'. In his final PMQs session, Blair was given a standing ovation by MPs, against House of Commons tradition.

Reflecting on his time in office, Blair recognised his personal development as Prime Minister as he grew in experience as a statesman and described how 'you start at your most popular and least capable and you end your least popular and most capable'. The Prime Minister's reform agenda also became bolder and more radical in his third term in office, spearheaded by the successful academies programme in education and the introduction of competition in the health sector through foundation hospitals. The eventual departure of such an electorally successful and politically astute Labour Prime Minister therefore presented a significant opportunity to the Conservatives.

The Brown years

Despite an initial bounce in popularity during a honeymoon period over the summer of 2007, Blair's successor, Gordon Brown, struggled to convey a clear sense of political direction and vision for the country as Prime Minister. The veteran Liberal Democrat MP Vince Cable later remarked that having spent ten years at the Treasury waiting to become Labour leader, Brown seemed to have 'run out of big projects' by the time he eventually stepped into the role.[1] Even the former US President Barack Obama observes in his memoirs that Brown 'lacked the sparkly political gifts of his predecessor'.[2] Without the natural charm and charisma Blair possessed, Brown proved less adept at fielding questions at Prime Minister's Questions sessions and lacked broad electoral appeal.

Part of Brown's difficulties as Prime Minister stemmed from knowing the extent to which he ought to differentiate from the Blair years. On the one hand, Brown was ideologically close to Blair and the differences between them related more to style and presentation than policy substance. It should not be forgotten that the New Labour project was as much Brown's vision for the Labour Party as it was Blair's and as young MPs in the 1980s and 1990s, the two men had developed a very close professional relationship based on a shared belief in the need for Labour to modernise. Furthermore, Brown had served as an incredibly powerful Chancellor for ten years under Blair. He had been given unprecedented authority across a range of domestic policies and was central to the Labour government after 1997 and could not therefore disavow that administration easily. On the other hand, like most new party leaders, Brown wanted to establish his own policy agenda as Prime Minister and distinguish himself as his 'own man'. By this point it was also clear that a section of the Parliamentary Labour Party wasn't going to tolerate 'continuity-Blair' and were looking to Brown to restore conventional state-led solutions in the health service and education, thus ending New Labour's experiment with market mechanisms in the public sector.

Without a fresh mandate from the electorate, Brown was arguably more reliant upon and constrained by the Parliamentary Labour Party than his predecessor. He provoked fury from his MPs when he set out a vision for 'modern manufacturing...drawing on the talent of all to create British jobs for British workers' in his first speech to Labour conference as leader in 2007.[3] The former Home Secretary, Charles Clarke, claimed that many colleagues were 'appalled' by the remarks and the Labour chair of the Commons home affairs select committee described the slogan as 'employment apartheid'. Later that summer, the Prime Minister's authority was further undermined when he attempted to extend the length of time terror suspects could be held by police without trial from 28 to 42 days. Although the vote narrowly passed in the House of Commons, 36 Labour MPs voted with opposition parties against the proposals and they were eventually defeated in the House of Lords.

Brown's political judgement and leadership skills were also increasingly called into question over the course of his premiership. During conference season in autumn 2007, the Prime Minister mistakenly allowed speculation to build about the prospect of an early snap general election later in the year. To dissuade Brown from banking his early popularity with the electorate, the Shadow Chancellor, George Osborne, planted a trap at the Conservative Party conference. To rapturous applause, Osborne pledged that a future Tory government would raise the tax-free inheritance tax threshold from £300,000 to £1 million, alongside a range of other fiscal goodies and tax reductions. Brown panicked and the snap poll was never called. The 'election that never was' did immense damage to the Prime Minister's personal reputation and standing, leading to him being dubbed 'bottler Brown'. Cameron later goaded him in the House of Commons, telling him he was the first Prime Minister not to call an election because he 'thought he was going to win it'.

As autumn turned to winter in 2007, the economy took a sharp turn south. With a large financial services sector, which had ballooned further under New Labour, Britain was particularly exposed to the effects of the unfolding international banking crisis. Given that New Labour's electoral successes after 1997 had been supported in large part by a reputation for economic and governing competence, the downturn undermined the party's electoral position. An already challenging set of circumstances were compounded by the fact that as Chancellor, Brown had spent the preceding decade proclaiming he had put an end to 'Tory boom and bust', something which appeared hubristic in the face of rapidly rising unemployment, business insolvencies and collapsing consumer confidence. David Cameron was able to combine personal attacks on Brown with a broader critique of Labour's management of the economy and told the Prime Minister in the House of Commons that 'you have had your boom and now your reputation is bust'. Government successes at the time, such as the role Brown played in coordinating a global response to the financial crisis at the G7 in London, were overshadowed by a growing public perception that Labour had lost touch with ordinary voters.

As Brown struggled to offer clear and decisive leadership in the face of economic turbulence, the Conservatives increasingly appeared as a government-in-waiting under Cameron's leadership. Since becoming leader in 2005, Cameron had set about detoxifying and modernising the Conservative Party brand to ensure its relevance in the 21st century by focusing on environmental issues and promoting the big society agenda. From late 2007, he established a lead over Brown on the metric of voters' preference for Prime Minister (Conservative leaders would maintain this lead over Labour until the early summer of 2020). Importantly, on economic competence, the Tories moved decisively ahead in summer 2008, gaining a commanding 16% lead over Labour according to IPSOS MORI polling data. To its detriment, the Labour Party, especially under Brown's leadership, was intimately associated with the economic downturn, what Cameron and the Conservatives labelled 'Labour's recession'.

The Labour brand was further damaged by the unfolding expenses scandal, which undermined the party's historic claim of being 'on your side.' Revelations that dozens of Labour MPs, including senior ministers in Brown's government, had for years been stretching the elasticity of an opaque system for parliamentary expenses to its limits, appalled the public at a time of falling wages and rising unemployment. In 2008, a mild-mannered Question Time audience member reflected the national mood when she asked the Labour Home Secretary, Jacqui Smith, 'Why is it one rule for you and one rule for everyone else?' The scandal damaged all political parties, but, as the governing party, it disproportionately affected the Labour Party and its MPs.

The effectiveness of the Conservatives as a party of opposition under Cameron's leadership also began to have a material impact at the ballot box by this point. In May 2008, Boris Johnson won the London mayoralty and unseated the incumbent, Ken Livingston. A colourful politician, Johnson demonstrated an ability to connect with London's ethnically diverse population and his victory in a Labour city helped establish a reputation for being the ultimate 'Heineken politician' who could reach parts of the electorate other Tories could never dream of reaching. The following year, the Conservatives won the European elections convincingly and UKIP, led at this point by Nigel Farage, pushed the Labour Party into third place, by winning 2.5 million votes. On the same day, local elections in England saw the Conservatives increase the number of councils they controlled to 30 and the Labour Party lost all its councils. Such was the extent of the electoral hammering that some local authorities were wiped entirely of Labour councillors. Sensing that their leader had become more of an electoral liability than an asset, the Work and Pensions Secretary, James Purnell, resigned from the Cabinet following the disastrous results and asked Brown to 'stand aside to give Labour a fighting chance of winning the next election.'

Changing voter priorities

Thirteen years of Labour government ended in the 2010 election. As Matthew Goodwin and Robert Ford argue, '[By 2010] concerns about the faltering economy now dominated British politics but immigration had become the second most important issue for voters, behind the economy and above unemployment.'[4] In practice, one could not neatly separate out the questions of immigration and the economy and many voters believed the two were intimately bound together as competition for jobs intensified. The charge that Labour had crashed the economy and opened the floodgates to mass immigration became embedded in the public imagination and was deeply damaging to the party's electoral prospects. As a result, in the run up to the election, Brown was unable to capitalise on the main advantage afforded to an incumbent Prime Minister. The public appetite was for change.

In a post-financial crisis economic environment, immigration went from being a second- or third-order issue to becoming among voters' top priorities. When New Labour came to power in 1997 just 3% of the public cited immigration as a key issue, but by the 2010 election that figure had risen to 45%. Voters expressed concern over the lack of control elected governments had over national borders, something which would become central in the EU referendum years later. There was also a feeling that having closed down debate over immigration for a decade, Labour was retrospectively asking for consent from the electorate for relaxed border policies. This was especially true given the 1997 election manifesto had committed to controlling immigration levels.

There was also a growing body of evidence by this point that white working-class communities in particular felt overlooked and ignored in the debate over immigration. In January 2009, a report for the Department for Communities and Local government based on interviews with voters in Birmingham, Runcorn and Widnes revealed a belief that the rules were being applied unequally to different groups in society. The report uncovered anecdotal evidence of refugees being able to find council accommodation more quickly than white working-class Britons, whose families had lived in the area for generations.[5] In focus groups, these voters expressed frustration at the way the government were too quick to 'shut down' an open conversation about immigration.

The Labour leadership found itself in a bind over the vexed immigration issue. Senior Cabinet ministers in Brown's government recognised the political sensitivities around mass immigration, especially in Labour's industrial and post-industrial heartlands. In 2009, the Home Secretary, Jacqui Smith, claimed that the 'cultural and emotional impact' of rapidly rising immigration had not been properly understood and the immigration minister Phil Woolas argued there was a need to find jobs for the 'indigenous population'. In his first speech as Prime Minister, Brown told delegates at Labour conference that immigrants need to 'understand their responsibilities to earn the right to settle in Britain.'[6] However, there were reasons to believe this change in tone from the Labour frontbench would not be sufficient to address the problems thrown up by immigration. By 2009, net migration had reached 229,000, a fivefold increase on the levels Labour had inherited 12 years earlier.[7] Such a sharp increase in the number of people entering the UK over this time caused net voter satisfaction with the government's handling of migration to fall as low as -60% in 2009. By the end of the decade, the Labour brand was inextricably linked to a liberal policy of relaxed borders and the party simply could not present itself as a credible advocate for robust immigration controls.

Labour's credibility on this issue was also undermined by the fact most of the party's MPs were visibly uncomfortable making the case for tighter border policies. In 2005, the Labour Party had condemned the Conservatives for proclaiming 'It's not racist to impose limits on immigration' and associated divisive rhetoric of this kind with the right of British politics. As we have seen, there was a backlash from the Parliamentary Labour Party following the Prime Minister's 'British jobs for British workers' speech. Rather than pander to UKIP, there was a belief among some MPs that the Labour Party ought to somehow stand above the dog whistle politics and demonisation of migrants, thus demonstrating moral leadership. Given the immigration issue wasn't about to disappear any time soon and the strength of feeling it aroused among a section of Labour's working-class voters, ignoring the problem was a strategy that carried great risks.

The 2010 election

Labour struggled to respond to changing voter priorities on the economy and immigration. Brown's natural preference was to migrate to political terrain upon which Labour were more comfortable. In theory, this meant focusing on domestic issues, such as the National Health Service and education reform, where the Conservatives remained vulnerable. In practice, though, there were important reasons why this was simply not going to be possible by 2010. Thirteen years into government, Labour was no longer able to shape and influence the political agenda as Blair had done to such a great effect a decade earlier; the party's authority had by this point been severely compromised by hang over effects from the Iraq War, a deteriorating economy in late 2007 and the unfolding MPs expenses scandal the following year.

On immigration, the Labour Party settled for a vague and non-committal stance that, in the words of the manifesto, 'we understand people's concerns about immigration.' Given the party's reluctance to actually do anything to reduce the number of people entering the UK in the preceding decade, this could easily be interpreted as saying we understand your concerns, but we are not going to do anything about it. Brown's infamous encounter with Gillian Duffy derailed the election campaign in the short term, but it also spoke to a wider challenge that Labour were facing in their industrial and post-industrial heartlands. In calling Duffy a 'bigoted woman' after she raised concerns about the number of immigrants 'flocking' into Britain, Brown confirmed a perception that the Labour leadership were somehow aloof and distant from the party's voter base.

Under Brown's leadership, the Labour Party was reduced nationally to just 29% of the popular vote in the 2010 election, its lowest share since 1983. A more catastrophic result was only avoided by the UK's first-past-the-post voting system, which protected the party's representation in the House of Commons and allowed Labour to return with 258 MPs (although this was still a considerable fall overall of 97 seats).

The Conservatives won an additional 96 seats, a significant increase to achieve within a single parliament and among the greatest increases in modern British political history. Many of the Conservative gains in 2010 were seats in Middle England that Blair had won for Labour in the 1997 election, such as Jacqui Smith's Redditch constituency in Worcestershire and the marginal Swindon seats in Wiltshire. Additionally, in a sign of the growing gulf the Labour Party was experiencing with working-class voters, several former mining areas fell to the Conservatives too: Cannock

Chase in Staffordshire was taken with a 14% swing, and nearby Sherwood in Nottinghamshire fell with a swing of 8%. Nationally, the working-class vote was split evenly between Labour and the Conservatives.

Cameron's internal party modernisation was also reflected in the number of female and ethnic minority Tory MPs elected in the 2010 election. The Women2Win campaign, pioneered by the Shadow Cabinet Minister Theresa May, helped MPs such as Amber Rudd and Andrea Leadsom, who would go on and serve in future Cabinets, into parliament.

The other big story of the election was the continued rise in support for the Liberal Democrat Party, driven by the phenomenon of 'Cleggmania'. The Liberals ended up with an impressive 23% of the popular vote and, importantly, were in the position to act as power brokers given that neither the Conservatives nor Labour had managed to win enough seats to form a majority government alone. As we shall see, Nick Clegg's decision to form a formal coalition with Cameron's Conservatives would have important consequences not just for his party but also British electoral politics more broadly in the years to come.

The Coalition (2010-2015)

Plenty of commentators expected the Conservative–Liberal Coalition to last only a matter of months and be over by Christmas, echoing the tragic predictions made in the summer of 1914 about the First World War. Instead, like the Great War, Cameron's government far outlasted expectations and the Coalition completed a full five-year electoral term.

The immediate and pressing task facing the new government involved dealing with the fiscal legacy bequeathed by the previous Labour government. In the final Labour budget in March 2010, the budget deficit stood at over £160 billion, the highest in peacetime history and the largest of all G7 countries. From the outset, Cameron and Clegg contrasted their economic policies with the profligacy and recklessness of the Blair–Brown years. Infamously, a handwritten note left by the outgoing Chief Secretary to the Treasury, Liam Byrne, to his successor David Laws was made public, explaining that, 'I'm afraid, there is no money left.' Although only a single note, it represented an embarrassing concession by a senior minister from the Brown government that Labour had left the public finances in a parlous state. Importantly, the note supported Cameron's argument that deep and painful public spending cuts were an economic *necessity* rather than a political *choice*.

Nonetheless, presiding over deep cuts to departmental government spending presented a particular challenge for a Conservative Party which, despite Cameron's efforts to de-toxify the brand, remained vulnerable on the moral question of fairness. Indeed, public spending cuts had the potential to have deeply regressive effects: hitting hardest lower-income households and vulnerable people who depended most on the services provided by central and local government spending. As a result, these cuts risked confirming a suspicion harboured by a section of the electorate that the Conservatives were still the 'nasty party' and thus undoing the work Cameron had done to re-brand the party since becoming leader in 2005. It was important therefore for the government to ensure their deficit reduction plan was both fiscally responsible and fair.

Staying on the right side of the line was arguably made more challenging by the Prime Minister's controversial decision to 'ring-fence' certain departments, such as health, education and international aid, and protect them from cuts. While protecting the most politically sensitive departments, especially the NHS, made electoral sense, ringfencing meant that the burden of spending cuts fell on a relatively small number of departments, such as local government, which covered libraries, social care services and welfare (excluding state pensions).

In the early years of the Coalition, painful cuts to government spending, coupled with a stagnating economy, put immense pressure on the government to change course. The Shadow Chancellor, Ed Balls, accused the government of cutting 'too far, too fast' and thus strangling a nascent economic recovery. The nadir of the government's fortunes came in April 2012, when Osborne delivered what was quickly dubbed an 'omnishambles budget', ridiculed for, among other things, the inclusion of a 'pasty tax', whereby hot takeaway food would be subject to VAT. At the Paralympics that summer, the Chancellor was met with a chorus of boos from the crowd before presenting medals to the competing athletes.

Opposing austerity

With a challenging economic backdrop and relative safety of the opposition benches under the new leadership of Ed Miliband, it might have been hoped that Labour would have the opportunity to regroup and unite against a new Conservative-led government. This was not to be. Miliband's efforts to turn a page on the divisive Blair–Brown years proved easier said than done. Having himself served in Gordon Brown's Cabinet, alongside other senior MPs on his frontbench like the Shadow Chancellor Ed Balls, Miliband struggled to detach himself from the perceived incompetence of the Brown government and its handling of the financial crisis. The Labour Party opposed what they called ideologically driven 'Tory austerity' and argued that Osborne's cuts had choked off the economic recovery; however, Miliband and his team faced great difficulties in presenting the Labour Party as a fiscally credible alternative.

Even during the challenging early years of the Coalition between 2010 and 2012, when the economic recovery seemed to have run out of steam and stalled, the Conservative Party remained ahead on the polling metric of economic competence. Voters wanted Cameron and Osborne running the economy rather than Miliband and Balls.

In opposition, Labour made only limited headway on the question of fairness, an issue upon which the Conservatives were clearly vulnerable. In the 2012 budget, for instance, a cut to the higher income tax rate from 50% for high earners at a time of public pay freezes and reductions to working-age welfare payments posed obvious questions about government priorities. However, Osborne's arguments, that income tax cuts actually raise overall revenues (thus making more funds available for public services) and that such reductions increased UK competitiveness, gained some traction. The case was easier for the Tories to make given that Blair had made similar arguments as Prime Minister and for much of Labour's time in government after 1997, the higher rate of income tax remained unchanged at 40%. Labour's moral authority on this question was further undermined by the relaxed tax practices of the 2000s under Brown's chancellorship, in which bosses of private equity firms were subjected to a lower rate of capital gains tax for a proportion on their earnings, resulting in a situation whereby their cleaners and administrative staff were paying a higher marginal rate of tax on their earnings.

Another headache for the Labour Party was that important aspects of the Conservative welfare reform programme were popular among their own voters, in particular the principle of 'making work pay'. A range of government policies, including a cap on benefits at £26,000 per year and Osborne's plan to limit child tax credit to two children, polled well and were viewed as important in restoring the incentive to work. The Conservatives were also able to draw a link between the introduction of universal credit, which was designed to simplify the benefit system and restore incentives to work, with the sharp fall in unemployment the government presided over after 2010. A dramatic fall in youth unemployment and the number of workless households allowed the Tories to present themselves as the party of the workers, while Labour's blanket opposition to reforming the welfare system left them vulnerable to the charge that theirs was the party of the 'shirkers'.

The politics of austerity

As Vince Cable argues in *After the Storm*, the Conservatives decisively won the political argument over fiscal consolidation primarily by insisting that spending cuts were 'difficult decisions' that needed to be taken given the state of the economy inherited from Labour in 2010.[8] However complicated the reality might have been, Cameron and Osborne successful located the causes of the 2008 financial crisis in Labour's fiscal mismanagement during the preceding decade. In doing so, they crafted a narrative, which senior Liberal Democrat ministers such as the Chief Secretary to the Treasury Danny Alexander and Deputy Prime Minister Nick Clegg were complicit in, presenting the Coalition as being on a stoic crusade to undo the damage of Labour's Great Recession. The government also successfully drew a politically expedient, albeit in several respects economically illiterate, analogy between public finances and the household budget to rationalise departmental spending cuts. Although spending cuts were a tough pill for the electorate to swallow, the government offered a clear and coherent political message that the country needed to live within its means.

The failure of Cameron and the Conservatives to win an outright parliamentary majority in 2010 also had an unintended political advantage as the government went about tackling the deficit. Because the spending cuts were in formal coalition with the Liberal Democrats, senior Liberal ministers, especially Danny Alexander and Nick Clegg, were highly visible figures at major budgets and fiscal events. This made it more difficult for their opponents to argue these were ideological spending reductions and also meant that negative political attention from unpopular policies, such as the trebling of university tuition fees, was directed towards the Liberal Democrats.

Beneath the tough talk on welfare and the need for economies to 'fix the roof while the sun is shining', Osborne's fiscal response after 2010 was in fact more flexible and pragmatic than is often thought; challenging the argument that the government's economic policies were ideologically driven. Like other Conservative Chancellors in the 20th century, Osborne presented himself as a steward of public finance while simultaneously running budget deficits year on year. In 2012, he quietly pushed back the year in which he aimed to balance the budget from 2015 to 2020, taking him closer to the fiscal plan that the outgoing Labour Chancellor, Alistair Darling, had envisaged in early 2010.

Where the cuts fell was also motivated by political calculation as much as economic realities. Recognising the political significance of the health service, Cameron moved to reassure voters that the NHS was 'safe with us' and spending accordingly rose in real terms over the course of the parliament. Despite raising further questions about the government's priorities, the portion of the welfare budget allocated to pensions was protected to accommodate the government's 'triple lock' pledge, whereby the state pension increased by the highest of prevailing inflation, average earnings growth or 2.5%. This policy insulated the non-working age, elderly population from the effects of deficit reduction and meant that the over-65s enjoyed among the quickest recovery in living standards of all demographic groups following the financial crisis. Along with the protection of universal winter fuel allowance, television licences and the Freedom Pass, the triple lock would feature in consecutive Conservative elections manifestos after 2015 and was important in allowing the Conservatives to build a formidable lead over Labour among older voters over the course of their time in government.

To soften the impact of spending reductions and facilitate the transition from a high-welfare economy to a low-tax, low-welfare economic model, Osborne looked for ways to reduce the tax burden on working families. From 2010, the government froze fuel duty for every year of the parliament, at a cost of around £9 billion per year to the Treasury. The tax-free allowance increased in consecutive years of the parliament and rose from £6,475 in 2010 to reach £10,500 five years later. This policy had the benefit of pulling 2.7 million of the lowest paid workers in the country out of paying income tax altogether, while also helping middle earners with tax relief too. Although increases in the tax-free allowance were a popular Liberal Democrat manifesto pledge, as Chancellor, Osborne was largely able to take credit for it.

Like his predecessors before him in the Treasury, Osborne looked for ways to raise much-needed tax revenues with minimal political damage. As Jean-Baptiste famously observed, 'The art of taxation consists of so plucking the goose as to obtain the largest possible number of feathers with the smallest possible amount of hissing.' An astute political tactician, the Chancellor recognised the advantages of the Conservatives being seen by voters as the party of low tax. Rather than increasing headline income tax rates, Osborne left unchanged the threshold at which individuals began paying those taxes, pulling in ever more people into the higher income tax band. Freezing tax thresholds helped raising billions of pounds in additional revenue for the Treasury.

Green shoots of economic recovery
The success of the Coalition government was tied inextricably to the performance of the UK economy. In the early years of the parliament, sharp reductions in capital and current government spending coupled with soaring energy prices, created inflationary pressures in the economy and choked off the nascent recovery that had begun late in Brown's premiership. However, from later 2012, the green shoots of a renewed recovery began to emerge. The Labour Party's attack line – focusing on the recklessness of austerity policies, which had purportedly strangled

the economic recovery – was rendered considerably less effective against a backdrop of rapidly returning business and consumer confidence in the private sector after the fourth quarter of 2012. The ONS would later revise economic growth in 2012, showing that the UK economy had grown by 0.2% and had therefore in fact avoided a double dip recession. Rising property prices underpinned improved consumer confidence; the collapse in the rate of unemployment was described by the Bank of England as 'nothing short of a miracle' and increased business investment supported a strongly growing economy. A sharp fall in oil and commodities prices after c.2014 pulled inflation down to almost zero and led to a boost in consumer spending. As a result, in 2014 the UK could boast the fastest GDP growth rates in the G7 and although London remained the economic powerhouse of the UK, a renaissance in manufacturing in the North and the Midlands supported a broad-based recovery from the crisis. After March 2013, the Conservative lead over Labour on the polling metric of economic competence increased to double figures.

Miliband's pivot to the 'cost of living crisis' agenda demonstrated political flexibility in the face of changing economic circumstances and recognised that there was a clear detachment between the UK's macro-economic performance at a national level and the experience for some ordinary working households following the financial crisis. At the Labour conference in 2013, Miliband told delegates that 'David Cameron talks about Britain being in a global race. But what he doesn't tell you is that he thinks the only way Britain can win is for you to lose.' Focusing on the fast-growing precariat part of the UK workforce, who were more vulnerable to low pay and insecure working contracts, represented a potentially profitable avenue for Labour to pursue politically.

The problem for Labour was using this line of attack to construct a broad voter electoral coalition. For many households, there was a mini boom in living standards and earning power after c.2013 and the Resolution Foundation argued at the time that 'Household income has been strong...driven by large falls in inflation and large increases in employment. In 2014-15, we know that median real household disposable income – the best measure of living standards – grew by 3.4%: the fastest increase since the early 2000s.'[9] Labour were talking to an important, but relatively small, proportion of the electorate who had been left behind by the economic recovery. Cameron accused Miliband and the Labour Party of constantly 'talking down' the UK economy and pointed out that most jobs created under his watch were full time jobs. He also argued that many workers on zero-hours contracts enjoyed the flexibility they offered, perhaps as a supplementary source of income or alongside other activities such as studying.

Although the Labour Party's diagnosis of problems in the UK economy resonated with a section of the electorate, the solutions offered seemed less credible. A pledge to freeze energy prices looked entirely rational in an environment of high prices when the policy was announced in 2013; however, against a backdrop of falling wholesale energy prices soon after, it seemed damaging and counterproductive. Cameron ridiculed Labour for advocating a policy that would have 'held up the price of energy' as well as wrecking jobs and investment in the sector. Miliband's interventionist policy proposals earned him the nickname 'Red Ed' in certain sections of the press, highlighting the importance of both the presentation and substance of policy.

Immigration

The issue of immigration continued to be a thorn in Labour's side after 2010. Like Brown before him, Miliband struggled to answer the charge that Labour had opened the floodgates to immigration in government. In 2015, the MORI polling series showed that voter concerns over immigration peaked and 45% of respondents recorded immigration as one of the most important problems facing the country. The Labour Party's preference, as in the 2010 election campaign, continued to be to engage on political terrain on which they felt more comfortable, such as the NHS or the cost of living. However, as in 2010, this was not going to be possible.

In a sign of problems to come down the line, the Shadow Attorney General, Emily Thornberry, was forced to resign in 2014 over an image posted on Twitter while canvassing in Rochester and Strood. The image showed a house with St George's flags hanging from the windows and a white van in the driveway, to which Thornberry added the tagline 'Image from #Rochester'. The incident provoked a furious backlash, including from within the Parliamentary Labour Party. Simon Danczuk, the MP for Rochdale, described the Tweet as 'derogatory and dismissive of the people'. In a further foreshadowing of the problems of later years, Danczuk observed that it was 'like the Labour Party has been hijacked by the north London liberal elite...and it's comments like that which reinforce that view.'[10] Incidents such as these, as with Brown's encounter with Duffy on the campaign trail in Rochdale, highlighted something deeper and more profound that was beginning to seriously affect the Labour Party: a profound disconnect between an institutional Labour Party based in London, and 'small-town' working-class voters across provincial England and Wales. Whether senior Labour figures were actually contemptuous of working-class communities or not was in some ways irrelevant. In blurting out that Duffy was a 'bigoted woman', or sneering at working-class patriotism, senior Labour figures were constructing and confirming a growing perception that they were out of touch with the issues ordinary voters cared about.

Miliband's efforts to reposition Labour in such a way that would address the concerns of working-class communities on immigration were ultimately unsuccessful. In the run up to the 2015 election, the 'Ed Stone', which was engraved with the key priorities of a future Labour government, committed to 'controls on immigration'. Similarly, the party's election manifesto pledged vaguely to 'secure reforms to immigration and social security rules'. It was not clear how such controls would work in practice, not least given that Labour policy firmly supported Britain's continued membership of the EU. Detailed policy commitments outlined in the manifesto, including that a Labour government would extend the period that EU jobseekers must wait before being able to claim out-of-work benefits and time limits for EU migrants to claim in-work benefits, failed to move the dial.

In fact, Miliband's strategy of talking tough on immigration not only failed to persuade sceptical voters, but it also had the effect of provoking a significant backlash from within his own party. When the Labour Party began selling red mugs with the words 'controls on immigration... I'm voting Labour' written on the side, it was met with derision by metropolitan MPs. The Labour MP for Hackney, Diane Abbott, described the 'shameful mug' as 'an embarrassment' and went on to say that 'the real problem is that immigration controls are one of our five pledges at all'. The Labour activist Owen Jones was equally dismissive, describing the gesture as 'Farage wannabe mugs.' Many in the Labour Party were deeply uncomfortable making the argument for tighter immigration controls.

Rise on the right

As Ford and Goodwin have shown in their research, right-wing parties, most notably UKIP, were making significant inroads into the Labour vote by this point. The authors describe how by-elections between 2011 and 2014 marked 'the first serious attempt by UKIP to win over a financially disadvantaged and working-class electorate'.[11] Nigel Farage's appeal was based on an ability to channel certain grievances felt by a constituency of Labour voters in provincial England and parts of Wales; grievances about declining national pride, a culture of political correctness and, arguably most of all, the scale of immigration.

The Conservative Party was also making a play for small-town Labour voters. In 2010, Cameron had successfully won back seats in Middle England that had been lost to New Labour in the preceding decade. In government, the Tories began to set their sights further afield. As early as 2013, senior Conservatives recognised the opportunity to reach deeper into Labour territory in Northern England, the Midlands and Wales. In an *Access All Areas* pamphlet, the Conservative MP and former miner Patrick McLoughlin wrote that 'our party should give no quarter to media stereotypes of leafy suburban gravel drives and the "Tory heartland"'.[12] The following year, the Conservative MP Neil O'Brien published a paper on regional growth policy entitled *Northern Lights*, signalling a growing interest in the changing electoral dynamic outside Southern England. O'Brien's identification of the increasing irrelevance of the North–South political divide and its replacement with a town–city divide represented early on how serious thinkers within the party were beginning to consider opportunities for the Conservatives to reach beyond Southern England.

Such thinking was also reflected in government policy. Osborne's political and economic project for a 'Northern powerhouse' envisaged a more regionally balanced economic growth model in which the gains would be shared more widely throughout the UK. Such policies, coupled with an appeal to more culturally conservative instincts of small-town voters on issues of law and order, immigration and British values, presented a clear political opportunity for the Conservatives. The party's 2015 election manifesto stated that 'Our plan to control immigration will put you, your family and the British people first' and the pledge to reduce net immigration to the 'tens of thousands', which critics derided as unachievable so long as the UK remained a member of the EU, continued to be official Conservative policy.

The 2015 General Election

The Conservative Party's electoral strategy ahead of the 2015 election was shaped by two important polling metrics: the clear and consistent lead David Cameron enjoyed over Ed Miliband as the party leader preferred by voters to be Prime Minister, and the Conservative Party's sustained ability to remain ahead of Labour on the metric of economic competence in the minds of voters.

As a governing party seeking re-election, the Conservatives would have to defend their record in office. Ordinarily this is a disadvantage for an incumbent Prime Minister, who would usually face criticism for decisions they have taken and mistakes they have made. For Cameron and the Conservatives in 2015, the task of winning a second term was made easier for three reasons. First, the Conservatives had formed a formal Coalition government in 2010 with the Liberal Democrats, thus distributing and in some cases entirely diverting attention from some of the more painful and controversial cuts, especially over tuition fees. Both Cameron and Clegg would have to defend and share responsibility for their record in office, and the Liberal Democrats could not serve their usual function as a protest vote against a Labour or Conservative government. Second, given the closeness of the Labour leader and many of his senior shadow ministers to the Brown government, Miliband was forced to answer questions about the fiscal record of the previous Labour government in the run up to and immediate aftermath of the financial crisis. Third, the Conservatives were helped by the relatively benign economic environment. Cameron pointed towards a robust recovery that stretched from late 2012 onwards with UK economic growth strong, unemployment low and falling rapidly, and, importantly, rising real wages giving consumers greater confidence.

In an appeal to the safety-first instincts of the British electorate, the Conservatives urged voters to stick with the government's 'long term economic plan', which by that point had reduced the budget deficit by one third and warned of the risks of a Labour government throwing the hard-won progress away. The low probability of Labour forming a majority government alone also led the Conservatives to talk up the prospect of a minority government supported by the SNP. For English voters, the spectre of a weak and impotent Miliband government, with Alex Salmond and Nicola Sturgeon calling the shots, provoked an intensely negative reaction. In the campaign the Conservatives presented voters with a blown-up image of Miliband in Salmond's shirt pocket to illustrate the Labour leader's weakness and the threat of a tie-up with the SNP.

Labour struggled to reassure voters that they could once again be trusted with the nation's finances. At the Labour Party conference in the autumn before the election, Miliband was criticised for failing to mention the budget deficit in a speech lasting over an hour, something Len McCluskey, Unite's General Secretary, described as a 'glaring omission'. The Conservatives branded the Labour leader a 'deficit denier' who had no credible plan to restore order to public finances. Lingering doubts about Labour's economic policies lasted right the way up to polling day. Because many senior members of the Shadow Cabinet team, including the Shadow Chancellor Ed Balls and Shadow Home Secretary Yvette Cooper, had served in the previous Labour government it would be difficult for Miliband to distance himself from the spending decisions of the Blair and Brown era. On a *Question Time* election special, Miliband was heckled by audience members as he attempted to defend the fiscal record of the Blair–Brown years. Asked by an audience member if he believed the last Labour government had 'spent too much', Miliband stated firmly, 'No, I don't,' to cries of derision.

While Labour's policies were individually popular, they were vulnerable to Conservative attacks. A mansion tax, which proposed an annual levy on properties worth over £2 million, for instance, was underpinned by the sound principle that the burden of taxation in the UK ought to be passed from earned income to unearned and accumulated (property) wealth, as well as a belief that the greatest burden should fall on those with the broadest shoulders. This was something most voters supported. However, the optics of such a major change in fiscal policy were more challenging. The Conservatives presented Labour's mansion tax as a raid on the family home and the caricature of an asset-rich, cash-poor 'little old lady' living in a family home all her life emerged. Miliband pushed hard against Tory claims that Labour's policy amounted to a cynical raid on the family home which hard working Britons had spent their lives saving for; however, policies such as the mansion tax gave the impression Labour was the same old party of tax and spend. The mansion tax policy also reflected the Labour Party's difficulties in taking individually popular policies and packaging them in such a way as to make them a credible prospectus for government.

The 2015 election result was a disaster for Labour. Defying opinion polling predicting a narrow result in the run up to the election, the Conservative Party ended up increasing their representation in the House of Commons by 24 seats and winning their first majority in over two decades. Despite inheriting a challenging economy in 2010 and presiding over five years of spending cuts, Cameron increased the Conservative national vote share (the first time an incumbent had achieved such a feat since Thatcher's 1983 landslide). With the exception of London, the Tories advanced across all parts of England, wiping the Liberal Democrats out in South-West England. In the North and the Midlands, a surge in the UKIP vote helped the Conservatives pick up small provincial towns such as the Shadow Chancellor's Morley and Outwood constituency. In Wales, the Tories won an additional three seats, including the Vale of Clwyd in North-East Wales.

Labour fought a losing conflict on two fronts: in England and Wales the party struggled against swelling support for UKIP and the Conservatives, while in Scotland, once a Labour heartland, the party was routed by a stunning surge in the SNP vote. The Labour Party's continued difficulties winning over aspirational working-class voters was made painfully apparent by the election, and the party's lead over the Conservatives among these voters vanished by 2015: split equally among the two main parties, with UKIP and the SNP picking up the remaining 30%. The loss of 40 seats in Scotland was a devastating blow in what was once one of Labour's heartlands and laid bare the difficulties facing Scottish Labour following the independence referendum.

The Corbyn experiment

The challenges facing whoever succeeded Miliband as leader in the summer of 2015 should not be underestimated. In the general election rout a few months earlier, Labour had been reduced to just 232 seats nationally, the party's lowest representation in the House of Commons since 1987. Despite presiding over five years of cuts to public spending, the Conservatives made advances into Labour territory across Northern England and parts of Wales, winning their first overall majority in two decades. In Scotland, another traditional Labour stronghold, the nationalists won all but one of Labour's seats – a devastating loss of 40 in the space of just five years.

The election defeat not only left Labour electorally vulnerable, but it also divided the party internally over how best to rebuild support and win back the millions of lost voters needed to form a majority government. Moderates, including the Blairite backbencher and leadership contestant Liz Kendall, argued that Labour should accommodate aspects of the Coalition's economic programme to restore the party's credibility. This might mean, for instance, adopting a more consensual approach to policies such as Osborne's new fiscal rules, which constrained public expenditure over the economic cycle. Cooper and Burnham, who stood as the Brownite candidates in the leadership contest, took a similar stance and saw the route to unlocking marginal constituencies, such as the bellwether seat of Nuneaton in Warwickshire, as being through regaining the public's trust to manage national finances and the wider economy. Burnham, for instance, spoke of the need for Labour to speak to the aspirations of the 'John Lewis shopper', implying that the 'Southern Discomfort' of the 1990s had once more presented a barrier to the party's electoral prospects in the 2015 election.

Adopting such an accommodationist approach, which might involve compromising on certain values and principles, was not a route Labour had been known to willingly go down in the party's 120-year history. With memories of Blair's hostile takeover of the party in 1994 following a fourth election defeat, Kendall's frank assessment of Labour's difficulties appalled many on the radical and even soft left of the party. What is the point of the modern Labour Party if it does not oppose the Tory's destructive programme of austerity? Moderates in the party spoke in Blairite terms of the need to rid Labour of radical extremists, thus preserving the party's socially democratic, left-of-centre tradition. However, that is not how the radicals saw it. Blair was the infiltrator who had turned the party into a neo-liberal Tory-lite party devoid of principle. Their responsibility was to preserve Labour's socialist principles at any cost.

The internal turmoil threw up an unlikely beneficiary: the relatively unknown backbencher Jeremy Corbyn. Corbyn entered the contest as the candidate of the left with a radical prospectus and unspun appearance. His perceived authenticity contrasted starkly with his competitors and, crucially, the purported betrayal of the Blair years. With no experience on either the opposition or government front benches, Corbyn was able to distance himself from both the fraught New Labour years and Miliband's ineffective opposition to austerity, offering a genuine alternative socialist vision for the party. Cooper, Burnham and Kendall, meanwhile, had served either in the Blair–Brown government or sat in Miliband's Shadow Cabinet, and their sudden criticisms of their former leader seemed shallow and opportunistic. Corbyn inspired and energised the party's base and his candidacy led to a swelling of new members, who for just £3 could have a say in the party's next leader. For his supporters – overwhelmingly graduate millennials living in metropolitan cities – Corbyn was a political symbol, the ultimate principled and incorruptible politician.

If in choosing Ed Miliband over his brother David for the leadership in 2010 Labour members were expressing a desire to turn a page on New

Labour, then Corbyn's rise to the top in 2015 represented an effort to actively repudiate Blair's legacy entirely. Corbyn himself had been a vocal critic of New Labour both in opposition in the 1990s when Blair had abolished Clause IV from the party's constitution, and also in government when, as a government backbencher, he voted against his own party no fewer than 428 times. Corbyn, and his parliamentary allies John McDonnell and Diane Abbott, were robust in their denunciation of the New Labour years, arguing that the previous Labour government had accommodated too much of the Thatcherite agenda, introduced market mechanisms into the National Health Service and taken the country to war illegally. During the leadership contest, when asked if Blair should be tried for war crimes at the International Court of Justice in the Hague, he replied, 'If [Blair has] committed a war crime, yes. Everyone who's committed a war crime should be [charged].'[13] Corbynism was as much about repudiating 13 years of New Labour as it was the Conservative governments led by Thatcher, Major and Cameron.

The prospect of a decisive lurch to the left further divided the Labour Party at a time when it should have been coming together in the aftermath of the general election defeat earlier in the year. As such, from the outset, Corbyn's strongest critics came from within the Labour movement itself. During the leadership contest, Blair had advised the centrist Progress group that 'If your heart is with Corbyn...[then] get a transplant.'[14] Moderates like Blair believed Labour had been here before and saw Corbyn's leadership ambitions straightforwardly as a rerun of the battles that had afflicted the party in the 1980s which had ended up consigning Labour to almost two decades in opposition. The only result of such a radical experiment would be electoral annihilation. The former Blairite Health Secretary, Alan Milburn, echoed the sentiment, telling the BBC, 'I'm afraid history tells a very brutal lesson about what happens when Labour lurches to the left... You are out of office, not for five years or ten, but for very many years... If the Labour Party really does have a death wish, then that is the way it will go.'[15]

Backbench Labour MPs, many of whom had served in the Blair and Brown governments, largely agreed with Milburn's analysis of the Corbyn experiment. As a result, few leaders have begun their time leading a British political party with so little support and such active hostility from their own backbenchers. Labour Party rules in 2015 dictated that in order to get onto the leadership ballot to members, an MP requires nominations from 15% of their colleagues (which amounted to just 35 MPs after the electoral rout in 2015). Helped by moderates like Margaret Beckett and Frank Field, who lent their nominations to Corbyn to broaden the debate and in the mistaken belief that he had no hope of winning, he managed (just) to secure a place on the ballot as the candidate of the radical left. Against expectations, Corbyn received overwhelming endorsement from the Labour Party membership and secured the leadership with a commanding 60% of the vote.

Converts to the cause

Jeremy Corbyn's political project inspired and energised the newly expanded Labour Party base (over 325,000 new members joined the party in the year after May 2015). As leader, Corbyn inspired thousands of young people to join the Party and become more engaged in a refreshing new brand of progressive, radical politics. At its peak, Labour Party membership under Corbyn's leadership numbered 564,443, making it the largest political party in Europe. His vision for a more equal and just society, in which the political interests of the many are placed above those of a rich and privileged few, had clear resonance in the economic environment created by the 2008 financial crisis.

When Corbyn became leader in 2015, rising asset prices, stagnant wages and a public pay freeze meant millions of young people were struggling to get a foot on the housing ladder, creating what the press called 'generation rent'. Even right-wing think tanks conceded that the UK housing market was deeply dysfunctional: a small handful of large housebuilders were able to generate huge profits as prices spiralled out of control. In 2017, the CEO of the FTSE 100 housebuilder Permission was the beneficiary of what was believed to be the UK's 'most generous ever' bonus scheme when he received a total of £128 million in cash and shares. Under Corbyn's leadership, the Labour Party positioned itself unapologetically against large, greedy corporations and exploitative landlords.

In his first speech as Labour leader, Corbyn spoke of how his party had 'grown enormously because of the hopes of so many ordinary people for a different Britain, a better Britain, a more equal Britain, a more decent Britain'. Unlike his opponents in the Labour leadership contest, Corbyn provided clear and staunch opposition to 'Tory austerity' and quickly established clear blue water between the opposition and government on fiscal policy. At a time when moderates within the Labour Party, led by the acting leader, Harriet Harman, were acquiescing to Osborne's welfare reforms, radicals asked what is the Labour Party for if it does not exist to oppose reductions in welfare spending? To the delight of members, Corbyn envisaged a more democratic Labour Party in which members debate and decide policy at conference, mirroring plans for an economy and society that works in the interests of millions of ordinary people rather than a privileged few.

On his becoming leader in September 2015, many in the Parliamentary Labour Party had not changed their minds about Corbyn. This was a man who was viewed as wholly unsuitable to lead a national party of opposition, let alone perhaps one day run the country. Having spent his entire political career as a rebellious and obscure backbench MP and a professional protester on the radical fringe of British politics, few Labour MPs believed Corbyn possessed the skills necessary to manage a mainstream political party, less still one capable of actually winning a general election. The Parliamentary Labour Party was allied with traditional Labour voters in their overwhelmingly hostility to Corbyn's leadership.

Although most Labour MPs, even on the left of the party, doubted the party could win a majority while Corbyn was leader, they stayed within the Labour tent out of loyalty to the party and in a belief that his enormous mandate from the members meant it was only right to suspend hostilities and 'give him a chance'. In the early months of Corbyn's leadership, respected MPs with broad appeal within the party, such as Hilary Benn and Andy Burnham, took high-profile roles in the Shadow Cabinet. Even figures that had served in the Blair government, such as Charlie Falconer, were given a spot at the top table and the moderate MP Angela Eagle was given Shadow First Secretary of State (meaning she would stand in for Corbyn at Prime Minister's Questions in his absence). As we shall see in the next chapter, the Brexit vote in 2016 would change this. After June 2016, the balance in the Shadow Cabinet shifted decisively against the moderates as they were either fired or resigned. In their place, Corbyn appointed loyalists such as Diane Abbott and Emily Thornberry to the top jobs.

Corbyn's policies

Corbyn's victory in securing the leadership brought clarity, if not electoral sanity, on a number of important political issues after the confusion of the Brown and Miliband years. On economic policy, Labour would be unambiguous in opposing Conservative austerity. Corbyn made the case strongly for reversing cuts to the welfare budget and drastically increasing spending on health, education and local government. In this respect, his economic programme resonated with many Labour MPs and voters, who wished to see a revival of investment in public services after five difficult years. However, the policy instruments underpinning Corbynomics were far from mainstream. During the leadership contest, Corbyn spoke of the need for 'People's Quantitative Easing' to finance investment through a new National Investment Bank, and there were apparently no limits on how much money a Labour government would need to spend in the welfare system. While Miliband had been cautious and apologetic about the need for wealth and income redistribution, Corbyn was neither. He identified with the economically and socially dispossessed and saw no difficulty with asking wealthy citizens to share the proceeds of their endeavours with the less fortunate in society.

Corbyn's position on the important immigration question was clearer than the vague rhetoric espoused by Brown and Miliband; however, it was unlikely to satisfy the millions of working-class Labour voters whose concerns over the issue were, if anything, intensifying further. Like many figures in the Labour movement, Corbyn struggled to condone what he regarded as draconian immigration controls. In line with his empathy for the most vulnerable in society, he identified with the plight of individual migrants and asylum seekers who sought a better life in Britain. After all, as he saw it, it was Blair's wars in the Middle East that had dislocated these people in the first place and created the conditions that drove these desperate families into Europe. Britain therefore had a moral obligation to support them and Corbyn opposed the way the media and Tory governments villainised migrants as being to blame for the country's economic problems.

Even more controversial than Corbyn's domestic agenda were his views on important foreign policy questions, which widened further the gulf with backbenchers and traditional Labour voters. Unsurprisingly, the most divisive episodes of Corbyn's early leadership, and the ones that ruptured most severely his relationship with backbenchers, came over issues of foreign policy. In his first ceremonial event as Labour leader, Corbyn refused to sing the national anthem at a Battle of Britain memorial service and his behaviour was branded 'disloyal' by a chorus of criticism from Conservative and Labour MPs, as well as military chiefs. Then, in November 2015, the Chief of the Defence Staff, General Sir Nicholas Houghton, told Andrew Marr that Corbyn's stance on Trident and nuclear weapons undermined the 'credibility of the deterrence'.[16] Strikingly, the Shadow Defence Secretary supported Houghton's right to 'express his doubts about her party leader becoming Prime Minister', revealing the tensions between mainstream MPs and their new leader early on. Extraordinarily, in a debate on military intervention in Syria in December 2015, the Shadow Foreign Secretary, Hilary Benn, spoke in favour of air strikes against the official position of the Labour leadership. To cheers from Conservative benches, Benn argued that 'as a party we have a responsibility one to another. We never have and we never should walk by on the other side of the road... It is time for us to do our bit in Syria'. Some 66 Labour MPs rebelled and voted with the government to support British military action.

Under Corbyn's watch, the Labour Party was left vulnerable once again to the charge that it would sooner support Britain's enemies than stand up for its country and its allies. Despite his purported pacifism and active role in the Stop the War coalition, Corbyn and his Shadow Chancellor, John McDonnell, had historically made supportive noises about the IRA and other dissident Republican organisations. In 2015, in an interview with BBC Radio Ulster, Corbyn was repeatedly asked to specifically condemn IRA bombing to which he replied in the generality, saying 'I condemn all bombing... I condemn what was done by the British Army as well as other sides as well.'[17] As we shall see in Chapter 5, other 'flash points', such as the Salisbury killings, highlighted the huge gap between Corbyn and moderate backbenchers further down the line.

Moderates in the Labour Party had little patience for Corbyn's posturing on serious foreign policy questions, providing them with yet more evidence of his unsuitability for high office. Under Corbyn's leadership, Labour was not returning to some pure and sacred moral position it had once held. On the contrary, the Labour Party had a long tradition of doing whatever was necessary to protect Britain's national security. After all, it was the Attlee government that had entered a coalition with the Conservatives in May 1940 to ensure that the national war effort could be waged as effectively as possible at home. Then, after the Second World War, it was a Labour government that had overseen the construction of Britain's independent nuclear deterrent, and a Labour foreign secretary, Ernest Bevin, who had insisted infamously: 'We've got to have the bloody Union Jack flying over it.'

The speed with which the Labour leader appeared to side with Britain's enemies abroad, including regimes with deeply questionable human rights records and democratic accountability, provoked outrage from moderate Labour MPs. It also planted a dangerous seed of doubt in the minds of voters about whether, as Prime Minister, Corbyn would do what was necessary to keep the country safe.

Responding to Corbyn

'He won't *actually* win, will he?' a bewildered David Cameron had asked colleagues in the summer of 2015 as the Labour leadership contest neared its end. If the surprise popularity of Corbyn presented an immense challenge to the Labour Party, then by that logic it offered the Conservatives an opportunity to consolidate their already dominant electoral position.

As we have seen, it was assumed, even by many in the Labour movement itself, that Corbyn's leadership would cast the Labour Party into a state of electoral irrelevance as Michael Foot's had in the early

1980s. Labour would not be able to win a majority in the House of Commons while Corbyn was leader because his radical economic prospectus would repel Middle England, and working-class voters in the North would baulk at his lack of patriotism. Before he became leader, Liz Kendall warned that a Corbyn leadership would be 'disastrous for the party, disastrous for the country – we would be out of power for a generation'. Under the terms of the Fixed Term Parliament Act, the next general election was set for 2020 and would, it was widely agreed, lead to a Conservative landslide if Corbyn were still leader. Surely, Labour had scored a massive own goal.

Having just been elected Labour leader, a snap ComRes poll showed that just 27% of voters surveyed believed Corbyn would make the best Prime Minister, compared with 44% for Cameron. Just one quarter of respondents believed Corbyn was fit to be Prime Minister. In a sign of the deep generational characteristics underlying British politics over this period, a majority of young voters (aged 18-34) chose Corbyn while an overwhelmingly high proportion of older voters (over 55) preferred Cameron.

At the same time though, Corbyn's victory in the Labour leadership contest also posed important risks to the Conservative Party. A weak and bitterly divided Labour opposition, led by an individual lacking support among his parliamentary party and the wider electorate, had the potential to undermine effective government by making the Conservatives complacent and less accountable for their actions. Such complacency was evident in March 2016 when George Osborne stood up at the dispatch box to give what would be his final budget. Among other things, the budget contained proposals to make a further £4.4 billion of cuts for disabled people (known as Personal Independence Payments). The depth of the cuts and the fact that they fell on the most vulnerable in society prompted the Work and Pensions Secretary, Iain Duncan Smith, to unexpectedly resign. In his resignation letter, Duncan Smith described the cuts as a 'compromise too far' and suggested there had been 'too much emphasis on money-saving exercises' by the Treasury at the cost of achieving fairness overall. Fortunately for Cameron, at the following PMQs session, Corbyn failed to take a shot at an open goal following a terrible week for the government. As the moderate Labour MP for Barrow-in-Furness John Woodcock wrote in *The Mirror*, 'Cameron [was] a sitting duck for interrogation over the most disastrous budget in living memory.' He asked in despair, 'how have we managed to turn one of the worst ever weeks for David Cameron's Tory government into another humiliation for the Labour Party?'[18]

The politics of spending cuts and austerity was also causing the government more difficulties by this point. Although Conservative MPs largely accepted the overall arguments in favour of fiscal consolidation, the impact being felt by the communities and constituencies they served was difficult to ignore or overlook. Families turning to food banks and an alarming increase in the rates of homelessness were among the most visible effects of the financial crisis, and subsequent reductions in central and local government spending following the formation of the Coalition. Government accountability and scrutiny was also greatly diminished by the absence of a credible and united Labour opposition. As a result, the government was forced into several embarrassing U-turns in the face of mounting backbench opposition to spending decisions. After the budget in 2016, Osborne scrapped the proposed cuts to PIP disability benefits and accepted that 'where we've made a mistake, where we've got things wrong, we listen and we learn'. As Corbyn pointed out at PMQs, the fact that the Chancellor had been able to quickly row back on the planned cuts rendered ineffective his initial argument that these were necessary reductions to restore order to public finances.

Corbyn threatened to expose the Conservatives as the 'nasty party' for other reasons too. A leader of the opposition seemingly so vulnerable on certain foreign policy issues, in particular his historic association with the IRA and other dissident terrorist organisations, made the temptation to engage in negative campaigning immense for Cameron. At the Conservative Party conference in autumn 2015, the Prime Minister described Corbyn as 'security-threatening, terrorist-sympathising and Britain-hating'. Many Conservatives might have agreed with the sentiment of Cameron's comments, but there was also concern that savage personal attacks might prove counter-productive, portraying the Tory Party as vicious or at least unkind. In the debate on Syrian air strikes,

Benn began his statement by urging the Prime Minister to apologise for personal attacks on Corbyn, describing him as a 'honest, principled and a good decent man'. Rather than directly attacking Corbyn and engaging in mud-slinging, some Tories felt it best to quietly get on with the important business of running the country and allow voters to work out for themselves the risks posed by the Labour leader to national and economic security.

By early 2016, there was a feeling that while Corbyn's Labour Party clearly faced immense difficulties in offering coherent and competent opposition, the Conservatives were having more than their fair share of problems in government. As we shall see in the next chapter, as the divisive EU question moved firmly to the centre of the political agenda, deep splits in both the main parties would be painfully exposed.

4

Surviving Brexit

(June 2016-July 2019)

The shock EU referendum result in June 2016 transformed the course of British politics. Both the two main political parties were forced to grapple with the enormous political consequences of the majority Leave vote. As the governing party, the Conservatives would have to negotiate and deliver Brexit as well as navigate the complex legal process of triggering Article 50. In opposition, the Labour Party would have to devise a strategy on Brexit while holding together a desperately divided voter coalition. It is no exaggeration to say that for both Labour and the Conservatives, the issue of Brexit would be a matter of survival.

It is argued here that Conservative divides were more manageable throughout this period because the Parliamentary Conservative Party was largely united on the overall principle that the referendum result ought to be respected and delivered, albeit Tory MPs struggled for a long time to agree the means by which that end should be achieved. This advantage allowed Theresa May to establish a coherent and unwavering political narrative through her premiership that her government was working to secure the UK's withdrawal from the EU.

The overall coherence of the government's effort to deliver the Leave result contrasted starkly with Labour's attempts to face both ways on Brexit. As leader, Jeremy Corbyn lacked the political authority within the Parliamentary Labour Party to lead a soft Brexit compromise based on a permanent customs union and close EU alignment, and many Labour MPs broke ranks to advocate a second referendum to stop Brexit. The decision of so many figures in the Parliamentary Labour Party to challenge the legitimacy of the 2016 referendum result, rather than accept it and move on, had important political consequences and further undermined Labour's standing in its industrial and post-industrial heartlands.

Trouble for Labour not the Tories?

In the end it was Labour and not the Conservatives, that struggled most with the issue of Britain's relationship with the EU as it became a live issue in British politics after 2015. Internally, it fractured the party along multiple fault lines, and electorally it eventually proved catastrophic. However, given the historic relationship between the two main parties and European integration, this is not necessarily what one might have predicted. After all, the Europe question had consumed and ultimately brought down every Conservative Prime Minister from Margaret Thatcher to Theresa May. Bitter internal party divisions in the 1990s, in which Tory backbenchers engaged in a form of parliamentary siege warfare against the Major government over Maastricht, were, to a large extent, responsible for the party's electoral rout in 1997. Through the early 2000s, persistent infighting over Europe on the opposition benches cast the Tories into the electoral wilderness as New Labour reigned supreme. Such was the toxicity of the subject that David Cameron felt it necessary to urge the party faithful in 2006 to 'stop banging on about Europe' if they wanted to see another Conservative government formed any time soon.

Labour's attitude to the issue of EU membership has a different history. In the 1960s, it was the Labour leader Hugh Gaitskell and trade union leaders who had opposed efforts by consecutive Conservative Prime Ministers to take the UK into the Common Market. In 1962,

Gaitskell told the Labour Party conference that British accession to the EEC would mean 'the end of a thousand years of history'. As late as 1983, the Labour election manifesto committed to unilaterally taking Britain out of the European Economic Community should the party win a majority. However, from the 1990s, under Tony Blair's leadership, the party wrapped itself in the European flag, even countenancing the possibility of joining the single European currency in the early 2000s. As Prime Minister, Blair sought to use the EU as a means of advancing his own agenda and values on the world stage. Fortunately for Blair, Europe was a third- or fourth- order issue for voters for much of his time in office and proved to be a formidable barrier to the Tories regaining office. For much of the 1990s and early 2000s, the Europe question constrained the Conservative Party, both dividing it internally and undermining its ability to connect on issues that most mattered to the electorate. Euroscepticism remained largely on the fringes of political debate for much of the New Labour era, and benign economic conditions helped suppress voter dissatisfaction with high levels of immigration coming from the EU.

It is striking that in the years running up to the referendum, of the two main political parties it was the Tories that appeared to be suffering more from divides over Britain's EU membership. As early as 2011, 81 Conservative MPs defied the party whip and voted for motion to grant a referendum on EU membership in a direct challenge to the Prime Minister's authority. A core group of MPs, known as the 'awkward squad', which included Steve Baker, Douglas Carswell and Peter Bone, used various parliamentary tactics to push the government in a more Eurosceptic direction. Reflecting on the Cameron years, Nick Clegg claims that the then Prime Minister came to 'loathe' some of his backbenchers because of their obstinacy over Europe.[1]

For various reasons, partly including the interest of party management, Cameron committed a majority Conservative government to a national referendum on EU membership after the next general election. At Bloomberg's London headquarters in 2013, he argued that 'Asking the British people to carry on accepting a European settlement over which they have had little choice [would make it] more likely that the British people will reject the EU.' Although this move was enough to pacify many of the critics within his party and offered an EU policy around which all could unite ahead of the 2015 election, it did not prevent the rebellious backbenchers Douglas Carswell and Mark Reckless resigning the Conservative whip to join UKIP in 2014. Cameron also recognised the high-risk nature of calling a referendum on EU membership at all, not least because of the unhealed wounds in the Conservative Party. When asked by his Director of Communications, Craig Oliver, for a reason why a referendum should not be called, the Prime Minister replied because 'you could unleash demons of which ye know not'.

During the referendum campaign, the Conservative Party appeared outwardly to be the more divided of the two major political parties. The official government position was to campaign for Britain's ongoing membership of the EU based on reforms that Cameron and his team had negotiated with Brussels in early 2016. Although many in the Parliamentary Conservative Party supported the Prime Minister, a significant minority of MPs on the government benches came out in support of the Leave campaign. In fact, of those who declared their referendum stance, 138 Conservative MPs supported Leave while 185 were in favour of Remain. The reforms negotiated were deemed unsatisfactory by leading Eurosceptics in the party: the backbencher Jacob Rees-Mogg told Cameron that 'the thin gruel has been further watered down'. To allow senior ministers to campaign for Britain to leave the EU, Cameron was forced to temporarily suspend Cabinet responsibility, and his close ally Michael Gove and the Tory mayor of London, Boris Johnson, joined the official Vote Leave team.

The government's tactics during the campaign deepened further the rift with Eurosceptic Tory backbenchers. Osborne's claims that a Leave vote would immediately cause house prices to slide by one third, unemployment to rise by 800,000 and necessitate a 'punishment' emergency budget infuriated many of his own MPs. Similarly, the Prime Minister's controversial claim that Brexit could endanger peace in Europe provoked accusations of scaremongering – what would soon be dubbed 'Project Fear' by Eurosceptics.

Labour appeared on the face of it to be more united than the Conservatives before the EU referendum. The overwhelming majority of the Parliamentary Labour Party fought hard during the referendum campaign for a Remain outcome. On economic grounds, Labour MPs argued that membership of the European Single Market generated employment and prosperity across the whole of the United Kingdom, and especially in manufacturing-intensive areas, many of them represented in the Midlands and North-East. On geo-political grounds, Labour argued that the UK's influence in the 21st century is best served through close co-operation with the country's European partners because challenges such as climate change and international terrorism transcend nation states. On freedom of movement, many Labour MPs stuck close to the New Labour-era consensus and regarded immigration as an immense benefit to the UK economy rather than a cost worth tolerating in exchange for Single Market access. As in previous general elections, there was little desire to engage with the immigration issue and move to address voter concerns about the scale and speed of immigration, something that had important consequences.

That the UK was fundamentally better off within the EU was a view held by a range of figures in the Labour movement – not just the majority of those in the Parliamentary Labour Party, but also trade unions, party members and former leaders such as Tony Blair and Gordon Brown. Although Labour MPs like Gisela Stuart and Kate Hoey were vocal advocates of the Leave cause, they represented a relatively small and somewhat marginalised group, drowned out by Remain voices within the party. Just ten Labour MPs (barely 4% of the Parliamentary Labour Party) formally supported the Leave cause, compared with 218 who officially declared their support for Remain. As a result, and unlike in the 1970s when towering figures such as Tony Benn on the left of British politics were making the case for British independence from a capitalist EEC, the Leave campaign became associated largely with the right (and in some cases the far right) of British politics. Leaving the EU was conceived as an opportunity to deregulate, to reduce bureaucracy and tariffs – what some described as a 'Singapore-on-Thames' economic model. Leading figures in the Remain campaign were keen to shape the debate in this way: Nick Clegg frequently used a drawbridge analogy to compare Brexiteers to 'Little Englanders' and draw a values divide between Leavers and Remainers. That the Leave campaign lacked high-profile figures from the left was to have profound consequences down the line, as it made it difficult for Labour MPs to reconcile themselves with Brexit.

Officially, the Labour Party leadership under Jeremy Corbyn was aligned with the Remain campaign during the referendum. Given his well-known personal reservations about the European project that went back decades, Corbyn articulated his position somewhat ambiguously as 'Remain and Reform' to reconcile his Euroscepticism with support for ongoing EU membership. His evasiveness on the Europe question would continue for three and a half years from the referendum all the way through to the election in 2019.

At times during the campaign, Corbyn struggled to disguise his long-held views on Europe, offering heavily scripted and non-persuasive speeches endorsing British membership, caveated with lengthy (and often more impassioned) criticisms of EU policy. Having spent almost his entire political career speaking at marches and rallies, the absence of conviction in making the case for Remain was palpable. He infuriated his colleagues in the parliamentary party by refusing to join over 200 Labour MPs in signing a letter stating the Labour Party's commitment to the UK's EU membership. Cameron goaded Corbyn on his performance in the campaign during his final PMQs session as Prime Minister immediately after the referendum, saying, 'I know the honourable gentleman says he put his back into it. All I'd say, I'd hate to see him when he's not trying.' Leaked emails and correspondence to the BBC suggested Corbyn and his advisor Seumas Milne had 'sabotaged' Labour Remain – purportedly refusing to attend events, share platforms with figures such as Tony Blair and Peter Mandelson, and omitting content from speeches. Alan Johnson, who had headed up the Labour IN campaign, described Corbyn's efforts to promote the advantages of EU membership as 'risible'.

Intriguingly, the two people who ended up leading the two main parties after the Leave result – Theresa May and Jeremy Corbyn – had adopted similar, ambiguous, positions during the referendum campaign. Like Corbyn, May had spent much of the campaign out of sight, keeping a low profile. She earned the nickname 'submarine May' from Cameron's team, who grew frustrated with her unwillingness to weigh in decisively on the merits of membership. As a result, both May and Corbyn could, albeit for different reasons, be described as reluctant Remainers.

The Leave Result

As results began coming through on the night of the referendum, it soon became clear that the margins of Leave victories were considerably larger than had been predicted. The referendum result was a political earthquake and represented a full-scale rebellion of voters against the official recommendation of all the main political parties (with the exception of UKIP). Overall, an estimated 64% of parliamentary constituencies (403) in Great Britain voted by a majority to Leave compared with just 240 for Remain. Once the results had been counted the electoral map displayed a sea of blue (Leave) across England and Wales, with yellow (Remain) pockets in London, Birmingham and Scotland. Britain's vote to Leave the EU would have profound consequences for both the main parties and electoral politics more widely.

The Labour Party was particularly affected by the vote. We saw earlier how important wedge issues such as the scale of immigration into the UK, questions of national identity and cosmopolitanism had for some time splintered and divided Labour's voter coalition; Brexit gave expression to that disconnect. Better-educated, metropolitan Labour voters based in urban centres and university towns overwhelmingly supported Britain's ongoing membership of the EU, while working-class voters living in regional towns and the suburbs of major cities came out strongly in favour of Leave.

It was Labour areas across North-East England, the Midlands and Wales, recording large majority Leave votes against the recommendation of their party, that helped create an overall majority for Brexit. Sunderland Central, one of the early declarers and home of the largest car plant in Europe, recorded a substantial 61% Leave vote against predictions of a narrow result. Once all the results had been declared, Labour ended up in what could be interpreted as a worst-of-all-worlds scenario: representing the parts of the UK that had most strongly voted Remain (constituencies in London and university towns like Cambridge) and those in Wales and

Northern England (their traditional heartlands) that had overwhelmingly opted for Leave. In total, an estimated 148 Labour constituencies had voted Leave (almost two-third of the total), compared with 84 for Remain. The strength of Euroscepticism across traditional Labour heartlands, expressed through the referendum, reflected a deep disconnect with liberal, metropolitan Labour voters in London and other big cities.

That the Leave vote came as such a surprise to so many figures in the Labour movement illustrates the extent of the gulf between the party machine and traditional Labour voters before Brexit had even happened. In *The New Working Class*, Claire Ainsley begins by describing the shock she felt while sitting in the Joseph Rowntree Headquarters in York on the night of the referendum. She explains how 'No one could quite believe it. York had voted solidly to remain in the EU, but it was only one of two places in the whole of North Yorkshire that did not vote to Leave.'[2] This reaction was mirrored across the country, not least in Labour's urban strongholds, such as London, where party establishment figures had (wrongly) assumed the economic merits of ongoing EU membership would be self-evident to their voters. Pundits and commentators had misread the mood of the country. The Labour Party had apparently misread the mood of its own voters.

The picture for the Conservative Party that emerged from the referendum was a different one. While around 80 Tory seats voted by a majority for Remain, largely in affluent parts of Southern England, the vast majority (247) had voted by wide margins for Leave. Given this disparity and the overall electoral geography in favour of Leave nationally, the most logical path was for the Conservatives to respect the referendum and deliver the result issued by the British people. Like-the-soon-to-be Prime Minister Theresa May, it seemed that plenty of Conservative MPs had been motivated to support the Remain cause not out of a particular affection for the EU project but out of loyalty to their leader and to keep the Cameron-Osborne show on the road. This made it much easier for Remain-supporting Tory MPs to throw their weight behind the Leave result than Labour MPs, who tended to be more passionate Europhiles.

The immediate effect of the referendum result seemed to be to unite the Conservative Party on the Europe question in a way it had not been united in 25 years. The parliamentary party swung behind a shared belief that the referendum result should be respected and delivered by a Conservative government. May's swift and convincing victory in the leadership contest suggested she was the right woman for the occasion: in her first Prime Minister's Questions session, she told Corbyn, to cheers from her backbenches, 'The Labour Party might be about to spend the next few months tearing itself apart, while the Conservative Party will be bringing the country back together.'

Through the difficulties of the years to come, the Conservatives enjoyed three advantages in formulating a response to Brexit. First, respecting the Leave referendum result made clear logical sense for the party. During the campaign, both the Remain and Leave sides had agreed that the result would be honoured. Thus, in the aftermath of the vote, it was less about whether one had supported Leave or Remain, but rather about democracy – a concept known as 'losers' consent'.

Second, given that many Conservative MPs who had campaigned for Remain during the referendum were no great fans of the EU, it would not be difficult for them to swing behind making possible Britain's exit from the bloc.

Third, the electoral geography supported the Leave vote: some 70% of constituencies were estimated to have voted by a majority to leave the EU. Early on, strategists in the Conservative Party recognised the once-in-a-generation opportunity presented by Brexit to re-draw the political map and make inroads in Labour Leave areas. It was also the case that a policy of delivering Brexit would unite a voter coalition of Leave voters and respect-the-referendum Remainers (some of whom might have reluctantly supported Remain).

Timeline: The Brexit years
(June 2016-July 2019)

June 2016   Theresa May replaces David Cameron as Prime Minister and promises to deliver on the result of the referendum, as well as stating that 'Brexit means Brexit.'

Jeremy Corbyn says in a television interview with the BBC that the government should trigger Article 50 immediately to begin the process of leaving the EU. The immediate effect of the referendum result triggers a massive rebellion against Corbyn from within the Parliamentary Labour Party.

Autumn 2016   Theresa May commits to trigger Article 50 by no later than the 29th March 2017.

John McDonnell says that Brexit means Britain must leave both the EU Customs Union and the Single Market. In November, McDonnell tells an audience that Labour would not seek to prevent or delay Brexit, describing those that would as 'on the side of certain corporate elites', and argued that his party 'should not try to re-fight the referendum or push for a certain vote'.

February 2017 A parliamentary vote authorising the government to trigger Article 50 passes by a massive majority of 384, thus beginning the legal process of the UK's exit from the EU.

The Labour leadership whips its MPs to vote with the government; however, 47 Labour MPs rebel.

June 2017   Conservative and Labour candidates stand on manifestos committed to respecting the outcome of the referendum.

The Labour manifesto states that the party 'respect[s] the result of the referendum and a Labour government would put the national interest first'.

The governing Conservatives remain the largest single party in the House of Commons, but their small working majority is wiped out.

October 2017   Theresa May re-commits to Britain leaving the EU by March 2019 and tells the Tory Party conference that she is 'confident we will find a deal that works for Britain and Europe too'. At the Labour conference, delegates vote to back the official Labour position on Brexit. The Shadow Brexit Secretary, Keir Starmer, outlines Labour's aspiration for 'a new progressive partnership with the EU' based on the exact same benefits of the Single Market, and suggests remaining in a customs union as 'a possible end destination for Labour'.

July 2018   Theresa May's Chequers proposals for a future partnership with the EU provoke the resignation of her Brexit and Foreign Secretaries of State. Corbyn says Labour will vote against the Prime Minister's proposals.

September 2018   Labour sets out six tests to determine whether the party would support a Brexit deal. While the conference prioritises bringing about a general election, an official motion is passed which pledges to 'support all options remaining on the table, including campaigning for a public vote'. Starmer gains a standing ovation when he tells Labour delegates that 'No one is ruling out the option to Remain.'

November 2018 The Prime Minister returns from Brussels with a withdrawal agreement, which Corbyn describes as 'half-baked' and pledges that Labour will oppose.

Jeremy Corbyn states categorically in an interview with the German magazine *Der Spiegel* that 'we can't stop Brexit' and argues that it is important to understand the causes of the referendum result. The Shadow Home Secretary, Diane Abbott, tells advocates of a second referendum in an interview to 'watch what you wish for', as it would likely result in another Leave victory.

January 2019 Meaningful vote 1 on the withdrawal agreement is defeated by a historic margin of 230. A total of 118 Tory MPs vote against a three-line whip to help opposition parties vote down the agreement.

In line with their conference policy, Labour table a no-confidence motion against Theresa May's government to bring about a general election. The vote is defeated 325-306 and Corbyn argues a 'damaging no-deal Brexit' should be taken off the table.

March 2019 The withdrawal agreement is defeated in a second meaningful vote by a margin of 149. A total of 17 Labour MPs defy the party whip and vote against a motion to hold a second EU referendum.

MPs vote down the EU withdrawal agreement meaningful vote for a third time (on 29 March, the day Britain had been due to exit), with Corbyn calling for legal commitments to a permanent customs union. Indicative votes are carried out at the behest of the Conservative backbench MP, Oliver Letwin. Corbyn whips Labour MPs to vote in favour of a permanent customs union, Common Market 2.0 and a public vote in indicative votes.

April 2019   Theresa May reaches out to the Labour frontbench to engage in cross-party talks and reaches consensus around a potential Brexit deal that might gain broad support across the House of Commons. These talks end without achieving the desired outcome.

May 2019   European elections lead to disaster for the main political parties. The Conservatives are pushed into fifth place and win just 9% of the popular vote (the worst result in a national poll since 1802), while Labour come in third (14% of the vote).

The day following the election result, Theresa May resigns as Prime Minister and leader of the Conservative Party.

July 2019   The Labour leadership adopt a second referendum as official party policy following pressure from trade unions, Shadow Cabinet ministers and backbenchers.

This timeline can be broken into three broad periods:

Part I (June 2016-June 2017): Before formal negotiations had begun. During this period, both the Conservative and Labour parties committed to respecting the referendum result. As the governing party, the Conservatives would have to deliver the result and negotiate the UK's withdrawal from the EU. Part I culminated in the 2017 election, which significantly affected and complicated the government's ability to deliver Brexit.

Part II (June 2017-March 2019): A minority Conservative government begins negotiations with the EU on the withdrawal agreement. During this period, the Labour leadership applied six 'tests' as conditions for their support for a government-negotiated agreement. Their principal demands are for the UK to be part of a permanent customs union with the EU, as well as legally binding protections for workers' rights and the environment to be written into the agreement.

Part III (April 2019-July 2019): Having failed to gain parliamentary approval for her withdrawal agreement, May engages in cross-party talks with the Labour leadership. In May, both Labour and the Conservatives suffer heavy losses in the European elections, pushed back to third and fifth place respectively. The following day Theresa May resigns. Labour adopts a second referendum position after the European elections, although Corbyn will not say whether or not he will support Remain or Leave.

Part I: June 2016-June 2017

The shock Leave result destabilised both the Conservative government and Labour opposition. Having strongly urged the UK to support ongoing EU membership based on the reforms he had negotiated, David Cameron resigned as Conservative Party leader and Prime Minister the day after the referendum. In a speech outside Downing Street, Cameron told the country that having voted by a majority to leave the EU, 'the will of the British people is an instruction that must be delivered [and that] the country requires fresh leadership to take it in this direction'. His swift replacement with Theresa May ensured a relatively smooth and orderly transition of power. May, who had earned the title of the longest-serving Home Secretary since the Second World War, appeared well suited at the time to the task of uniting the Conservative Party and the wider country. She had supported Remain during the referendum, but not enthusiastically. May also earned the respect of MPs in her years as Home Secretary for her quiet determination to deliver results without the need for media attention or constant praise. As Prime Minister, she assembled a Cabinet team to negotiate a withdrawal agreement with the EU, putting key Brexit-supporting MPs in senior positions, including Boris Johnson at the Foreign Office, David Davis at the newly created Department for Exiting the European Union, and Liam Fox at the Department for International Trade.

The Conservative Party's relatively swift transition of leadership contrasted with the machinations in the Parliamentary Labour Party. Corbyn's perceived failings during the referendum campaign had the immediate short-term effect of triggering a massive rebellion from within the Parliamentary Labour Party. The Labour MP for Stockport, Ann Coffey, tabled a motion of no confidence against her leader, expressing 'ang[er] beyond belief' at the referendum result and suggesting that when it came to making the case for Remain, Corbyn's 'heart wasn't in it.' In an indiscreet dig at Labour MPs, Corbyn told the House of Commons that 'Our country is now divided, and the country will thank neither the benches in front of me nor those behind me for indulging in internal factional manoeuvring at this time.' In late June, no fewer than 21 members of the Shadow Cabinet resigned in a period of just three days, including the Shadow Foreign Secretary, Hilary Benn, and the Shadow First Secretary of State, Angela Eagle. Many Labour MPs had been not just surprised but also deeply disappointed by the Leave result, and Corbyn, who many already had scant regard for, offered a useful scapegoat. On 28 June, 172 Labour MPs voted at a Parliamentary Labour Party meeting for Corbyn to go, while a mere 50 colleagues supported him.

The absence of a credible alternative candidate weakened those vying to see Corbyn gone, however. Angela Eagle and Owen Smith's coup ended disastrously, with the eventual consequence of consolidating Corbyn's position in the party. In the leadership contest in September 2016, 62% of members backed Corbyn over Smith (which was an actual increase of 2%, equivalent to 62,000 votes over a year earlier when he was first elected leader). Despite his lamentable performance in the referendum, the members weren't ready to give up on their hero just yet.

The mass resignations that immediately followed the referendum result radically transformed the balance between radicals and moderates in the Shadow Cabinet from the summer of 2016. Loyalists, such as Emily Thornberry and Diane Abbott, were moved to the top posts of Shadow Foreign and Home Secretary respectively, while Rebecca Long-Bailey was handed the Shadow Business brief. The former Director of Public Prosecutions, Keir Starmer, was given responsibility for shadowing Davis at the Department for Exiting the European Union.

In the immediate aftermath of the referendum and in the months that followed, the official Labour position was to accept the Leave result and allow the government to proceed with a negotiated departure from the EU. On the morning of 23rd June, Jeremy Corbyn enthusiastically told a BBC interviewer that the government should immediately commence the legal process of the UK's departure from the EU, arguing that 'The British people have made their decision... We must respect that result and Article 50 has to be invoked now.' He could barely hide his emotions as Piers Morgan assumed in a Good Morning Britain interview that he would be disappointed after 'a bad night for everyone on the Remain side'. Corbyn's enthusiasm to begin the process of withdrawal surpassed that of even some of the most prominent figures from the Leave camp, who recognised that a period of reflection might be needed as the Conservative Party elected its new leader and the country recovered from the ordeal of the prior months.

For much of Brexit Part I, between June 2016 and June 2017, a majority of MPs appeared to have accepted the referendum result. During the campaign, both the Leave and Remain sides had promised to respect and enact the result, whatever the outcome – something that would later become known as 'losers' consent'. Given many MPs (including plenty of Labour MPs) also found themselves representing constituencies with large Leave majorities, it would have been difficult at such an early stage to have been seen to challenge the authority of the referendum result before the government had even had the opportunity to enact it by beginning formal negotiations with the EU. The huge parliamentary majority for triggering Article 50 in February 2017 implied there was cross-party support for delivering Brexit across the House of Commons. Under a three-line whip, Labour MPs voted by a margin of over 3:1 with the government to allow Theresa May's team to formally begin negotiations with the EU.

The main contention in public debate during this period was less a question of whether or not Brexit would happen (that had been dealt with during the referendum), but rather what form it would take. One could credibly argue that what had not been settled by the binary Leave/ Remain referendum was the type of relationship the UK would have with the EU outside the bloc: would the UK follow the Norway associate membership model and remain part of the EU Single Market, or pursue a looser relationship based on a Canada-style Free Trade Agreement? Down the line, supporters of a second referendum would use this distinction as an argument for going back to the people for another public vote because of the purported ambiguity of what people had voted for in 2016.

May's government signalled its intent to pursue a looser EU relationship, with the UK outside the Single Market and customs union. In her Lancaster House speech, the Prime Minister set out a 'Plan for Britain', in which she set out a priority to control immigration levels after Brexit and promised to negotiate towards the 'freest possible trade' with the EU.

Because many Labour MPs had supported Remain during the referendum campaign, it is unsurprising that opinion in the Parliamentary Labour Party largely preferred a closer future relationship – what became known euphemistically as a 'soft Brexit'. The former Labour leader Ed Miliband argued in late 2016 that the UK should remain inside the Single Market and customs union to prevent making Leave voters 'poorer... with less money for public services'.[3] Maintaining close economic and political ties with the EU might offer a means of unifying the country and respecting a decisive, but close, Leave result. For Labour, an EEA-style Brexit might also provide a convenient means by which to both respect the referendum result and protect ties with the EU after Brexit, satisfying both parts of the party's voter coalition. As always, the issue of immigration would complicate things. Would a soft Brexit compromise respect the referendum result, given that – apart from an ambiguous 'break' on immigration – EEA countries such as Norway accept freedom of movement rules? Fortunately for Corbyn, at this stage in the process, Labour could fudge the technicalities.

In principle, many Labour MPs were reconciled to the fact that Brexit would happen during Part I. Labour unified in opposing what was termed an ideological 'Tory' Brexit that might endanger people's livelihoods, undermine links with Britain's European partners and harm living standards.

There were already signs in late 2016 and early 2017 that Brexit was shaping and influencing voter behaviour. In December 2016, the Liberal Democrats overturned a 23,000 Conservative majority in the affluent, Remain-voting London seat of Richmond Park and unseated Zac Goldsmith. Then in February 2017, the Conservative candidate Trudy Harrison defeated Labour in a by-election in Copeland – the first time a governing party had gained a seat in a by-election since 1982. In opinion polls, the Conservatives enjoyed a consistent lead over Labour of 15 points suggesting that if a general election were called, May would win a landslide majority.

2017 General Election

In terms of navigating the UK's exit from the European Union, as well as the course of British politics more broadly, the 2017 election changed everything. By depriving Theresa May of a working majority in the House of Commons, the election drained the considerable political authority she had previously enjoyed as Prime Minister. Prior assumptions that Brexit would happen in some form or another (and likely in a form of government's choosing) were dramatically thrown into question by the surprisingly narrow result.

During the campaign, Corbyn skilfully disarmed May on the divisive Brexit question by stating in the Labour manifesto that the party 'accepts the referendum result and a Labour government will put the national interest first. We will prioritise jobs and living standards, build a close new relationship with the EU, protect workers' rights and environmental standards, provide certainty to EU nationals and give a meaningful role to Parliament throughout negotiations'. This was a clear and coherent policy position which succeeded in temporarily bridging Labour's divided voter coalition.

By taking the issue of Brexit 'off the table', Labour was free to focus on domestic issues around which the party could more easily unite. Corbyn was judged to have performed well in the campaign and he benefited from the election becoming more a verdict of seven years of Conservative austerity than being about his personal suitability for high office or the ability of his Shadow Cabinet to govern. The Westminster Bridge terror attack brought into focus cuts to police numbers under May's six year long tenure as Home Secretary; extraordinarily, a Corbyn-led Labour Party bested a Conservative government on issues of law and order, and even issues of national security. Given how his party was polling ahead of the election, the Labour leader also enjoyed an outsider advantage. Rather than putting Corbyn into Downing Street, a vote for Labour could be presented as a means of preventing the Conservatives from winning an unassailable majority in the House of Commons.

Corbyn managed to achieve a 40% vote share and increased Labour's representation to 262 seats in the House of Commons (an increase of 30 from 2015). The swing against the Labour Party in the North, the Midlands and Wales was contained, and the damage limited to a relatively small number of seats. In London, Labour successfully united the Remain vote and won a slew of seats, including former Tory strongholds such as Kensington and Battersea, as well as picking up the marginal seat of Croydon Central.

Beneath the surface though, the election revealed Labour's vulnerabilities. Despite the Conservatives fighting a very poor campaign in which the party manifesto imploded weeks before polling day, Labour had managed to return to where it was in 2010 in terms of seats – a modest achievement after seven years in opposition. Like many in the Parliamentary Labour Party, working-class voters had not actually changed their view of Corbyn during the 2017 election. The Labour candidate for the marginal seat of Barrow-in-Furness in North West England, who held his seat by just 209 votes, told his constituencies he would never 'countenance voting to make Jeremy Corbyn Prime Minister'. Many working-class voters in Labour heartlands might have swallowed voting for Labour in 2017 out of a belief (which at the time seemed rational) that he could not win power. Equally, Leave voters who wished to see the referendum result enacted might have felt safe voting Labour given the party's manifesto contained no mention of a second referendum or stopping Brexit.

Labour's impressive 40% vote share also did not change the party's fundamental dilemma over Brexit. In fact, if anything, it complicated it further. The Labour Party had won so many votes by sewing together a fragile coalition of traditional working classes, who were promised in the manifesto that Labour respected result of the referendum, and thousands of young voters who used a vote for Labour as a bulwark against Brexit. It was clear that some voters had sided with Labour out of a belief that the party would not obstruct the course of Britain's exit from the EU, while others had done so for precisely the opposite reason: to stop it. One group would have to be disappointed.

Although May had failed to convert many of these seats into Tory gains, there had been a considerable swing in Labour Leave areas to the Conservatives. Constituencies like Mansfield had turned blue for the first time in their history, and North-East Derbyshire returned its first Conservative MP since 1931. Overall, the Conservative vote share increased 6% (the equivalent of 2.4 million additional votes), a significant advance for an incumbent party seeking a third term in office. As some commentators have since pointed out, May's efforts in 2017 helped lay the groundwork for Johnson's landslide two years later.

Deadlock

In the UK's majoritarian parliamentary system, political parties must win a working majority to deliver on manifesto commitments and to get their business through the House of Commons. The parliament that was returned in 2017 proved almost uniquely hostile to the executive. Not only was it the case that May no longer possessed a majority in the House of Commons and therefore could not form a government alone, but she had to rely on the support of the Democratic Unionist Party through a supply and confidence arrangement. The role of the DUP posed several peculiar challenges for May's new government. The fact that the DUP was a Northern Irish party undermined the government's ability to negotiate a withdrawal agreement with the EU because Ireland and the Irish border were at the epicentre of Brexit. Furthermore, the DUP was not a national party (unlike the Liberal Democrats, who had entered government in 2010 with the Conservatives), which meant that Northern Ireland received disproportionate attention in the supply and confidence agreement: the DUP secured an extra £1 billion of funding for Northern Ireland, largely focused on health, infrastructure, and education budgets.

The close election result led to a brief period of enthusiasm for a cross-party approach to deliver a form of Brexit that would gain broad support across the House of Commons. In the absence of an overall majority, it became clear that there would need to be Labour support for a Conservative-negotiated withdrawal agreement. Ruth Davidson, whose Scottish Conservative MPs now numbered 13 in the House of Commons, told May to 'reach out' to other parties and 'work with others on Brexit'. The senior Labour MP Yvette Cooper wrote in the Guardian, 'We should set up a small cross-party commission to conduct the negotiations and have a clear and transparent process to build consensus behind the deal.'[4] The election had also strengthened the position of ministers in government keen to limit the economic damage of Brexit; the Chancellor, Philip Hammond, who it was rumoured May had planned to remove from his post had she won a majority, was reportedly in favour of a cross-party approach and a softer Brexit to limit the impact on business.

Desirable as such cross-party cooperation might have seemed at the time in principle, there were considerable barriers to achieving such an outcome in practice. First, Cooper's call for a commission to negotiate Brexit was unrealistic: the European Union has always negotiated and conducted its business with executives and not legislatures. The triggering of Article 50 in February 2017 had given the British government the authority to begin negotiations, not parliament as a whole (whose function it was to scrutinise the executive branch of government, not become it).

Second, the UK's adversarial political system, with its winner-takes-all electoral model, is not well designed to encourage and facilitate cross-party cooperation. There is little peacetime precedent of continuous and sustained cooperation on this basis in the UK. May was hardly going to invite Corbyn to join her Cabinet.

Third, whoever was leader of the two main parties, such cooperation was difficult to imagine. And given that it was May and Corbyn leading the government and official opposition, it became even harder to envisage. May was a conventional Conservative figure and Corbyn a radical from the left of the Labour Party. Despite their relative closeness on Brexit, their political differences made the space for compromise extremely limited. Besides, in the aftermath of the 2017 election it was not inconceivable that the government could at any time collapse, and the assumption remained in the autumn of 2017 that another snap poll would advantage Corbyn – who seemed as close to Downing Street as had ever been previously imagined. Far better to let the Conservative government tear itself apart over Europe than for the leader of the opposition to engage constructively with May on Brexit at that point.

In some ways it is ironic that it was the 2017 election, in which the two main parties with between them 579 seats (90%) in the House of Commons and both committed in their manifestos to delivering the result of the referendum, that ended up endangering Brexit most of all. In practice, in a winner-takes-all system, combined seats in the House of Commons make little difference. After 2017, Theresa May did not have the working majority she required in the Commons to realise a version of Brexit in her image and could not be sure her agreement would gain parliamentary approval. While the Labour manifesto claimed to respect the referendum result, the party's position was vague and non-committal, envisaging a close future partnership with the EU based on dynamic regulatory alignment. It was unlikely that an acceptable Labour Leave option would be compatible with mainstream opinion in the Parliamentary Conservative Party, which favoured a clean break.

Brexit Part II: June 2017–April 2019

During Brexit Part II, the government struggled to deliver its headline Brexit commitments contained within the Conservative's 2017 election manifesto.

Before the general election, the Brexit Secretary, David Davis, had hoped to negotiate the withdrawal agreement (pertaining to Britain's outstanding legal obligations) and a future relationship (including trade and security) simultaneously, and he predicted that the timetable of the talks would be the 'row of the summer'. In an early sign that the government's negotiating position had been weakened by May's domestic position after the election, UK negotiators accepted that the 'divorce bill', citizens' rights and Northern Ireland border would be agreed first. The UK would also seek a stand-still transition or implementation period, during which the future relationship could be negotiated and business would have time to prepare for the new trading relationship with the EU.

Importantly, the election caused a shift in the balance of power within the new government, which in turn affected the course of Brexit negotiations. The previously powerful Number 10 unit was weakened by the Prime Minister's diminished political authority and by the departure of her co-chiefs of staff, Nick Timothy and Fiona Hill, upon whom May had depended heavily. The influence of the Treasury, and in particular the Chancellor of the Exchequer Philip Hammond, was correspondingly enhanced, making a 'softer, business-friendly' departure from the bloc more likely. The trade-off between economics and sovereignty was central to the Conservative Parliamentary Party's internal divisions over how the Leave result should be prosecuted. One Eurosceptic Cabinet minister, who sought a looser political and economic arrangement with the EU after Brexit, briefed the press that Hammond was part of an attempt 'by the establishment' to prevent Britain leaving the EU at all.

The shift in emphasis of the government's vision for Britain's future outside the EU was reflected in the Prime Minister's Chequers proposals, announced in the early summer of 2018. Under the 'Chequers arrangements', the UK would effectively remain part of the EU's Single Market for goods, underpinned by a 'common rule book'. The proposals provoked outrage from within the parliamentary Conservative Party and prompted the resignation of the Foreign Secretary and Brexit Secretary. In his letter of resignation, Davis expressed concern with the way the proposed arrangements would 'make the supposed control by parliament illusory rather than real… The common rule book policy hands control of large swathes of our economy to the EU and is certainly not returning control of our laws in any real sense'. Despite a large publicity push over the summer, which included the Prime Minister writing to Conservative members, Eurosceptics within the party overwhelmingly urged May to 'chuck Chequers'.

May's decision to pursue the Chequers arrangements was a political miscalculation, though not necessarily because the substance of the proposed EU relationship envisaged was particularly damaging to UK economic or geopolitical interests. The mistake was exhausting scarce reserves of political capital seeking approval for a UK-EU relationship that was simply not available. Because Chequers was a form of 'cakeism', which envisaged the UK maintaining access to the Single Market for goods and returning border control to Westminster, it was met with overwhelming hostility from EU member states. In the early autumn, President Macron rejected the proposals at a conference in Salzburg and restated that the four freedoms enshrined in the Single Market were 'indivisible'.

The Conservative Party's divisions over how to prosecute the Leave referendum result reflected the fundamental trade-offs thrown up by Brexit. A looser relationship with the EU, styled on Canada, would meet Eurosceptic demands for the restoration of British sovereignty and political independence; however, in at least the short term it would cause economic disruption.

While May struggled to manage tensions within her party after the 2017 election (as any Conservative Prime Minister would have), she was helped by two important factors. First, because the Conservative Party was overwhelmingly united in the overarching principle that the referendum result should be respected and delivered, May could present a clear political narrative about the need for the UK to leave the EU and make a success of Brexit. Second, May could take some comfort in the fact that for all her government's problems with this issue, the Labour Party was struggling just as much (and arguably more) over how to respond to Brexit.

Wait and see

To manage a divided and restless Labour Party, Corbyn adopted a position of creative ambiguity in the months and years following the general election. It became a common refrain to ask, 'Just what is Jeremy Corbyn's position on Brexit?' It was a question that eluded many. Personally, Corbyn was clearly unenthusiastic about the European project. For his entire political career as a Labour backbencher, he had been a vocal critic of the European integration. Like his political mentor Tony Benn, Corbyn had opposed British entry into the European Economic Community in the 1960s and 1970s, and he voted against the Maastricht and Lisbon treaties. As we saw earlier in the chapter, his performance during the referendum campaign was at best half-hearted, and, according to senior LabourIN figures, deliberately attempted to sabotage the Remain cause. In an appearance on Channel 4's *The Last Leg* shortly before the referendum, he infuriated Remainers by describing himself as about '7 or 7.5 out of 10' on the EU, and added with a smirk, 'I'm not a big fan.' Corbyn's influential director of communications, Seumas Milne, was also a life-long Eurosceptic.

Despite his historic Euroscepticism, it is debatable whether Corbyn was particularly interested in the opportunities leaving the EU presented to the UK. After the 2017 election, the prospect of forming a Labour government rose markedly, and the Labour leader treated Brexit tactically to destabilise a struggling Conservative administration and sweep to power, rather than an opportunity to transform British society. It has even been suggested that allies of Corbyn were willing a no-deal Brexit outcome because the political and economic dislocation such an event would cause might create exactly the conditions in which the British people would be forced to turn to a radical Labour government and Corbyn could sweep to power. Indeed, radical socialist thinkers have long recognised that to achieve fundamental reforms to the capitalist economic model, a full-scale crisis might be needed, something the French economist Thomas Piketty argues in *Capital*. Such thinking was also reflected by John McDonnell's response to the 2008 financial crisis, when he told an interviewer, 'I've been waiting for this moment my entire life.' For Corbyn and McDonnell, Brexit seems to have been of secondary importance to the opportunity to win power and deliver a transformative economic programme.

Fortunately for Corbyn, being in opposition, it was possible to face both ways for a long period of time on Brexit, indulging in the very real splits running through May's administration and opposing every proposal her government came forward with. Optimistically, Brexit might even present an opportunity to destabilise and undermine the government as they entered what would inevitably be difficult negotiations with the EU.

It suited the Labour leadership for a diminished Conservative Prime Minister to take control of the negotiations, weakened by splits on the government backbenches. In opposition, it was possible to peddle vague platitudes about the need to oppose the government's proposals and instead call for a 'jobs first' Brexit because that is an advantage afforded by not being in government. That the Labour leadership had little intention of engaging seriously and constructively on Brexit was made apparent when the party agreed the 'six tests' at the party conference upon which a withdrawal agreement would be judged to determine Labour support. Although Labour's 2017 manifesto clearly stated that the party 'respect[ed] the referendum result', almost any version of Brexit the government produced would be incompatible with Labour demands. The tests reflected the ambiguous approach the leadership would take towards Brexit, treating it as a tactical issue to weaken May's government:

Labour's six tests

- Does it ensure a strong and collaborative future relationship with the EU?
- Does it deliver the 'exact same benefits as we currently have as members of the Single Market and customs union?
- Does it ensure the fair management of migration in the interests of the economy and communities?
- Does it defend rights and protections and prevent a race to the bottom?
- Does it protect national security and our capacity to tackle cross-border crime?
- Does it deliver for all regions and nations of the UK?

Labour's tests were simultaneously vague ('ensure a strong and collaborative future with the EU') and specific ('exact same benefits'). Such ambiguity in Labour's demands suggested to many commentators that there were almost no circumstances in which the party would have supported a Conservative-negotiated agreement. It also reflected the party leadership's strategy on Brexit – to ostensibly respect the referendum while at the same time destabilise May's government.

Few Shadow Cabinet ministers believed Labour's 'six tests' were serious. At a private meeting in Brussels in 2019, the Shadow International Development Secretary, Barry Gardiner, described the 'exact same benefits' test as 'bollocks... Always has been and remains it'. It was impossible to have the 'exact same benefits' outside the Single Market and customs union as being inside, not least because it would completely defeat the object of membership. For a time, the Labour leadership seemed to entertain the notion that it would be possible to be inside *a* customs union with the European Union while still maintaining an independent trade policy. As May discovered when she presented her Chequers proposals to EU heads of state, there was no appetite for offering the UK a tailored, hybrid deal that preserved access to the Single Market while guaranteeing controls over migration.

Asked about the controversial 'exact same benefits' condition, the Shadow Brexit Secretary, Keir Starmer, claimed it had been lifted from the promises made by the Vote Leave campaign during the referendum campaign. Such a defence was hardly compelling: the illusion of exact same benefits did not stop being 'bollocks' once it migrated from Vote Leave propaganda to Labour policy!

Although Labour's evolving Brexit position in the months and years following the 2017 election was subjected to significant criticism and at times ridicule, a policy of creative ambiguity was in many respects entirely rational for a party whose voter coalition was so deeply divided. Prioritising efforts to destabilise a weak and divided Conservative government made tactical sense and helped unite the Labour Party. Tactically, by adopting a position that was not so close to May's stance that he would have to support the Prime Minister's agreement, but simultaneously not so far away that it seemed outlandish, Corbyn was able for a long time to occupy a position that both destabilised May's government and held his own party together. Given May's vulnerability and the high likelihood that the Conservative Party might implode on the issue, it made tactical sense to adopt a 'wait and see' approach. Were the UK to leave the EU without a withdrawal agreement, for instance, then the political turmoil that followed could provide exactly the conditions for a radical Corbyn government to be swept to power and be given the keys to Number 10.

Corbyn's intense resistance to adopting a second referendum position, much to the consternation of Labour members, was a display of strong leadership in the face of intense internal pressure. This was especially true given he owed his position as leader to precisely this group within the Labour Party.

Likewise, Labour's central Brexit demand for a permanent UK–EU customs union, underpinned by environmental protections and safeguards for workers' rights, represented a sound basis for a soft, moderate Labour Leave option. A customs union offered a means of bridging divides in a fractured parliament, as well as offering a compromise future relationship that might unite a divided nation. Maintaining frictionless trade with the EU after Brexit would limit potential economic damage to manufacturing-intensive regions in the UK most exposed to the effects of Brexit, something the Confederation of Business Industry and other business organisations supported. A customs union also offered a permanent solution to the challenge of avoiding the need for a hard border on the island of Ireland, thus respecting the Good Friday peace agreement. For these reasons, Corbyn's soft Brexit compromise Leave option was supported by respect-the-referendum Labour MPs, many of whom represented majority Leave seats.

Strategically, it was entirely rational for Labour to adopt a moderate Brexit policy to hold together a divided voter coalition and oppose an ideological 'Tory Brexit'. After all, some of the most heavily Leave-voting areas in the EU referendum were recorded in Labour's post-industrial heartlands. The 2017 Labour election manifesto, upon which all the party's MPs were elected, clearly stated that 'Labour accepts the referendum result' and made no reference to the need for another confirmatory public vote. By skilfully disarming May of Brexit as an issue of contention in the election campaign, Corbyn led his party to a commanding 40% vote share and won 262 seats in the House of Commons. It is estimated that some 4 million Leave voters supported Labour in 2017; presumably, many of these voters were kept in the Labour voter coalition in the belief that their party would honour their manifesto commitments and not stand in the way of Brexit.

Labour divides

Corbyn's ambiguity over Brexit attracted significant criticism from colleagues in the parliamentary party and the wider commentariat. It became a well-known trope for Labour MPs to snipe at their leader's ambiguous stance by saying 'If you walk in the middle of the road, you get run over.' *The Economist* wrote disparagingly that 'It is a measure of Mr Corbyn's leadership ability that he has managed to take a moderate position on the one subject, Brexit, where extreme positions are popular, and extreme positions on everything else.'[5] There was little recognition of the immense challenge any Labour leader would have faced managing such a restless and divided party, or credit given for the compromise policy position he adopted. Corbyn exhausted every ounce of his political authority and capital in the Labour Party to push back against backbenchers, Shadow Cabinet ministers and party members who desperately wished for Labour to become a party of Remain. In this, it was arguably Labour moderates that were more liable to misread the public mood and ended up adopting the more extreme second referendum position to try and reverse the 2016 referendum.

Over time, discipline within the Parliamentary Labour Party broke down and a growing number of Labour MPs threw their weight behind a second referendum position. Splits within the Parliamentary Labour Party centred around differing interpretations of the 2017 Labour manifesto they had been elected on. Respect-the-referendum Labour MPs representing majority Leave seats in England and Wales stuck closely to the party's official permanent customs union position, recognising that to hold their seats in 2017 they had promised their constituents not to stand in the way of Brexit. On the other hand, metropolitan Labour MPs representing heavily Remain-voting seats had stood on a manifesto containing Brexit commitments they had little intention of following through. Moderate Labour MPs also used their advocacy of a second referendum to channel a wider dissatisfaction with Corbyn's leadership.

In reality, Labour divisions went far beyond Brexit by this point and the honeymoon period Corbyn had briefly enjoyed after the surprise election result began to wear off through late 2017 and 2018. A series of 'flash points' over important foreign policy questions exposed the yawning gap between the leadership and moderate Labour backbenchers. When in March 2018 a former Russian military officer and his daughter were poisoned in Salisbury, Corbyn's failure to condemn Russia caused

Labour MPs to round on the leadership and shout 'shame' as he rose to the despatch box in the House of Commons. In *Left Out*, Pogrund and Maguire recall a parliamentary session where 'so overpowering was the disgust of the Labour benches that Eleanor Laing, overseeing proceedings as Deputy Speaker, was forced to intervene: "We can't have both sides of the House shouting at the leader of the opposition!"'[6] Despite the overwhelming evidence that this was an act of Russian state-sponsored terrorism on British soil, Corbyn suggested that samples be sent to the Kremlin to be verified. The Labour leader's defence of the Russian government was not borne out of a particular affection for Putin's regime. Rather, his view of the world, as so often, was to side with America's enemies – in this case the Russian state. To rub salt in the wounds, some Labour MPs even praised May's response in the Chamber and Ben Bradshaw, the Labour MP for Exeter, said, 'Can I assure the prime minister that most of us on these benches fully support the measures she has announced.' The chasm between moderates in the Parliamentary Labour Party and the leadership had become unbridgeable.

Then, in April 2018, dozens of Labour backbenchers supported the government in responding to Assad's use of chemical weapons with targeted military action in Syria. The Labour MP Chris Leslie argued that 'a policy of inaction also would have severe consequences' and went on to criticise his own leader's response, saying, 'Those who would turn a blind eye, who would do nothing in pursuit of some moral high ground, should also be held accountable for once today as well.' The moderate Labour MP Mike Grapes told his Twitter followers, 'Sorry to say my party is led by a man who questions Russian responsibility for Salisbury, who rejects action to stop Assad's use of chemical weapons, who opposes humanitarian intervention and gives Russia a veto on UK action #NotInMyName.'

The withdrawal agreement

Theresa May returned from Brussels with a UK–EU–negotiated withdrawal agreement in the winter of 2018. The legally binding agreement guaranteed the rights of EU and UK citizens; accepted a divorce bill payment of £39 billion; and included a 21-month transition period during which the future relationship would be negotiated. Contentiously, to avoid the need for physical customs infrastructure on the island of Ireland and thereby respect the integrity of the Good Friday peace process, the agreement also contained proposals for a UK wide 'backstop'. Under the terms of the backstop, the UK would remain part of the EU customs union until such a time as alternative arrangements could be found to avoid the need for customs checks on the island of Ireland. If the backstop came into effect, Northern Ireland would also remain closely aligned to the regulatory arrangements of the EU Single Market.

May's agreement and the proposals contained within it provoked significant backlash from Conservative MPs, the DUP and opposition parties. Resistance focused on the proposed Irish backstop. Unionists argued that were the UK to enter the backstop, Northern Ireland would remain in regulatory alignment with the EU Single Market while the rest of Great Britain would be free to diverge thus undermining the integrity of the internal market of the United Kingdom. Eurosceptics also feared the absence of a unilateral mechanism by which the government could exit the backstop, could leave the UK 'trapped' in a customs union arrangement with the EU without legal recourse and therefore the means to escape.

The Prime Minister struggled to articulate the merits of the withdrawal agreement she and her team had negotiated even though there was a strong case to be made. This was the only deal on the table and would allow the UK to safely depart from the EU, thus minimising economic disruption for business. The agreement held the United Kingdom together and the backstop contained provisions for a UK-wide backstop rather than the Northern Ireland only arrangement that the EU had proposed. This had been a significant negotiating achievement on the British side, and yet the Prime Minister was unable to receive, or obtain, credit for it. May also failed to reassure her colleagues that rather than being a 'trap', the Irish backstop was an insurance policy to preserve peace in Ireland and was a temporary expedient in the event that alternative arrangements could not be found during the 21-month transition period. Ironically, the Eurosceptic MPs who feared the backstop most were also the same MPs who believed alternative arrangements were readily available, including technological solutions, to prevent a hard border on the island of Ireland.

May's internal party management difficulties were painfully exposed in December 2018 when, fearing a disastrous defeat on her deal in the Commons, the Prime Minister pulled a vote on the agreement to secure further concessions from the EU. A leadership challenge followed, and fully one third of the parliamentary party voted to remove the Prime Minister from her post.

Although the government's position in late 2018 and early 2019 appeared untenable – and indeed in many respects it was – the Prime Minister enjoyed an important advantage. The failure of her opponents within the parliamentary Conservative Party to remove her in December reflected the absence of credible and workable alternative solutions to the agreement that had been negotiated: it was the 'only deal in town'. There were also no obvious figures on the government backbenches to replace May, nor did a Corbyn-led Labour opposition appear to be a government-in-waiting.

Labour's efforts to bring down the government rather than address the substantive Brexit question also had the unintended effect of stabilising May's administration at a time of apparent weakness. In January 2019, the first meaningful vote on the withdrawal agreement went down to a historically large defeat in parliament and no fewer than 118 Conservative MPs voted against a three-line whip to oppose the deal. Ordinarily, a defeat of such significance and magnitude would have likely spelled the end of the government; however, the confidence motion that followed had the effect of uniting the Tory tribe against Jeremy Corbyn. After six hours of parliamentary debate, Labour MPs watched grim-faced as Michael Gove delivered a well-scripted evisceration of the leader of the opposition in his closing statement. To cheers from government backbenchers, Gove told the Commons that a Corbyn government would mean 'no allies, no deterrent, no army… No way can this country ever allow that man ever to be Prime Minister and in charge of national security'. The government defeated the motion comfortably and it became apparent that a significant minority of Labour backbenchers did not want Corbyn to become Prime Minister any more than the Tories did.

Corbyn's refusal to engage in cross-party talks after the heavy defeat of the withdrawal agreement provided further evidence of the Labour

Party's short-term, tactical approach to Brexit. In practice, there was little that was substantive in the agreement that Labour could object to. The deal included non-regression clauses on workers' rights and environmental protections. It also introduced a structural bias towards a customs union in the UK's future relationship with the EU because of provisions of the Irish backstop. At one point, Corbyn criticised the backstop as it might leave the UK 'trapped' – trapped in a customs union he had been calling for! Cross-party talks were an opportunity to win important Labour concessions on the withdrawal agreement that could be sold as a victory and one which the leadership passed on.

Labour's deepening divisions

The Labour Party's ability to offer effective opposition was further undermined by deepening divisions over how best to configure a suitable Brexit policy of their own. While the official Labour position was to advocate for a soft Labour Leave option, underpinned by a permanent customs union, an ever-growing number of MPs were calling for a public vote on the withdrawal agreement as a condition for their support. In February, seven Labour MPs resigned the party whip to form the new political party Change UK and explicitly called for a second referendum on EU membership.

Labour MPs shared a belief by 2019 that wrangling over Brexit had become a damaging distraction from important domestic issues, such as the health service. They differed substantively on what to do about it. Advocates of a second referendum believed that holding another public vote would settle the Brexit issue decisively and allow politicians to go back to talking about the substantive issues the public cared about. Respect-the-referendum Labour MPs, whereas, argued that the Leave vote ought to be enacted via a negotiated withdrawal agreement to allow the country to move on.

The louder and ultimately more influential pressure group within the Parliamentary Labour Party were those MPs seeking to push official Labour policy in the direction of supporting a second referendum. Given the size of the Labour Leave vote and therefore the electoral risks posed, why did so many Labour MPs encourage the party leadership to support another Brexit vote? It is worth pausing to consider this important question.

From the moment the Leave vote had been declared in June 2016, there had always been an argument that another referendum might be needed on the terms of the agreement negotiated by the government. Although relatively few articulated this view so soon after the referendum, the Labour MP Owen Smith argued during his leadership challenge to Jeremy Corbyn in September 2016 that 'the people should be given another chance to vote...when the terms [of a deal] are clear'. A second referendum might be portrayed less as a concerted effort to overturn Brexit, but rather an opportunity for the public to pass judgement on the substance of a withdrawal agreement. How, one might ask, could voters object being given a final say given the enormity of the issue at stake? Advocates of this course of action liked to quote the Brexit Secretary, David Davis, approvingly when he had said in 2012, 'If a democracy cannot change its mind, it ceases to be a democracy'. Furthermore, far from being an affront to democracy, it was repeatedly stated that, 'You can't undermine democracy with more democracy.'

Unlike many Conservative backbenchers, Labour MPs struggled to reconcile themselves with the Brexit vote. They did not tend to be reluctant Remainers – they had campaigned passionately for a Remain outcome during the referendum campaign and continued to believe, irrespective of the Leave result, that continued EU membership was best for the country and their constituents. Reconciling themselves with the reality of Brexit was therefore going to be immensely difficult, especially if it was a form of Brexit negotiated and delivered by a Conservative government.

The opportunities leaving the EU offered, such as regaining control of national borders, reducing the regulatory burden on business or the restoration of parliamentary sovereignty had limited appeal to many in the Labour movement. Most Labour MPs supported immigration and identified with the plight of immigrants and refugees seeking a better life. The Windrush scandal, in which a post-war generation of migrants were threatened with deportation, and the purported 'hostile environment' that had been deliberately created at the Home Office compounded a belief on the Labour benches that the debate around immigration – which were intimately bound up with Brexit – was nasty and divisive.

Opponents of Brexit were emboldened by the narrow election result in 2017 and the fragmented parliament it produced. That the Labour Party successfully stemmed the Conservative tide in the election might have given some figures in the party a false sense of security about their position in Leave-voting areas; suggested a degree of stickiness about the Labour vote. The Conservatives failed to convert target seats such as Sedgefield, Darlington and Stoke-on-Trent – all of which were held comfortably by Labour, some with healthy four figure majorities. At the time, this might have encouraged a long-held belief that while traditional Labour voters might drift to UKIP or abstain, they would not ultimately return Conservative MPs to Westminster. This argument persisted all the way up to the 2019 election.

As negotiating an orderly withdrawal from the EU became an increasingly fraught exercise through 2018 and 2019, Labour MPs might have felt they were channelling their constituents' frustrations with the government's handling of negotiations by calling for a public vote. Far from being the 'easiest deal in history' to negotiate, delivering Brexit had become a political psychodrama, provoking open warfare on the government backbenches. Between 2017 and 2019 there were no fewer than 16 Cabinet and 60 ministerial resignations. Parliament was deadlocked and seemed unable to resolve the issue. In early 2019, May's government had suffered historically large defeats trying to pass her withdrawal agreement through the House of Commons. Going 'back to the people' with another public vote could be framed as the only viable option left, given parliament's failure to reach a consensus on how to move forward on the issue.

Given the challenges of negotiating and delivering the Leave result, it was common to believe, based on limited and often impressionistic evidence, that millions of Leave voters had changed their minds about Brexit. For Europhiles it seemed obvious that the public would be suffering from buyer's remorse as the realities of leaving the EU became apparent. Economic impact assessments of May's withdrawal agreement showed that the UK's economic growth path would be far lower than compared with a Remain scenario. These assessments also indicated that manufacturing-intensive Labour Leave areas in South Wales, North-East England and the Midlands were most exposed to the effects of a hard Brexit. Labour MPs might have asked why they should support Brexit given it would make their constituents and the country poorer.

Labour MPs might also have underestimated the depth of feeling aroused by Brexit and genuine Euroscepticism in Labour Leave areas across the North, the Midlands and Wales. The Leave vote was frequently misdiagnosed as being a result of voters reacting against Cameron-era austerity or a cry for help from those who felt left behind by decades of globalisation and de-industrialisation. The implication was that many people had voted for Brexit for reasons that essentially had nothing to do with the European Union itself. Labour under-estimated the strength of Euroscepticism in Labour Leave-voting areas at their peril. Given working-class voters had been overlooked, even ignored, for decades, how would they feel if the Labour Party once again disregarded their vote in the referendum too? The more opponents of Brexit, both inside and outside of the Labour movement, challenged the legitimacy of the referendum result or disparaged Leave voters for their economic illiteracy, the more determined Leave voters became that Brexit should happen.

Respect-the-referendum Labour MPs

Some Labour MPs understood the potential consequences for the party if they were seen to be obstructing the course of Brexit. Another, far smaller, caucus of MPs in the Parliamentary Labour Party put pressure on the leadership to resist calls to make a second referendum position official party policy. Instead, they argued, Corbyn should compromise with the government to allow a deal to pass the House of Commons. Many of these respect-the-referendum Labour MPs represented Leave-voting constituencies (some of which had recorded very large Leave majorities in 2016) and feared the electoral repercussions if the party was seen to obstruct Brexit.

In February 2019, Caroline Flint claimed around 40 Labour backbenchers could vote for the Prime Minister's withdrawal agreement. In mid-March, when Corbyn whipped Labour MPs to abstain on a vote on whether to hold another referendum, a handful of Shadow ministers resigned to vote against the motion. In her resignation letter, the MP for East Barnsley (Leave, 71%), Stephanie Peacock, wrote: 'I was elected on the Labour manifesto that pledged to respect the result of the 2016 EU referendum. The people of Barnsley elected me to honour that promise... I believe the people spoke in 2016 and we need to enact that decision.'[7] The MP for the Leave-voting constituency of Stoke-on-Trent-North, Ruth Smeeth, also resigned and said at the time 'This was a difficult decision, but I have a duty to support the will of my constituents. We need to leave and leave with a deal that works for the Potteries.' In effect, these MPs were signalling to their leader and their constituents that there were almost no circumstances in which they would support another EU referendum.

The third meaningful vote
On the day the UK was supposed to have been leaving the EU (29th March), the government was defeated on the third meaningful vote by 58 votes. Some 34 Conservative MPs voted against a three-line whip and opposed the agreement (which included 10 Europhiles calling for a second referendum and 24 'Spartans'). As Tony Blair pointed out, in their bitter opposition to the withdrawal agreement – especially the contentious Irish backstop – the Tory Party indulged in 'something which my party [Labour] typically succumbs to…[which] is ideology'.[8] The labelling of the agreement 'May's deal' did not help. Those on the Conservative benches who had long before come to resent May's premiership channelled their frustrations into opposing the agreement and the Irish backstop.

A caucus of respect-the-referendum Labour MPs, many of whom represented constituencies with large Leave majorities, came close to voting with the government on the third meaningful vote. Lisa Nandy (MP for Wigan, 63% Leave) and Gareth Snell (MP for Stoke-on-Trent, 72% Leave) even put down an amendment ahead of the vote to make it more palatable to Labour MPs. The amendment aimed at giving parliament a greater say in the next phase of the negotiations by, among other things, 'empower[ing] the House of Commons to pass a resolution or resolutions setting out the negotiating mandate for the future relationship...and requi[ring] the Prime Minister to report at least every three months on the progress of negotiations.' The Speaker of the House of Commons, John Bercow, did not call this amendment, and therefore it was never voted on; however, the attorney general, Geoffrey Cox, agreed to incorporate the substance of the amendment into the withdrawal bill. Nevertheless, neither Nandy, nor Snell, voted with the government. In the end, only five Labour MPs did so.

It seems reasonable to question why more Labour MPs didn't vote with their conscience on this issue and support the government given there were sound political reasons for them to do so. The withdrawal agreement May's team had negotiated was compatible with many Labour demands and there was little in terms of the substance of the agreement that they could disagree with. The agreement guaranteed citizens' rights; included a two-year implementation period to negotiate the future relationship and contained non-regression clauses on workers' rights and environmental protections. The Irish backstop was designed to prevent a hard border on the island of Ireland and thus protect the integrity of the 1998 Good Friday Agreement; hardly something the Labour Party could object to. The backstop also introduced within the withdrawal agreement a structural bias toward a customs union in the future relationship, which was Labour's preferred future UK-EU relationship and their central Brexit demand. In many respects, May's deal was the ultimate compromise that should have united the House of Commons.

The reluctance of Labour MPs to break a three-line whip and support the government on Brexit legislation was even more surprising given that parliamentary rebellion had become habitual since Corbyn had become leader. Conventional party discipline had virtually broken down since 2015 and Labour backbenchers had routinely rebelled and voted with their conscience on a range of issues, such as Trident missile renewal or military intervention in Syria. These MPs could have framed their decision not as rebelling or voting with the government, but rather honouring the promises they had made in the 2017 election that they would not attempt to obstruct Brexit.

Some Labour MPs, including Gloria De Piero and Sarah Champion, have since expressed regret for not voting for May's deal in March 2019 and it seems there were several important factors that stopped them from doing so at the time. Firstly, and most importantly, they did not believe the agreement would pass. Because the DUP had signalled that they could not support the withdrawal agreement and the ERG were split down the middle, the parliamentary arithmetic was moving away from the Prime Minister. This in turn created a negative feedback loop whereby Labour MPs anticipated that the agreement would not pass and therefore would not lend their votes to support it, thus further reducing the chances of it passing. Anthony Seldon records in *May at 10*, how on the day of the third meaningful vote, 'A group of ten Labour MPs slipped into the PM's room behind the Speaker's Chair... Some were in tears, all were fearful, vexed, aware of the risks they were taking in supporting the motion.' They told May bluntly, 'If we can be certain the vote will be won with our help, then at least we'll be risking our careers for something, but if it goes down, we'd have run that risk for no benefit at all.'[9] Gavin Barwell, the Prime Minister's Chief of Staff, recalls how 'In the end, she simply couldn't give them the assurances they sought.'[10] Would-be Labour rebels, who had every intention on supporting the agreement, stepped back from the brink because they calculated their intervention would not make the crucial difference in helping the meaningful vote pass.

A second formidable obstacle that prevented the Prime Minister winning sufficient support for her withdrawal agreement lay in the difficulties offering assurances that would satisfy her own backbenchers, while simultaneously trying to reach across to opposition backbenchers. Before the third meaningful vote, for instance, May told a 1922 Committee meeting of Tory backbenchers that should the agreement gain parliamentary assent, she would step down as Prime Minister and allow another leader to oversee the next phase of negotiations on the future relationship. While this had obvious appeal to Conservative MPs like Boris Johnson (for personal political reasons) and Jacob Rees-Mogg (who had long grown impatient with May's premiership), it had the effect of repelling Labour MPs. The risk for Labour MPs was that in voting for the withdrawal agreement, they might be indirectly voting to put a hard Brexiteer like Boris Johnson into Downing Street.

Brexit Part III: April–July 2019

The defeat of the third meaningful vote on the withdrawal agreement in the early spring left the government struggling for direction. Passing Brexit legislation to secure the UK's legal departure from the EU had been the central preoccupation of May's government for almost three years following the referendum. In total, the Prime Minister had promised no fewer than 108 times that the UK would leave the EU on 29th March. Having staked its political credibility since 2016 on respecting and delivering the result of the referendum, it would be difficult for the Conservative government to evade responsibility for this failure and pin the blame on opposition parties. This was especially true given that 34 Conservative MPs had voted against the withdrawal agreement, including 28 'Spartan' Eurosceptic MPs.

It was often claimed at the time by Eurosceptics that the 2017-19 parliament was a 'Remainer parliament', hellbent on stopping Brexit at all costs. Although it is true that most MPs elected in 2017 had supported Remain during the referendum; there was in fact a Brexit majority in the House of Commons and a majority of members respected the Leave result and believed it ought to be enacted. Indeed, the vast majority of the Parliamentary Conservative Party, the entire Democratic Unionist Party as well as perhaps some 25 Labour and Independent MPs favoured this outcome. There was a majority for delivering Brexit. The problem was that in the UK's partisan political system it proved virtually impossible to organise a cross-party caucus of MPs to agree and deliver an acceptable withdrawal agreement that would secure the UK's departure from the bloc. Between January and March 2019, meaningful votes on May's deal were defeated by historically large margins. In April, when parliament seized control of the order paper and carried out indicative votes on a range of Brexit options, including a permanent customs union, public vote and Single Market membership, they were all defeated. There was no majority in parliament for the negotiated withdrawal agreement, nor for any other option such as exit without an agreement, a second referendum, a permanent customs union, retaining common market access or revoking Article 50.

Government efforts to re-engage in cross-party talks with the

Labour frontbench in April ended indecisively. The Labour Party continued to make its support for any withdrawal agreement conditional on the future relationship containing legally binding commitments to a permanent customs union with the EU, as well as demanding dynamic alignment between the UK and EU to minimise friction at the border. Most backbench Labour MPs, and frontbenchers such as the Deputy Leader Tom Watson, had gone much further and by this point and were arguing forcefully for a confirmatory referendum on the Prime Minister's agreement.

The European elections

The European elections in the spring of 2019 were highly unusual, both because of the circumstances in which they were held and because the UK was supposed to have left the EU by that point and they therefore should not have been happening.

The overall beneficiaries of such a febrile environment were the Brexit Party, which had been formed by Nigel Farage just a few months earlier to make the case for a 'clean-break Brexit.' The party won the election convincingly with 30% of the national vote. In second place were the Liberal Democrats on 20% of the vote, helped by the crude 'bollocks to Brexit' slogan. Voters frustrated with the government's failure to deliver Brexit by the end of March channelled their dissatisfaction into supporting Farage's party, while those seeking an unambiguous commitment to another referendum to undo Brexit backed the Liberal Democrats. The two main parties were squeezed, and Labour and the Tories fell into third and fifth position respectively.

Superficially, the Conservative Party emerged from the election fatally damaged. May had led her party to its lowest national vote share in over two hundred years (9%) having failed to secure the UK's withdrawal from the EU under the timetable she had set herself. Across England and Wales, the Conservative Party lost ground to the Brexit Party and the Liberal Democrats.

Beneath the surface, though, the Conservatives could take comfort in the fact that the message from their voters was clear: deliver Brexit. While voters furious with the government for failing to deliver Brexit might have voted for Farage to register a protest, the Conservatives remained the only party that could practically give effect to the Leave vote. A Leave voter coalition existed for the Conservative Party to mobilise, they just needed to find a way, and a leader, to mobilise it.

In many respects, the elections were more damaging for the Labour Party. Other than the referendum itself, no single event or moment crystallised more clearly the extent of Labour's Brexit divisions than the European elections. The results presented a worst-of-all-worlds scenario for the party leadership, just as the referendum had three years earlier. In urban centres and university towns, the Liberal Democrats made substantial advances at Labour's expense. In Central London, for instance, the Liberals won three MEPs with 27% of the vote, including a majority of votes in Islington (the part of North London Jeremy Corbyn and Emily Thornberry represented). In Labour's heartlands across the North of England and Wales, the Brexit Party made impressive gains and hoovered up the Leave vote.

While most Labour MPs agreed that the party could prevaricate no longer on Brexit, they were fundamentally divided about how to respond to the European elections. Metropolitan MPs representing Remain-voting seats pressed for an unambiguous commitment to a second referendum position and Thornberry told her followers on Twitter, 'I'm sorry... We should have been clearer.' Respect-the-referendum MPs representing Leave seats, meanwhile, doubled down in opposition to a second referendum and became more resolute in the belief that Labour must not stand in the way of Brexit. Lisa Nandy, whose Wigan council area had voted by a majority (41%) for the Brexit Party in the election, argued that if Labour adopted a second referendum position, it would represent 'a final breach of trust with voters' and argued if anything the shift had been 'towards no deal' in Labour Leave areas.

In July, despite the runaway success of the Brexit Party in the election, Labour officially adopted a second referendum as party policy. The pressure from within the shadow Cabinet, parliamentary party, Labour member-ship and trade union movement had become irresistible for Corbyn. It was an unsurprising, if not inevitable, evolution in Labour policy and it had important consequences for British electoral politics thereafter.

Evaluating the Brexit years
(June 2016– July 2019)

As national political parties with broad voter coalitions, both the Conservative and Labour parties were divided over how best to respond to the shock Leave vote. Ultimately, though, the fact that Conservative splits pertained overwhelmingly to the means by which the Leave vote should be prosecuted, rather than the end of whether the UK should remain in the EU or not, allowed the government to present a coherent political narrative about the need to deliver Brexit and allow the country to move forward.

The Labour Party's divides, whereas, related to the fundamental question of whether to accept the referendum result and move on or attempt, via a second referendum, to prevent Brexit from happening. This compromised Corbyn's ability to formulate coherent opposition to the government.

The Conservative Party

As the party that had called for the referendum in the first place, it would be the Conservatives that would have to deliver the mandate set by the British people in 2016 and take responsibility for its consequences in the years that followed. As we have seen, divisions within the Parliamentary Conservative Party centred largely around whether the opportunity to achieve political independence and enhanced national sovereignty by exiting the bloc should be prioritised over the need to mitigate the economic impact of Brexit. These divisions manifested themselves in opposition to the Prime Minister's Chequers proposals in the early summer of 2018, which envisaged the UK remaining part of the EU Single Market for goods and maintaining frictionless trade in goods with the European market. Similarly, the historically large defeats the government suffered in meaningful votes on the withdrawal agreement in early 2019 were driven by a fear among Conservative Eurosceptics that the Irish backstop provision was part of EU efforts to keep the UK 'trapped' within its regulatory sphere.

Despite these divides, the overwhelming majority of the Conservative Parliamentary Party were united on the broad principle that the UK should leave the EU. Most Conservative MPs respected the

2016 referendum result and wanted to the UK to get on with making a success of Brexit. Discipline within the Conservative Party was also maintained after the 2017 election by the prospect that should the government collapse, there was a real possibility that Corbyn might enter Downing Street, aided by the SNP.

Of the 317 Conservative MPs elected in the 2017 election, the majority respected the referendum result:

Conservative Remainers (3%)

Relatively few in number (around just 8 MPs), the 'Conservative Remainers' favoured a second EU referendum, presumably with the aim of stopping Brexit. Three Conservative MPs, Heidi Allen, Anna Soubry and Sarah Wollaston, resigned the Conservative whip in February 2019 to join Change UK and actively campaign for a people's vote. This group also included the former Attorney General, Dominic Grieve and former Universities Minister Jo Johnson. These MPs all voted against the Prime Minister's withdrawal agreement on three occasions.

Common Market 2.0 (12%)

Just 37 Conservative MPs voted in indicative votes for Nick Boles' proposal for Britain to temporarily join the European Economic Area and a customs union with the EU. Importantly, Boles and many of the MPs in this group supported May's withdrawal agreement.

Prime Minister's withdrawal agreement (87%)

In total, 277 Conservative MPs supported the Prime Minister's agreement in the third meaningful vote in March 2019. Among them were prominent members of the European Research Group, such as the Chairman Jacob Rees-Mogg as well as Eurosceptics such as Dominic Raab, Iain Duncan Smith and Boris Johnson.

Spartans (9%)

In total, 28 Conservative 'Spartan' Eurosceptic MPs voted against the Prime Minister's withdrawal agreement in the third meaningful vote in March 2019. They included ERG members, including the Deputy Chair,

Steve Baker, Mark Francois and the veteran Eurosceptic Bill Cash. Their principal objection to the deal centred on the provisions of the Irish backstop and a fear that the UK could remain 'trapped' within the regulatory sphere of the European Union. These MPs largely believed the UK should pursue a no-deal Brexit alternative.

The Labour Party

Labour's divides over Brexit were fundamental. The institutional Labour Party – including most Labour MPs and a large section of the party membership – struggled to reconcile itself with the Leave result, less still a form of Brexit negotiated by a Conservative government. As we have seen, Corbyn's efforts as leader to construct a nuanced Labour Brexit policy, based on the principle of closer regulatory alignment with the EU and underpinned by a permanent customs union, were undermined by the decision of many Labour backbenchers to unilaterally advocate for a second referendum.

The Parliamentary Labour Party can be divided into five groups:

'Second Referendum' (76%)

By 2019, the largest single group of Labour MPs were those who formally favoured a second referendum to break the parliamentary deadlock. While some, including the Labour MP for Tottenham David Lammy, wanted to essentially turn the Labour Party into a Remain party (i.e. use a second referendum to overturn the 2016 vote), others such as Liz Kendall, who represented the Leave seat of Leicester West, were keen to articulate the vote as being confirmatory (i.e. giving the people another verdict). Ultimately, though, few were in any doubt that the intentions of those advocating a second referendum was to overturn the Leave vote in 2016; supporters of another public vote were no friends of Brexit or the cause of the UK leaving the EU.

In February 2019, a small caucus of backbench Labour MPs resigned the party whip to form a new political party, Change UK. These MPs were moderate Remainers, such as Chris Leslie, Chuka Umunna and Luciana Berger, who abandoned Labour over issues of anti-Semitism, Corbyn's leadership and to forcefully make the case for a second EU referendum.

In the indicative votes in March 2019, 198 Labour MPs voted for Margaret Beckett's proposal for a public vote on the withdrawal agreement that had been negotiated with the EU. Labour MPs representing seats in heavily urbanised areas such as London, or in university towns, needed not fear the repercussions of such a Brexit policy. On the contrary, in some of these constituencies, they might have worried that Labour was not being unambiguously Remain enough; the Liberal Democrat and Green parties were both strongly committed to a second referendum position, potentially outflanking Labour on this issue.

'Ambiguous on Brexit' (~20%)

Some Labour MPs, many of whom represented seats with large Leave majorities, took an ambiguous position on Brexit, neither explicitly supporting the withdrawal agreements brought before the House of Commons in meaningful votes by Theresa May and Boris Johnson, nor throwing themselves behind a second referendum. Like almost all their colleagues they opposed a no-deal but were not willing to vote for a deal either, and these MPs were not signatories to the letters delivered to Corbyn by the 'MPs for a deal' group.

A number of senior figures within the Parliamentary Labour Party, including the party's former leader Ed Miliband and former Shadow Home Secretary Yvette Cooper, can be categorised in this group. Miliband opposed May's withdrawal agreement on all three occasions and argued that a public vote could be needed as 'a last resort'.[11] Miliband's Doncaster North constituency recorded among the highest Leave votes in the country (72%). Cooper showed similar ambiguity on Brexit, neither voting for a withdrawal agreement nor explicitly advocating another referendum. Like Miliband, Cooper represented a constituency with a large Leave vote (Normanton, Pontefract and Castleford, 69%).

'Labour MPs for a deal' (8%)

The next group of Labour MPs were those who favoured an orderly exit from the EU and respected the result of the 2016 referendum but did not vote with May's government in meaningful votes on the withdrawal agreement.

These MPs explicitly opposed a second referendum, arguing that it would be divisive and would not allow the country to move forward. In a letter to Corbyn in April 2019, MPs from this group urged the Labour leader to engage in cross-party talks to reach a deal because 'Delaying for many months in the hope of a second referendum will simply divide the country further and add uncertainty for business.' Many of these MPs became members of a formal cross-party group called 'MPs for a deal', which was formed in September 2019 and would go on and signal their support for Boris Johnson's renegotiated withdrawal agreement in October.

This caucus consisted largely of Labour MPs who represented Leave seats in the North of England, the Midlands and Wales, such as Melanie Onn (MP for Great Grimsby, Leave 71%), Laura Smith (MP for Crewe and Nantwich, Leave 60%) and Emma Lewell-Buck (MP for South Shields, 62% Leave).

'Respect the Referendum Remainers' (2%)

The next group of Labour MPs, who were also relatively few in number, were those who respected the result of the referendum and were willing to put this into practice by voting with the Conservative government to deliver Brexit. Having themselves campaigned for Remain, they believed the best course forward for the UK was a negotiated exit from the EU through a withdrawal agreement. Their commitment to achieving this end was demonstrated by their willingness to defy a three-line party whip and vote with the government in one or more of the meaningful votes on the withdrawal agreement brought before the Commons by Theresa May in early 2019.

Of these, the former Europe Minister and MP for Don Valley, Caroline Flint, was perhaps the most vocal. Her constituency recorded a 68% Leave vote in the referendum. The others were Kevin Barron, the long-standing MP for Rother Valley (67% Leave), who voted for the Prime Minister's Withdrawal Agreement on all three occasions, and Rosie Cooper, the MP for West Lancashire (55% Leave), who voted with the government on the third meaningful vote. However, not all of the MPs in this cohort represented Leave seats. The MP for Poplar and Limehouse

(66% Remain), Jim Fitzpatrick, voted for the Prime Minister's withdrawal agreement on the third meaningful vote in March 2019.

In the third and final meaningful vote on the May deal, which was held on 29 March 2019 (the date legally Britain had been supposed to leave), just five Labour MPs walked through the division lobbies with the government and broke a three-line whip.

'Avowedly Eurosceptic' (2%)

The final, relatively small group in the Parliamentary Labour Party, were those Eurosceptic MPs who had actively campaigned for Leave during the 2016 referendum. The official Labour Leave group in 2016 had been led by the relatively unknown MPs Graham Stringer, Kelvin Hopkins and Roger Godsiff. However, this caucus also contained better-known backbenchers, such as the MP for Birkenhead, Frank Field, the veteran MP for Bolsover, Dennis Skinner, and Gisela Stuart, the chair of Vote Leave. Few in number, these MPs were closer to traditional Labour voters on a range of issues, not merely in their belief in Britain's place outside the EU, but also on immigration policy. Many of these MPs came from a different tradition of Labour politics to careerists of the Blair and Miliband years. Dennis Skinner, for instance, had been a miner in Chesterfield before representing the seat of Bolsover for 49 years.

In response to Brexit, almost all of these MPs were committed to delivering the Leave result and some would go on to vote with the government and help facilitate Britain's exit from the EU. In a customs union debate in 2018, Kate Hoey, John Mann, Graham Stringer and Frank Field voted with the government. During the meaningful votes on the EU withdrawal agreement in early 2019, Field and Mann voted with the government.

Where did it all go wrong for Labour?

In three years, between June 2016 and July 2019, the Labour Party's official Brexit position shifted dramatically. In the immediate aftermath of the Leave vote, Corbyn called for the government to trigger Article 50 and the vast majority of the Parliamentary Labour Party respected the referendum. The debate at the time largely centred on the question of what type of relationship the UK should form with the EU, rather than whether the UK should leave. Following the close 2017 election result, a growing number of Labour MPs seized the opportunity to make the case for another referendum with the aim of stopping Brexit. Eventually, despite fierce resistance, the Labour leadership succumbed to pressure from backbenchers and after July 2019 argued in favour of public vote, with a Labour-negotiated Leave option and Remain on the ballot.

Appraisals of the Labour Party's response to Brexit have been characterised by extremes. On the one hand, it is sometimes suggested that *if only* the leadership had reached a clearer policy position, such as an unambiguous second referendum Remain position, sooner, then the electorate would have rewarded the party's clarity (the silver bullet thesis). On the other hand, it is possible to regard Labour's difficulties with Brexit as being the product of a divided national voter coalition, a problem for which there were no easy answers available (the inevitability thesis). In practice, neither of these positions are satisfactory.

The silver bullet thesis is, for several reasons, disingenuous. It is not clear how a moderate leader, such as Owen Smith, positioning Labour as an unambiguous Remain party, could have better managed the difficulties thrown up by Brexit. Tony Blair has claimed that 'if the Labour Party had taken a strong position on Brexit…[which stated that] if they [the government] come up with a bad agreement, we're going to say that you put it back to the people. If we'd said that right from the beginning we'd have got through it.'[12] It is impossible to know whether this is true. However, given the strength of Euroscepticism in Labour Leave areas, it would have been difficult to have challenged the authority of the 2016 referendum result so soon after it had been announced.

Equally, though, the inevitability thesis, which implies that the Brexit vote made Labour's electoral annihilation unpreventable, suffers limitations too. There were several important contingencies in the years following the referendum that could have brought about a significantly different outcome. Had the Labour leadership engaged constructively in cross-party talks, for instance, then Corbyn could have claimed credit for winning concessions on the withdrawal agreement on issues of workers' rights, environmental protections or trade.

Alternatively, had a caucus of 'respect-the-referendum' Labour MPs chosen to support the third meaningful vote on the withdrawal agreement in March 2019 and it had passed into UK legislation, then the process of Britain's exit from the EU would have been thrown in a different direction, as well as the political dynamic within Britain's domestic political system. The Labour Party would have been well positioned to push for an early general election. Such an election, with Phase I of Brexit 'done', could have been used as a democratic mandate for negotiations on the UK's future relationship with the EU – with the Labour Party perhaps standing on a manifesto committed to a permanent customs union and the Tories advocating a looser arrangement via a Free Trade Agreement.

For several reasons, such circumstances would have been politically disadvantageous to the Conservatives.

First, it would have made it more difficult for the Conservatives to convert Labour Leave voters in the election because the issue of Brexit Phase I would have been settled and the UK would have legally left the EU. Labour MPs in Leave seats who had voted with the May government on the third withdrawal agreement could claim they had honoured their 2017 election manifesto promises, and not stood in the way of Brexit. The circumstances in which the election would eventually be fought – with Brexit Phase I incomplete or still to be resolved – were immensely important. In this an analogy can be drawn to the 1945 general election, in which Churchill's Conservative Party was roundly defeated by Attlee. Had the election been held with the Second World War still being waged and not 'done', voters might have been inclined to vote for Churchill and the Tories. Instead, the electorate was casting its vote after the war had ended, so it voted for the party better placed to 'win the peace'. The electorate does not use elections to express gratitude for what politicians have done in preceding years, it takes what is given and looks forward to who can give it more of the things it wants.

Second, Corbyn could have argued that he had done everything in his power to prevent the May deal from passing the Commons, allowing him to save face with the Europhile membership. However, with Phase I of Brexit settled, he could make an argument for a longer transition period, a customs union and single market alignment. He might also have been better able to pivot to important domestic issues, such as the National Health Service, on which the Tories would be more vulnerable.

Third, if May's deal had narrowly gained parliamentary approval with a handful of Labour votes, it is conceivable that the provisions of the Irish backstop would have split the Conservative Party.

It is ironic, then, that Labour MPs who might have been minded to vote with May's government in spring 2019 did not do so for partisan reasons, and to avoid the perception that they were bailing out the Conservatives. However, as we shall see in the next chapter, they helped create the conditions in which Boris Johnson could come to power and win a big parliamentary majority with Brexit undelivered.

5

End Game

(July-December 2019)

Boris Johnson's election by party members as Conservative leader and therefore British Prime Minister in July 2019 came at a time of crisis for the Conservative Party. The failure of the May government to secure the UK's exit from the EU on schedule, coupled with the unwillingness of parliament to countenance a no-deal exit or for the EU to consider re-opening the withdrawal agreement, created a paralysis. Blame for this failure was laid firmly with the government itself by voters and in the European elections the Conservatives won barely 9% of the national vote share and finished in fifth place. In the immediate aftermath of those elections, the Brexit Party and Liberal Democrats were leading in a series of shock national polls – the first time in recorded history that two political parties had come ahead of the Conservatives and Labour.

From the moment Johnson entered Number 10, his government's expressed aim was to regain the initiative on Brexit. In his first address to the nation as Prime Minister, he acknowledged the need to 'fulfil the repeated promises of parliament to the people and come out of the EU on October 31… No ifs or buts'.

In a sign that his government's domestic policy programme would mark a decisive shift from that of predecessors, the Prime Minister promised to 'make your streets safer...and begin with another 20,000 police on the street'. He also committed to 'start [work] this week with 20 new hospital upgrades' and pledged to 'level up per pupil funding in primary and secondary schools.' The speech was littered with active verbs and reflected a sense of Johnson's urgency to deliver on several key policy priorities. As a result, the 2019 election campaign *de facto* began in July, and one could argue that the starting gun of the campaign was fired on the steps of Downing Street when Johnson set out the ambitions of the new government.

This chapter begins at a time when the Conservative Party seemed to be in total disarray having won the support of just 9% of voters in the European election and ends six months later with Johnson winning for his party its largest parliamentary majority in a generation with 44% of the national vote.

Two massive and interdependent tasks were assigned to Johnson when he became Conservative Party leader: to keep Nigel Farage 'down' and to keep Jeremy Corbyn 'out'. The first required the Prime Minister to manage the nascent threat posed on the Conservatives' right flank by Farage's Brexit Party, which would need to be strangled in the cradle to restore the Conservative Party's electoral position. As we have seen, the Brexit Party won millions of votes in the European elections, including across traditionally Conservative-voting parts of Southern and Eastern England, as well as battering the Labour Party in its Northern and Welsh heartlands (parts of the country the Conservatives would need to win over in the event of an early general election). If the Brexit Party could be reduced to the low single digits in opinion polls, it would be possible to complete the second task: preventing Corbyn from entering Downing Street as Prime Minister. The route to Conservative victory in an imminent general election would, as Johnson and his team understood, be through uniting the Leave vote under a single banner.

The nature of these formidable tasks helps explain in large part why Johnson succeeded so convincingly in the party leadership contest, despite the suspicion and sometimes active hostility he aroused among many

Conservative backbenchers. Having been one of the leading figures in the 2016 Vote Leave campaign, Johnson was well positioned to restore Conservative credibility as the party to deliver Brexit. His unique personal and political brand also suggested he might be able to succeed where his predecessor had failed and in unlocking the parliamentary stalemate over Brexit. Johnson's credentials as the ultimate 'Heineken politician', who could reach sections of the electorate other Conservatives would struggle to reach, had been established in 2008 and 2012 as the twice-elected mayor of London in a Labour city, and made him a potential asset to the party. During the leadership contest, three 'rising stars' in the Parliamentary Conservative Party – Oliver Dowden, Rishi Sunak and Robert Jenrick – intervened to endorse Johnson's bid. In an article entitled 'The Tories are in deep peril, only Boris Johnson can save us', they wrote that 'these are not normal times, and we need a leader who can engage everywhere, energetically advocate our cause and win people over. No Conservative is better placed to do this than Boris Johnson. He will take the fight to our opponents – Farage and Corbyn – and we will win.'[1] Their endorsement has since been considered pivotal in unlocking the support of wavering Conservative MPs, thus enabling Johnson to overcome the most formidable obstacle he faced to becoming leader. The Conservative Parliamentary Party, as so often in history, prioritised the electoral demands of the time over personal loyalty to any one leadership candidate.

Johnson's official campaign film demonstrated an astute under-standing of what was needed to rescue the Conservative Party from its predicament and set out his priorities were he to become Prime Minister. He was filmed speaking to a wide range of voters about restoring police stop-and-search powers to address spiralling knife crime in the Capital, the urgent need to deliver the referendum result and funding for the NHS and the education system. One voter, who confessed they would not ordinarily vote Conservative, was asked by Johnson whether she 'would consider voting for me', to which she replied affirmatively.

As Prime Minister, Johnson's determination to deliver the result of the referendum and ensure the UK's departure from the European Union by October 2019 was *the* central policy of his new government. To restore collective Cabinet responsibility and discipline in the parliamentary party, all new ministers signed up to the Prime Minister's pledge that the UK would leave the EU with or without an agreement by October. Prominent Eurosceptics were given big portfolios, such as the Home Secretary, Priti Patel (one of a handful of Tory Spartans who had voted against May's withdrawal agreement on the third meaningful vote in March), and the Foreign Secretary Dominic Raab, who, during the party leadership contest, had refused to rule out proroguing parliament if necessary to deliver Brexit. The Chancellor of the Duchy of Lancaster, Michael Gove, was given responsibility for handling no-deal preparations and chaired a daily Brexit Cabinet committee to this end, while the enigmatic figure of Dominic Cummings, who was credited for pioneering the successful Leave campaign in 2016, was brought in as chief adviser to the Prime Minister, along with other Vote Leave alumni from the referendum.

Although the government's Brexit stance benefited from being clear, unambiguous and above all easily communicated to the electorate, such a strategy was not without risks. Rumours that Johnson was not seriously engaging in negotiations with the European Union and, under Cumming's advice, was pursuing a no-deal exit, unnerved colleagues in the Conservative Parliamentary Party. In the summer, the popular and charismatic Scottish Conservative leader, Ruth Davidson, resigned, surprisingly. While the official stated reason for Davidson's departure was to spend more time with her young family; few were in any doubt, giving the timing, that the Prime Minister's Brexit policies had played a role in driving her decision to step down. Other Brexit 'doves' in Johnson's Cabinet were also placed on resignation watch by journalists, including the Work and Pensions Secretary Amber Rudd, who, during the 2016 referendum campaign, had infamously described Johnson as 'the life and soul of the party...but not the man you want driving you home at the end of the evening'. The Prime Minister's brother, Jo Johnson, who had campaigned for a People's Vote since resigning as a minister from May's government a year earlier, and the Culture Secretary, Nicky Morgan, were both also thought to be close to resigning.

In a sign of the government's determination to deliver on its Brexit commitments, parliament was prorogued in September on Johnson's advice. This was a controversial and provocative move, which critics of the

159

government dismissed as at best reckless and at worst unconstitutional. It was widely believed the move had been lifted directly from the Cummings' playbook.

There were several important reasons why Johnson might want to marginalise the role of parliament at this time. First, prorogation aimed at signalling to EU negotiators that parliament would not stand in the way of Brexit and force a delay to Article 50 as it had in the early Spring, thus strengthening the UK's negotiating position. Second, it demonstrated that the government was doing everything within its power to deliver the referendum result, thereby countering the threat posed by Farage and the Brexit Party. Third, prorogation was designed to expose the domestic enemies of Brexit, especially within parliament and on the Labour benches.

This final point was particularly important. In the run up to the prorogation, the backbench Labour MP, Hilary Benn, introduced a bill – what would become known as the Benn Act – that required the Prime Minister to request a further three-month extension to Article 50. Labour was playing into the government's hands and Johnson dismissed the 'surrender bill' as part of an effort to undermine the UK's negotiating position. That the Supreme Court voided the prorogation only supported the Prime Minister's argument that his government was being undermined and thwarted by those – in the House of Lords, the Courts and in the establishment more generally – who had never accepted the referendum result.

When 21 Conservative MPs, including the former Conservative Chancellor Ken Clarke and grandson of Winston Churchill, Nicholas Soames, voted with opposition parties to allow the passage of the Benn Bill into legislation, Johnson stripped them of the party whip. Such a move signalled the Prime Minister's intent to restore discipline to a Conservative Party which had grown increasingly troublesome in the preceding years. Rudd resigned from the Cabinet and surrendered the Conservative whip to sit as an Independent, citing a belief that the government's 'main objective was a no-deal Brexit', while Jo Johnson described an 'unresolvable tension' between family loyalty and the national interest and departed from the Cabinet as well.

Labour's struggles

Johnson's leadership was both an opportunity and a threat for the Labour Party, which had also emerged badly bruised from the European elections in July. The Prime Minister was a divisive figure in the House of Commons and provoked far greater animosity on the Labour benches than Theresa May ever had. His personality and style of premiership, coupled with the government talking up the prospect of a no-deal exit, went some way in uniting a fractured Labour Party. Over the summer of 2019, Corbyn focused on working with other opposition parties to prevent a no-deal outcome, which he argued would be disastrous for the British economy – something most Labour backbenchers and a significant minority of Conservative MPs agreed with.

Equally, though, May's departure from Downing Street and replacement with Johnson posed potential risks for Labour. As we have seen, Johnson won the Conservative leadership convincingly because he was a distinctive, charismatic politician bolstered by a strong electoral record and reputation as a political campaigner. The Prime Minister's determination to deliver Brexit at a time when Labour had shifted to endorsing a second referendum threatened to unite the Leave vote decisively behind the Conservative banner and rout Labour in in their Northern heartlands. Pledges to increase police numbers, restore stop-and-search powers for police and inject cash into the National Health Service also signalled that the government was establishing a new centre ground on domestic policy. Johnson was making a hybrid political offer to the electorate, shifting leftward on the economy with an interventionist levelling up agenda and investment in public services while at the same time showing a strong determination to deliver Brexit and establishing a more robust stance on issues of law and order.

Corbyn's eventual, albeit reluctant, migration of official Labour policy to a second referendum position antagonised respect-the-referendum Labour MP's representing seats in Northern England. Desperate to distance themselves from the leadership over Brexit, many took matters into their own hands. In August, Sarah Champion, told the *Daily Politics* show that she would sooner see a no-deal outcome over 'no Brexit at all', and John Mann, who had supported May's withdrawal agreement, insisted he would 'never vote to stop Brexit' even if it meant the UK exiting the bloc without an agreement.[2] The Labour MP for Wigan, Lisa Nandy, said she had 'changed her mind' and would now vote for a withdrawal agreement if given another chance. In September, the Labour MP for South Shields, Emma Lewell-Buck, told the ITV 'Acting Prime Minister' podcast that if forced to choose she would sooner see Labour enter government with the Brexit Party than a party seeking to overturn the referendum result, i.e. the Liberal Democrats.[3] The Tory strategy of promising to deliver Brexit whatever the cost was at last forcing Labour MPs to make difficult choices.

Corbyn's leadership continued to divide the Parliamentary Labour Party too. The splits brought about by his leadership – broadly between Labour moderates and radicals – cascaded and intersected with the splits generated by the Leave result in 2016 – over whether Labour MPs respected the 2016 referendum result or not. Figure 1, below, illustrates that the Parliamentary Labour Party can be divided into four 'camps' depending upon their response to the twin challenges of Brexit and Corbyn's leadership:

Figure 1 Parliamentary Labour Party, 2019

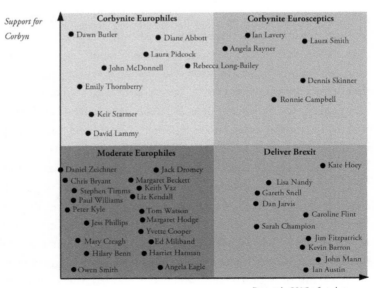

Corbynite Europhiles: Corbyn allies and loyalists, most of whom sat in the Shadow Cabinet or held Shadow ministerial positions. Many, including the most senior members of Corbyn's team, were Europhiles keen to see Labour adopt an unambiguously Remain position.

Corbynite Eurosceptics: Relatively few in number, these MPs were both loyal to Corbyn and were committed to delivering the referendum result.

Moderate Europhiles: By far the largest caucus in the Parliamentary Labour Party. These MPs objected to Corbyn's leadership and also opposed Brexit, favouring a second referendum.

Deliver Brexit: A relatively small cohort, these Labour MPs were moderates who believed the referendum result should be respected and honoured.

Figure 1 illustrates that the two main wedge issues within the Parliamentary Labour Party by 2019 were over Corbyn's leadership and divisions over how to respond to the 2016 Leave vote. These deep and complicated splits fundamentally compromised Labour's ability mount effective opposition to the government. In the summer of 2019, the party's official position was for a Labour government to renegotiate the withdrawal agreement and place a 'credible Leave option' on the ballot along with Remain in a public vote. However, a small caucus of respect-the-referendum Labour MPs, fearing the electoral consequences of Labour becoming a party of Remain, vowed to support a withdrawal agreement if it was brought back before the House of Commons.

    With a general election likely imminent, it was problematic that so many Labour MPs were either in the 'Corbynite Europhile' or 'Moderate Europhile' camps. The 'Corbynite Europhiles' were supporting a leader who was repellent to many voters and were also keen to move Labour to a Remain (second referendum) position, which carried any number of electoral risks. Likewise, the 'moderate Europhiles' held an equally challenging position. By opposing Corbyn, often loudly and publicly, they were undermining their own leader and fostering internal disunity within the party. Going into a general election, this meant they were urging people to vote Labour despite not actually wanting Corbyn to be the Prime Minister themselves. On Brexit, MPs in this group were also in the electorally contentious position of advocating a second referendum.

'We have a deal'

It is undoubtedly the case that Johnson's single greatest achievement in his first term as Prime Minister was persuading the European Commission to re-open the withdrawal agreement his predecessor had negotiated. As was so often the case, his political opponents inflated further his achievement by claiming for months that it would be impossible to do this, let alone possible to amend the agreement in such a way that could gain parliamentary assent. Returning triumphantly from Brussels with a deal also confounded critics in the moderate wing of the Conservative Party who had come to believe that the government had no intention of negotiating further with Brussels. The new withdrawal agreement united the Conservative Party not merely on the principle of leaving the European Union but how that end could be achieved. Every Conservative MP, including members of the European Research Group, agreed to vote for the agreement, thus making credible the claim that it was Labour and opposition parties, rather than ideologues in the Tory party, that were obstructing the course of Brexit.

Circumstances also gave the Prime Minister momentum to build cross-party support for the new deal. By autumn 2019, many MPs across the House of Commons were suffering from Brexit-induced exhaustion (Brex-austion). Three years of divisive national debate over the status of UK's relationship with the EU and how to respond to the surprise Brexit vote had taken its toll on parliamentarians, who found themselves at the epicentre of the crisis. A caucus of Labour MPs publicly stated their intention to vote with the government, despite, from a Labour perspective, Johnson's agreement being inferior in a number of ways to the version May's team had negotiated a year earlier. Explaining her decision to support Johnson's withdrawal agreement, the Labour MP for Great Grimsby, Melanie Onn, wrote in *The Guardian* that MPs ought to 'use this unique chance to help us move on and get back to helping our constituents' by voting for the deal.[4] The heightened risk of a no-deal

Brexit scenario placed pressure on Labour MPs that favoured a managed withdrawal from the EU. In an open letter to her Rotherham constituents, Sarah Champion wrote, 'The indications from the European Union are they are unlikely to accept a further delay to Britain's exit...even with an extension I do not believe it is feasible to simply delay indefinitely.' Cross-party support for the Prime Minister's agreement gave it additional credibility and made Labour attack lines on the substance of the deal more difficult to make.

Despite mounting expectations that the parliamentary arithmetic had shifted decisively towards the government, the 'Super Saturday' parliamentary session – which had been dubbed as a historic opportunity for parliament to express support for the withdrawal agreement in a meaningful vote and at last allow the country to move forward – ended in gridlock and disappointment.

General Election 2019

The Fixed Term Parliament Act allowed a government, which having removed the whip from 21 of its own MPs was operating with a *de facto* negative 46 majority, to continue functioning. However, the failure of parliament to decisively coalesce around a withdrawal agreement on four separate meaningful votes and thus allow the government to enact its central policy of securing the UK's exit from the European Union made calls for a general election increasingly difficult to resist.

The circumstances in which the election was called – especially the fact that Phase I of Brexit had not been resolved and the UK had not legally left the EU – significantly advantaged Johnson and the Conservatives. The Labour leadership ostensibly resisted going to the polls until a no-deal Brexit had first been 'taken off the table'. In practice, Corbyn's team were resistant to an early election because they feared it would result in a disastrous defeat.

Conservative strategy
During the campaign, the Conservative Party deployed a tripartite strategy in which they effectively fought three separate regional campaigns with

the aim of winning an overall majority in the House of Commons. In the Midlands, Northern England and Wales, the Tories planned an offensive into former Labour heartlands by promising to 'Get Brexit Done', defeat Corbyn and deliver an ambitious levelling-up agenda. In Southern England, they would have to defend affluent, Remain-voting seats from the resurgent Liberal Democrat Party by highlighting the risks posed by a Corbyn premiership propped up by the Scottish nationalists. Finally, in Scotland, the Conservative Unionists were tasked with protecting 13 Tory-held seats from a renewed SNP advance by focusing their campaign on the constitutional issue of Scottish independence, as well as the threat of a Corbyn-led government to national and economic security.

The first component, which was central to the party's prospects of winning an overall majority in the House of Commons, aimed at winning a slew of Labour Leave seats across provincial England and Wales. Since the UK had voted to leave the EU, Tory strategists had recognised that the referendum might bring about a once-in-a-generation electoral re-alignment based around newly formed Brexit loyalties. This might allow the Conservatives to reach low income and working-class Leave voters in Northern England and Wales who had previously been thought unreachable. In calling a snap election in April 2017, Theresa May had hoped to capitalise on precisely this opportunity and move dozens of Labour Leave seats in England and Wales into the Tory column. As we saw in the previous chapter, the Prime Minister failed to redraw the political map, however, she did achieve a considerable swing towards the Conservatives in these areas and picked up five 'Red Wall' seats in the process. To build on the foundations May's team had laid down two years earlier, it was hoped that Johnson's charismatic leadership and political magnetism might help voters overcome the historic aversion to the Conservative Party in these areas and tip them over into the Tory column.

Johnson's team was starting to 'think the unthinkable' by heavily targeting seats that had never been represented by a Conservative MP, such as Bishop Auckland in County Durham, and the market town constituency of Bolsover in Derbyshire, represented by the veteran Labour MP Dennis Skinner. There were several reasons to think these seats might be fruitful targets for the Conservatives. Many had recorded large Leave majorities in the 2016 EU referendum. They contained an above average proportion of older and retired households. Instinctively, these voters were culturally Conservative, deeply patriotic and proud of the local area. Importantly, as Steve Rayson has argued, they were more likely to 'identify as English rather than British.'[5] Their historic tendency to vote Labour was driven more by habitual voting over generations rather than a particular affinity for the 21st century Labour Party.

By promising to 'Get Brexit Done', the Tories offered an end to the political stalemate and a route through which the country could at last move forward, in stark contrast to Corbyn's Labour which would undertake a three-month re-negotiation with the EU and carry out another national referendum.

By drawing a line under years of austerity and committed to an ambitious levelling-up agenda, in which billions of pounds of public investment would be diverted outside of London and the South-East, Johnson established his as the beginning of a new government rather than a fourth term following a decade of Conservative rule. Pledges to build 40 new hospitals and hire thousands of new nurses also represented a concerted effort to be on the front foot on the NHS. Finally, Johnson sought to re-establish the party's reputation on issues of law and order by committing to hire an additional 20,000 police officers in the next parliament and restoring the power to stop-and-search, which had been outlawed by his predecessor. Matthew Goodwin argues that low-income voters became 'up-for-grabs' by the time of the 2019 election because they were 'cross-pressured by their strong desire for greater economic redistribution but also support leaving the European Union.'[6]

The second regional campaign was fought in affluent Remain-voting seats in South and South-West of England against a resurgent Liberal Democrat threat. A handful of these seats had recorded large Remain votes during the referendum and although these voters were naturally inclined to vote Conservative, they might object to the reckless way in which the government had gone about delivering the Leave result, especially under Johnson's leadership. Some of the seats in the South-West had been held by the Liberal Democrats during the Blair years. To counter this threat, the Tories emphasised the threat a Corbyn-led government would pose to national and economic security. It was hoped that Liberal Democrat tactical voting could be minimised by appealing to the 'safety first' instincts of middle-class voters, who might calculate that a managed Brexit via a withdrawal agreement could be a price worth paying if it meant preventing Corbyn from entering Number 10.

The final part of the Tory electoral strategy centred on defending the 13 Scottish seats Ruth Davidson's team had won for the party in 2017. By making the election a judgement on the constitutional question of whether there should be a second independence referendum in Scotland, the Conservatives once again sought to establish themselves as *the* party of the Union. Although Davidson had stepped down as the Conservative leader in August 2019, she remained an important figure in Scottish politics and her face appeared on election literature in marginal Tory–SNP target seats. She was also active on the campaign trail. This was important for the Conservatives. Had Davidson resigned explosively over the Prime Minister's handling of Brexit and refused to be involved in campaign, the party would have been deprived of their most popular and successful figurehead north of the border. Instead, Davidson could be used once more as a means by which to rally and unify the Unionist vote behind the Conservative banner.

Labour strategy
Labour's electoral strategy was comparatively defensive, and especially so for a party that had spent a decade on the opposition benches. Corbyn and his team had for months resisted the Prime Minister's efforts to hold a general election to break the parliamentary gridlock caused by Brexit. The primary reason for this was because they had Johnson 'trapped' and many figures close to Corbyn, including his influential communications director Seumas Milne, believed Labour would lose badly.

The route to an outright Labour majority was fraught. By 2019, Corbyn's personal popularity rating among voters had slumped to new lows and the Conservatives enjoyed a consistent and healthy opinion poll lead. In *Left Out*, Pogrund and Maguire reference a 20,000-sample size YouGov MRP model that was shown to Corbyn and senior Shadow Cabinet ministers at Labour conference in September 2019. The poll suggested that in the event of an early election Labour would be reduced to a mere 138 MPs, the lowest since the First World War, and that strongholds like Vauxhall would fall to the Conservatives as the Liberal Democrat vote split the Remain vote.[7]

Another reason for Labour's defensive posture was that the party began the election campaign from a relatively strong position. In 2017, Corbyn had out-performed expectations and won a respectable 260 seats with a formidable 40% national vote share. Given the difficulties he had experienced in the intervening years and the likelihood that 'peak Corbyn' had long passed, Labour's best hope by autumn 2019 was to shore up its electoral position by holding onto as many seats as possible and contain the Conservative advance as they had two years earlier. To repeat the success of 2017, Corbyn's team attempted to pivot towards domestic issues upon which Labour tended to be more trusted accordingly to opinion polls, such as investment in the NHS. This, it was hoped, might prove a profitable way of dissuading lifelong Labour Leave voters from turning to the Tories. A bad outbreak of flooding early in the campaign also presented an opportunity to remind voters of the effects of a decade of public spending restraint, highlighting chronic under-investment in regional flood defences to protect local homes and businesses.

Unusually, given the stage in the electoral cycle, there were limited opportunities for Labour to advance and there were just a handful of target seats that the party might realistically stand a chance of winning. These included relatively affluent, Remain-voting constituencies in Southern England, including Iain Duncan Smith's Woodford Green constituency, the Central London constituency Cities of London and Westminster, and even the Prime Minister's West London seat of Uxbridge and South Ruislip. Strikingly, the Conservatives were trying to win among the most socially and economically-deprived seats in the United Kingdom, while the Labour Party set its sights on affluent Europhile voters in Southern England.

Brexit
From the outset of the election campaign, the unresolved issue of Britain's relationship with the EU loomed large in the public imagination – something which advantaged Johnson and the Conservatives. Like his

predecessor in spring 2017, Johnson had pushed for a snap vote to win a sufficiently large majority to break the deadlock over Brexit and translate the national Leave majority into parliamentary representation. Unlike in 2017, the merits and necessity of an election were considerably more persuasive this time around. Three years of wrangling over Brexit, or what Johnson termed 'dither and delay', were beginning to take their toll on the electorate. Not only were voters tired of the Brexit psychodrama, but the parliamentary gridlock was consuming so much time and energy that other domestic priorities, including the National Health Service and the education system, were scarcely being given the attention they deserved.

By late 2019, the Prime Minister's promise to 'Get Brexit Done' appealed to an electorate tired with and frustrated by years of indecision over how to give effect to the 2016 referendum. This catchy soundbite was central to the Conservative campaign and it had not been dreamed up by strategists in CCHQ or Dominic Cummings; rather, it came from the mouths of voters themselves. In focus groups, people spoke of a desperate desire to see the psychodrama 'done' so the country could return to some semblance of normality and move forward. The endlessly repeated soundbite 'Get Brexit Done' was emblazoned on the side of Conservative campaign buses and literature, bringing to mind Blair's adage that 'just when you are fed up to the back teeth of hearing a message, that's the moment when voters are just starting to hear it.' In north London, Johnson visited a Jewish bakery and handed out doughnuts to enthusiastic customers who called back, 'Get Brexit Done.' The Prime Minister's deal united Leave voters who were furious with parliament for failing to decisively resolve the issue with 'respect-the-referendum' Remainers who recognised that the country needed to move forward.

Of course, the 'Get Brexit Done' message would get a harder hearing in some parts of the UK. In Scotland, the Conservative Party was fighting to defend seats from the SNP in a country that was overwhelmingly hostile to both Brexit and Johnson's leadership. Likewise, in Southern England, the Conservatives held dozens of affluent Remain-voting seats that were vulnerable to a resurgent Liberal Democrat vote. The 2017 election had demonstrated that the realignment of voters around Brexit loyalties was not a one-way street as affluent middle-class constituencies such as Canterbury and Kensington fell to Labour.

Ultimately, promising to deliver Brexit was a calculated risk for the Conservatives. Given the electoral geography favoured Leave, it seemed a sound one. The European elections had shown that voters rewarded parties with a clear and coherent Brexit strategy.

The Labour Party's Brexit position, although theoretically coherent, failed to strike a chord at a time when the electorate desperately sought a decisive route forward on an issue they had long ago tired of. There was little to recommend the proposition that a Corbyn-led Labour government would return to Brussels for further rounds of negotiation and within three months put a Labour Leave option against the option of Remain in a public vote. Corbyn, who many voters did not believe was fit to run the Labour Party let alone hold the office of Prime Minister, offered further uncertainty and delay where the British people sought clarity and resolution.

From the European elections in the late-spring of 2019 onwards, senior Labour figures had anticipated that the greatest electoral vulnerability was in Liberal Democrat-facing seats in big cities and university towns. It was these elections that had at last tipped the leadership into adopting a second referendum position as official Labour policy. Only mid-way through the election campaign itself, when a YouGov MRP showed Johnson on course for a large majority and the Conservatives were poised to make deep inroads into Labour Leave areas across the North, the Midlands and Wales, that Labour finally acted. Lacking big beasts in the Shadow Cabinet with robust Brexit credentials, the party Chairman, Ian Lavery, was despatched in what looked like a desperate last-ditch attempt to shore up their electoral position in the Red Wall. It was too little, and it was too late.

Leadership

Although Johnson was himself a divisive leader, the potential lines of attack a Labour frontbench might make against him were rendered ineffective by the inadequacies of their own leadership. For instance, the Prime Minister was clearly vulnerable on the question of trust. However, given Labour's relationship with the Jewish community had been severed under Corbyn's leadership, it would be difficult for the party to make a moral critique of the Conservatives and their leader. Similarly, given his own perceived limitations, Corbyn was not in the position to capitalise on the Prime Minister's relative lack of experience in government and administrative deficiencies.

Leadership was central to the Conservative electoral strategy and Johnson's ability to transcend his party's traditional association with the interests of the rich few and appeal directly to ordinary voters was crucial. Johnson's leadership represented a stark change in tone and style compared with his predecessors. As Prime Minister, he returned the party to a tradition of 'boisterous Toryism' which favours individual responsibility over state interference and rejects the notion that people cannot be trusted to control their own lives. This tradition had long appealed to a certain section of aspirational working-class voters and it seems possible that Johnson's colourful private life, littered with personal indiscretions and infidelities, enhanced rather than hindered his chances of reaching these voters. On the campaign trail, the ITV national editor Allegra Stratton reportedly came across voters in Red Wall seats explaining their intention to vote 'for Boris' rather than the Conservatives and a group of builders stood proudly by a 'We Love Boris' sign in the North-West.

Labour went into the general election with a leader who not only lacked the support of many of his colleagues in the parliamentary party, but who was also deeply unpopular among the wider electorate. One IPSOS MORI poll indicated that Corbyn's net approval rating had collapsed to -60, lower than any party leader in modern history and worse even than Michael Foot's ratings in 1982. On the doorstep, Labour candidates standing in constituencies across Leave seats were time and again confronted with voters who simply could not countenance the notion of Jeremy Corbyn being Prime Minister. Rather than being an asset to be exploited, Corbyn was an enormous liability to be managed during the election campaign and Labour candidates standing in Northern constituencies explicitly excluded reference to Corbyn in their election leaflets.

Some former Labour MPs even urged voters to support the Conservatives in the election. The MP for Dudley North, Ian Austin, who had served as a minister in Brown's government, gave an interview to Sky News at the beginning of the campaign in which he described Corbyn as 'unfit to lead the Labour Party...and certainly unfit to lead the country.' Together with the former MP for Barrow-in-Furness, Austin launched a campaign against extremism to oppose Corbyn's bid to become Prime Minister. Ivan Lewis, the Jewish MP for Bury South, told his constituents that 'institutional racism' within the Labour Party meant that while voting Conservative would 'require much soul-searching... It is the right thing to do'. On the campaign trail in County Durham, the former Vote Leave Chair, Gisela Stuart, urged her Labour colleagues to 'bring the country together by vot[ing] for Boris Johnson and for Brexit'. These extraordinary interventions reflected the extent to which Corbyn's leadership, and the Leave vote had upended traditional party affiliations and loyalties.

Shifting allegiances
Following a six-week campaign in the middle of winter, voters went to the polls on December 13th (the first time an election had been held in December in almost a century). At 10pm, the major news outlets broadcast the exit poll to the nation. According to the poll, Johnson and the Conservatives were on course to win a resounding victory and voters awoke the morning after a dramatic election night to survey the effects of the political earthquake that had shaken the nation overnight. Once the votes had been counted, the Conservatives had increased their representation in the House of Commons by 47 seats and their national vote share rose to 44%, an impressive achievement after almost a decade in government and higher even than the share Tony Blair managed to achieve in 1997. The electoral map was awash in a sea of blue. In England, the Conservatives consolidated their already dominant electoral position and after the election held twice as many English seats than Labour, with a commanding 47% share of the vote. In Wales, the Tory party achieved its highest seat count in a generation. Even in Scotland, where Johnson was personally unpopular and where the Conservatives lost a number of seats to the SNP, the party's vote share held up at 25%.

Labour ended election night with 60 fewer seats – most of which had been lost to the Conservatives in England and Wales, and to the SNP in Scotland. The so-called 'Red Wall', which once ran across North-East England, the West Midlands and North-East Wales, was demolished and reduced to a pile of rubble. In Staffordshire, for instance, all twelve MPs elected were Conservative – the first time ever. Those bricks left standing in the Red Wall were precarious. Ed Miliband's once-safe Doncaster North seat was reduced from a 14,000 majority to a marginal 2,370 majority and the Labour majority in Normanton, Pontefract and Castleford, represented by Yvette Cooper, collapsed to just 1,276.

Much attention has been given by journalists and commentators to the lifelong Labour seats that returned Conservative MPs for the first time ever, such as Bishop Auckland in County Durham and nearby Blythe Valley, which was perhaps the biggest shock of the night. In the end, around one third of Conservative 2019 gains were seats like this that had never been blue before. A further 39% of them had been Conservative seats in the previous century, including many that Margaret Thatcher had won in the 1980s, such as Darlington or Bridgend in South Wales. The remainder, around 30%, were seats that had been lost since 2010 and were re-gained from Labour, such as Bury North and High Peak.

Labour consolidated support among a core voter base of graduate millennial voters living in urban centres and overwhelmingly in the private rented sector of the housing market. The party's single gain of the night was the affluent South-West London seat of Putney, a reflection of the dramatic realignment underway. In Scotland, Labour was reduced to its lowest vote share in over a century (barely 19%) and was once again left holding just a single seat; the student-heavy constituency of Edinburgh South. In Wales, the party was reduced to 22 seats, its lowest representation since 1983. Labour's retreat from its heartlands in the Celtic fringes meant that after the election it was more of an English party than at any time in its history.

Worse even than the damage to Labour's electoral standing was the judgement cast on the party by its own voters. Yvette Cooper recalled an encounter in which a constituent 'broke down in tears' because she felt the party had given her no choice but to vote Conservative and a furious lifelong Labour voter in Wigan told the candidate Lisa Nandy, 'I haven't left the Labour Party, the Labour Party has left me.' Ruth Smeeth, whose Stoke-on-Trent seat fell to the Conservatives, stated simply: 'We don't represent the people we were created to represent' and told a reporter on election night that 'We are the nasty party.'

The blame game

Explanations for Labour's defeat began almost from the moment the exit poll revealed that the Conservatives were on course for a landslide victory. In the immediate aftermath of the result, attention inevitably turned to the role played by Jeremy Corbyn's leadership of the Labour Party and the divisive Brexit issue, which had been central to the campaign.

Labour moderates largely interpreted the election result as vindication of their long-standing opposition to Corbyn's leadership. In a lecture celebrating the 120-year anniversary of the Labour Party, Tony Blair described 'Our latest defeat [as] entirely predictable and predicted. We went into an election with a Leader with a minus 40% net approval rating, on political terrain chosen by our opponents, with a manifesto promising the earth but from a planet other than earth, and a campaign which substituted a narcissistic belief in our righteousness for professionalism.'[8] Blair added that it would have been better for Labour 'if a moderate' had been leading the party, suggesting that Corbyn was the decisive factor in bringing about the party's defeat. On the night of the election, the former Labour Home Secretary Alan Johnson described how 'Corbyn was a disaster on the doorstep… Everyone knew that he couldn't lead the working class out of a paper bag.' Mary Creagh, whose Wakefield seat fell to the Conservatives, laid blame for the defeat with the leadership and described Corbyn as 'guilty of preening narcissism' and suggested he was too 'slow to accept responsibility' for the fact that 'on his watch, a lot of very bad things have happened in the Labour Party'. The former Foreign Secretary Jack Straw went further and told Sky News that he was 'relieved' Johnson had won the election and said he 'had this worry that the country could be in really dangerous hands' if Corbyn had won. Straw added that Corbyn was an 'apologist' for terrorist groups.

Allies of Corbyn in the Labour Party, on the other hand, were quick to locate the causes of the defeat with the divisive Brexit issue. In their version of events, Corbyn and the policies he espoused were inherently popular, as demonstrated by the 2017 election result. The politics of Brexit poisoned the well and hijacked an energising Labour manifesto, in turn causing the loss of dozens of Red Wall seats in Northern England and Wales. The Shadow Equalities Minister and close ally of Corbyn, Dawn Butler, told the BBC that the cynical and populist 'Get Brexit Done' soundbite had cut through among a certain section of the electorate and derailed the Labour campaign and the left-wing commentator Grace Blakely pointed out that 'If you look at where we lost seats, it was because we came out for a second referendum.' Jon Landsman, whose Momentum organisation was vital to the Corbyn project, said, 'We've seen an election that is incredibly polarised because of Brexit... We've seen large numbers of working-class voters...voting for the most right-wing government since Chamberlain.' According to Labour radicals it was Brexit, rather than Corbyn's leadership, that had upended traditional party loyalties and thus handed Johnson dozens of Labour Leave seats and a landslide victory.

Figures from within the Labour Party itself are in many respects the wrong people to diagnose the causes of the defeat. They were too close to events and the key decisions that directly led up to the election and therefore cannot offer a dispassionate analysis. Their explanations suffer from over-simplification, are often motivated by a political agenda and focus too heavily on identifying 'culprits'. It seems conceivable, in practice, that both the divisive and unresolved issue of Brexit and the Corbyn's leadership were each themselves sufficient conditions for the Conservative Party's electoral victory. In combination, they proved devastating for Labour. Lifelong Labour voters who might otherwise have felt uncomfortable with voting Conservative could justify their decision on the basis that it was a vote for Brexit and to stop Jeremy Corbyn entering Downing Street.

Both moderate and radical figures must accept their share of responsibility for Labour's electoral problems. It was moderates in the party, including from the New Labour era, who more than any others made a forceful case for a second EU referendum position in an effort to undo the 2016 Leave vote. This damaged the Labour brand and suggested to Leave voters what they had long believed, that their views were secondary to metropolitan Remain voters. Equally, though, Corbyn's leadership made Labour's ambition to form a majority government virtually unachievable. Time and again Labour candidates were met on the doorstep with voters explaining they simply could not vote for the party while Corbyn was leader.

Long-term roots

As the dust has settled, accounts of Labour's devastating election defeat have rightly moved beyond a narrow focus on issues of leadership and the divisive Brexit issue. It is increasingly recognised that the roots of the 2019 election result go deep and that the Labour Party's drift away from its industrial and post-industrial heartlands had begun long before Corbyn became leader in 2015 or the Leave vote the following year. The foreword of the official *Labour Together* review of the 2019 defeat captures this spirit when the authors describe the election as 'a historic defeat, a long time coming, a mountain to climb', and state that 'our report lays bare that our defeat had deep roots'.[9]

Some former Red Wall MPs recognised the complicated and nuanced political story that had led Labour to its worst electoral defeat since 1935. Caroline Flint, whose Don Valley constituency turned blue for the first time in a century, argued that Labour had started 'listening too much to the metropolitan cities and university towns', while the former MP for Stoke-on-Trent, Gareth Snell, suggested that Labour's 'policies [were] developed by people living in cities and therefore not relevant for the concerns of people living in towns'.[10] The detachment of the institutional Labour Party from communities in Northern England and Wales was reflected not just in the policies adopted by the Westminster leadership, but also at a local level too. The former Redcar MP Anna Turley claimed that Labour 'never spoke to the pride of local areas' and Snell lamented that too often his party simply said, 'Isn't it awful here', with few ideas about how to improve the prospects of the local community.[11] Deborah Mattinson's polling of Red Wall voters in the months following the election echoes these sentiments, and voters complained bitterly that 'Labour has no aspiration for our areas.' Given that Labour's political roots lie in communitarian organisations and institutions, underpinned by the notion of 'being on your side', the detachment from local communities in Northern England and Wales was devastating.

Many figures in the institutional Labour Party, as well as the mainstream media, were shocked by the election result. In many respects, their shock merely reflects the extent to which they had become detached from what was going on in the ground outside London. For those paying attention, the fall of the Red Wall in 2019 was not a bolt from the blue – it had been crumbling for decades. The Conservative mayor for the Tees Valley region, Ben Houchen, observed in 2020 that 'If you look at every general, local or European election since 2005, Labour have gone backwards in every region [of the North East of England].'[12] In 2017, Houchen himself beat the Labour favourite to become Tees Valley mayor – a sign that the tectonic electoral plates were moving in the North-East of England. Rachel Burgin, who had stood as the Labour candidate in the Copeland by-election in early 2017, said that the Conservative Party's victory in a seat that had been held by Labour since its creation in 1983, 'should have sounded the alarm bell that Labour was getting things very, very wrong'. The warning signs were there, too few senior Labour figures chose to pay attention.

6

Electoral trends

(2007-2020)

As we have seen in this section so far, the Conservative Party's fortunes dramatically recovered over the course of the long decade from c.2007 to 2020 following the prolonged malaise experienced during the Blair years. In the 2010 General Election, the Conservatives ended thirteen years of Labour government and went on to win four consecutive electoral victories, increasing the party's national vote share on each occasion. This chapter examines the underlying trends that underpinned and help explain Conservative electoral success over this period.

After 2007, Conservative leaders enjoyed a consistent and at times commanding poll lead over their Labour opponents on the question of voters' preference for Prime Minister, underpinning more presidential campaign strategies in general elections. Likewise, on the polling metric of economic competence, the Tories were consistently more trusted than Labour by the electorate from the summer of 2008 onwards. The Labour Party struggled to move on from the devastating political damage of the 2007-8 financial crisis which severely damaged the Labour brand. Following the crisis, a succession of Labour leaders and their Shadow

Chancellors were unable to reassure voters they could be trusted to manage national finances and the economy.

The Conservative Party's voter base widened considerably over the long decade and a series of dramatic events, most obviously the Brexit vote in 2016, coupled with changes in the leadership of the two main parties, caused the demographic profile of its voters to change considerably. By the end of the decade, the Conservative Party was almost unrecognisable from the one Cameron had led into the 2010 General Election; older, more socially and economically diverse, and enjoying far better representation across all parts of England, as well as Wales and Scotland too. Over the same period, the Labour Party's political appeal narrowed considerably. Under Miliband and Corbyn, Labour strengthened its grip on younger voters in big metropolitan cities and university towns, but this has been to the overall detriment of its support base in provincial England and Wales. In another heartland, Scotland, the Labour Party was almost entirely wiped out.

A question of leadership

Tony Blair's departure from frontline politics in the early summer of 2007 marked an important turning point for the Labour Party's political fortunes. Consecutive leaders thereafter struggled to match the electoral successes of their predecessor and achieve broad, widespread political appeal. This is reflected in the fact that from late 2007, Conservative leaders enjoyed a consistent, and at times commanding, poll lead over their opponents on the question of voters' preference for Prime Minister until April 2020.

In general elections, Cameron, May and Johnson benefited from an incumbency advantage and were considered more prime ministerial than their Labour counterparts in part because they already held the office of Prime Minister and, as incumbents, they could use the infrastructure of the Downing Street operation, such as the podium outside Number 10, to project their authority to the nation. Conservative Prime Ministers were also able to frame their role as being partly about preventing Labour leaders, such as Miliband and Corbyn, who purportedly posed a threat to national and economic security, from entering Downing Street. The threat of the unknown and appeal to the 'safety first' instincts of the electorate helped the Tories establish electoral hegemony after 2010.

The gap in voter perceptions between the leaders of the main parties was consistently exploited by the Conservatives in general election campaigns. In the 2015 election, they contrasted the 'competence' of Cameron's leadership with the 'chaos' a Miliband administration would cause. Similarly, in 2017, May's team attempted (albeit with considerably less success) to contrast 'strong and stable' Conservative leadership with a Corbyn-led radical Labour Party. By the 2019 election, Corbyn's popularity had diminished to such an extent that his net satisfaction had slumped to negative 60 – lower than any leader of the opposition in recorded history.[1]

Figure 2 Voter preference for Prime Minister (2008-2019) *Source*: YouGov, British Electoral Survey

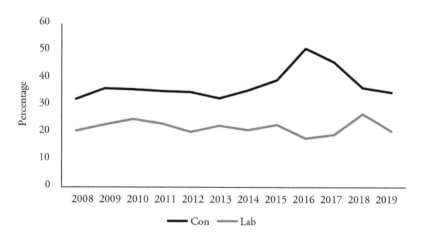

Figure 2 shows us that Conservative leaders enjoyed a substantial polling lead over their Labour opponents during the long decade from 2007. This lead extended to as much as 39% in April 2017, the month in which Theresa May called a snap general election. Strikingly, the Conservative lead on this metric was sustained against a backdrop of internal disunity over a range of domestic policy issues such as welfare cuts during the Cameron years and open civil war in response to May's withdrawal agreement in late 2018 and 2019. Despite the challenges Conservative Prime Minister's faced in office – not least over the Europe question – the public still overwhelmingly preferred them over the Labour alternative.

Each of the three Conservative leaders contributed in different ways to the expansion of the party's voter base and continued electoral success over this period.

David Cameron

David Cameron's victory in the Conservative Party leadership contest in 2005 represented an important step for the party on the path back to electability. Cameron inherited a party that, having suffered three consecutive general election defeats, still seemed far from close to winning back power. In the 2005 election, the Conservatives had won just 198 seats, located overwhelmingly in the Southern English shires. As leader, Cameron returned his party to the role it had historically fulfilled, as a pragmatic and electorally responsive political operation capable of challenging the New Labour fortress and eventually forming a government.

There were always those within the Parliamentary Conservative Party (largely on the Eurosceptic wing) who were uncomfortable with Cameron's modernising agenda. This was a relatively young MP who, having only been elected to parliament four years earlier, was seeking to radically shake up a party that was struggling to adapt to the 21st century. The Eurosceptic former prisons minister, Ann Widdecombe, reflected this sentiment when she described how, 'Mr Cameron, for heaven's sake, had only been there five minutes and suddenly he was standing for the leader of the party.'[2] While Cameron's victory in the leadership contest against his rival David Davis was emphatic, there were those within the party who distrusted a Europhile moderate in the Blairite mould intent on doing whatever was necessary to make the party relevant again. His message to the party faithful in 2006, that the Conservatives needed to stop 'banging on about Europe', however accurate it might have been, was a tough pill to swallow.

Nonetheless, Cameron's sceptics were willing to go along with his leadership because, having lost badly in three consecutive elections, they recognised the need for change if the party were to start winning again. By 2005, the party was at last ready to change.

Two strategic prongs underpinned Cameron's political project. The first, which is commonly associated with his personal style of leadership and political philosophy, was primarily aimed at detoxifying the Conservative brand. This involved making the party more middle class and comfortable with modern Britain. Cameron recognised that it would be necessary to occupy a socially liberal and economically moderate position to reconnect with voters in a fast-changing British society. Electorally, the principle aim of this strategy was to win back the seats and voters in Middle England that had been lost to New Labour and the Liberal Democrats since 1997.

The second strategic prong, which in some respects pulled in the opposite direction to the first, focused on capitalising on traditional Conservative political strengths. In government, the Conservatives adopted a tough stance on issues of law and order and a more robust approach to immigration under May's tenure as Home Secretary. Cameron also moved to restore the party's reputation on economic competence. Addressing the spiralling welfare budget under Blair and Brown's watch, the Tories consciously positioned themselves as the 'workers party' by introducing welfare policies in government to 'make work pay'. The benefit cap, which set an upper limit of £26,000 on annual household welfare payments, typified this. This part of the Cameron project involved making a play for aspirational working-class voters, recognising that consecutive Labour leaders, including Blair, Brown, and Miliband, had neglected a constituency of voters in Northern England and Wales.

Capping benefits polled well among the wider electorate, in particular Labour voters. It also spoke to the government's wider ambition to restructure UK labour markets and create a 'high-skill, high-pay and low welfare economy'. In the 2015 budget, Osborne introduced a national living wage to raise the incomes of the lowest paid and the tax-free income tax allowance rose to £12,500, lifting millions of low paid workers out of paying tax altogether. For his years as Prime Minister, contrasting the Conservatives as the 'party of the workers' against Labour as the 'party of the shirkers' suited Cameron's political narrative well and mobilised a broad coalition of middle-class and aspirational working-class voters.

Ambitions to expand the party's political appeal beyond traditional strongholds in Southern England and the rural shires can also be seen in George Osborne's political and economic project to create a 'Northern powerhouse'. Derided by some as little more than an opportunistic slogan, Osborne's efforts to divert private and public sector investment, including foreign direct investment from emerging economies such as China, into the North of England represented a concerted effort to rebalance the economy after decades of London-centric growth. After decades of under-investment in what would become known as 'left behind' towns outside Southern England, including through thirteen years of a Labour government, the fact that a Conservative Chancellor was making the case for geographical redistribution of economic activity was itself significant.

Electorally, Cameron's strategy paid dividends. In the 2010 General Election, the Conservatives won an additional 96 seats, including dozens of seats in Middle England that had been lost to Blair in the preceding decade. Five years later, the party increased its vote share and won an overall majority by pulling middle-class Liberal Democrat voters in suburban London and South West England into the Conservative electoral coalition. Although Cameron's electoral successes can largely be explained by the conversion of predominantly middle-class English voters, the drift of working-class voters towards the Conservatives can be seen this period too. In 2015, the Tories defeated Labour in a slew of seats across Northern England and the Midlands. In Wales, Cameron increased his party's seat total by three.

Theresa May

The departure of Cameron from Downing Street and his swift replacement with Theresa May in the summer of 2016 illustrated once more the responsiveness of the Conservative Party to rapidly changing political circumstances. A competent and hard-working Cabinet minister, who had kept a low profile during the referendum campaign, May seemed at the time well placed to unite the country and get on with the job of delivering the referendum result. As the longest serving Home Secretary for almost a century, she had demonstrated a sturdy resilience in the face of bitter opposition from establishment figures, something it was hoped would serve the country well, ahead of challenging negotiations with Brussels.

Early on, Conservative strategists, including the Prime Minister's Chief of Staff Nick Timothy, recognised the political opportunity presented by the surprise Leave vote in June 2016. We saw in Chapter 4 how millions of traditionally Labour-leaning voters across Northern England, the Midlands and Wales had helped deliver the surprise Leave result. A Conservative Party determined to honour the referendum result, and led by a politician with May's background, might have been gifted a once-in-a-generation opportunity to reach deep into Labour Leave-voting areas. In her first speech as Prime Minister on the steps of Downing Street, May articulated a route for her party to reach these voters, who she identified as 'just about managing' and for whom 'life is tough'. Crafted by Timothy, the speech recognised very soon after the referendum some of the underlying factors that had caused the Brexit vote. Under May, the Conservatives embarked on a more interventionist economic policy programme, proposing energy price controls, racial and gender pay audits and the option of workers sitting on company boards, a clear departure from the Cameron years.

Although May failed to achieve her primary objective of securing the UK's departure from the European Union, history might eventually be kinder to her premiership. As Prime Minister, she worked tirelessly to deliver the referendum result, while simultaneously preserving the integrity of the internal UK market. In her first speech as Prime Minister, May reminded the nation that 'The full title of my party is the Conservative and Unionist Party, and that word is "Unionist" is very important to me... The precious, precious bond between England, Scotland, Wales and Northern Ireland.' Significantly, her first trip on becoming Prime Minister in July 2016 was to Scotland, highlighting the importance of the Union to her personally. The Prime Minister's Unionism and determination to maintain the integrity of the internal market of the United Kingdom helped the Conservatives to win their highest number of seats in Scotland in a generation (13) in the 2017 election. It also manifested in the substance of the withdrawal agreement negotiated by May and her team, which included UK-wide customs arrangements in the event that the backstop was triggered, rather than the Northern Ireland backstop proposed by the EU.

May's efforts as Prime Minister laid critical foundations upon which her successor would build. In the 2017 election, there was a substantial swing towards the Conservatives across the North, the Midlands and Wales in a prelude to the more dramatic gains Johnson would make two years later. After the 2019 election, Caroline Flint pointed out that, 'Theresa May sowed the seats in reducing majorities in my seat and elsewhere.'[3] Similarly, The *Labour Together* report acknowledges that 'the Conservatives had already paved the way to victory in these seats back in 2017.'[4] Overall, May increased the party's national vote share by 6%, a total of 2.4 million voters and the first time in recent British history that a Prime Minister had increased their party's vote share for a third consecutive national election.

The 2017 election also caused the Conservatives to swing leftward on economic policy, something which is given relatively little attention. Long before Johnson entered Downing Street, May had already begun to move her party away from the fiscal constraints of the Cameron–Osborne years. Although the appointment of the fiscally hawkish Chancellor, Philip Hammond, made a major step change in public spending more difficult, May announced on the 70th anniversary of its creation that the NHS would receive its largest ever cash injection in its history, totalling £6 billion. Corporate reform policies, including pay audits of listed companies and energy price freezes, suggested May's government was more comfortable using the levers of the state to intervene in dysfunctional private sector markets and correct market failures than her predecessor.

The Prime Minister ultimately lacked the ability to gain parliamentary approval for the withdrawal agreement negotiated by her government, however the deal provided the basis for the re-negotiation her successor would undertake with Brussels. Given much of the substance of the original legal text remained, it can be argued that the UK's exit from the EU was secured because of the joint efforts of both May and Johnson's administrations.

Johnson's premiership signalled a decisive change from his predecessors, both in style and substance. As Prime Minister, he immediately recognised that the Conservative Party had staked its political credibility on delivering the referendum result and securing the UK's departure from the EU. Therefore, to eliminate the nascent threat posed by Farage's Brexit Party, his government would have to regain the initiative on Brexit and enact the Leave result, whatever the cost.

The government's domestic policy programme also signalled a decisive break from the fiscal rectitude of the Coalition years and was more ambitious than anything May attempted in government. If Cameron had set about to de-toxify the Conservative Party in 2005 on certain social and cultural issues, Johnson aimed to de-toxify the party brand on economic issues by decisively turning a page on austerity.

Recognising his limitations as an administrator, the Prime Minister constructed a team to deliver his political objectives. Dominic Cummings, who was a strategic thinker and had played a central role in the Vote Leave campaign, was installed as Chief of Staff, while Michael Gove, who had established a formidable reputation as a delivery-focused minister in Cameron and May's Cabinets, was given responsibility for no-deal Brexit planning. The new Chancellor, Sajid Javid, who had been a long-standing advocate of using large scale infrastructure projects to stimulate growth, was fully signed up to Number 10's fiscally expansionist levelling up agenda.

In the space of just six months, Johnson achieved the two tasks assigned to him as in the early summer of 2019: to keep Farage down and to keep Corbyn out. In October 2019, Johnson confounded his critics by persuading the EU to re-negotiate the withdrawal agreement and returned from Brussels in October 2019 with a new deal. With the contentious backstop provision removed from the agreement, the Prime Minister secured the support of the entire Parliamentary Conservative Party for his deal.

In December 2019, the Conservatives won the largest parliamentary majority in a generation and the party's national vote share rose to 44%. As a result, Johnson is the first British Conservative Prime Minister to have triumphed over the Europe Question, where his predecessors Thatcher, Major, Cameron and May could not.

Following Blair's departure in 2007, a succession of Labour leaders struggled to achieve widespread electoral appeal and, after 2010, to offer a credible alternative to the Conservative government of the day. In general elections, Labour leaders tended to be more of a liability to be managed than an asset to be exploited, encouraging the Conservatives to make elections more presidential.

Gordon Brown

As the longest-serving Chancellor of the Exchequer since 1832, Brown appeared to be uniquely well qualified for the role of Prime Minister and was heir apparent for the leadership. He was considered a more strategic thinker than Blair, and it had been assumed by some figures in the Labour Party that Brown and not Blair had been the natural successor as leader in 1994.

After 1997, Brown earned a formidable reputation as the 'Iron Chancellor', presiding over a long period of stable macroeconomic conditions, and redistributing the economic gains from a growing financial services sector to fund investment in public services. His interventionist economic policy programme and political abilities provided Brown with a strong personal power base within the parliamentary party.

Brown's strengths lay in administrative competence and an enormous capacity for hard work; however, he struggled with some of the presentational aspects of being Prime Minister. He suffered unfortunate comparisons with his predecessor and was unable to match Blair's abilities as a political communicator. Under Cameron's leadership, Brown faced an increasingly formidable Conservative opposition and consistently poor performances at Prime Minister's Questions undermined his support on the Labour backbenches.

The rapid deterioration of the UK economy from the middle of 2007 undermined the Prime Minister's hard-won reputation for economic competence and severely damaged the Labour Party brand. His handling of the immediate emergency crisis in 2008 at the G8, which included coordinating a major global stimulus package, was overshadowed by a perception that 'Labour's recession' had been brought about by overspending in the preceding decade.

In the 2010 election, Gordon Brown led his party to its lowest vote share in a generation (29%) and the Labour brand became tainted by the perceived fiscal recklessness of the preceding decade.

Ed Miliband

There are two principal functions of the leader of Her Majesty's Opposition. The first is to scrutinise the government of the day and hold them to account. The second is to offer voters a plausible replacement to the government if, at any time, it should fall. While many judged that Miliband was effective in carrying out the first of these functions, and his leadership helped make the Coalition government function better as a result, few considered him to be the leader of a government-in-waiting after 2010.

The Labour leader's net satisfaction remained negative for most of his years in opposition and in November 2014 fell to a record low of negative 44%.[5] He struggled to address a perception among voters, reinforced by many of the broadsheet newspapers, that Labour had crashed the economy and opened the floodgates to immigration during their time in government. As Figure 2 shows, Cameron enjoyed a consistent poll lead over Miliband on the metric of voters' preference for Prime Minister. In the 2015 election, the Conservatives were able to turn Cameron's leadership ratings to their advantage by making the campaign presidential.

The 2015 election result was a disaster for Labour. Under Miliband, the party failed to regain the trust of Middle England to manage the economy, haemorrhaged support among aspirational working-class voters in provincial England and Wales, and were wiped out in Scotland by the SNP.

Jeremy Corbyn

Corbyn's surprise victory in the leadership contest in the summer of 2015 posed an unprecedented challenge to the Labour Party. At the time of his becoming leader it was widely believed, including by many figures within the Labour movement itself, that Corbyn would spell electoral catastrophe for the party because the British people would never countenance making him Prime Minister.

Against expectations, Corbyn performed well in the 2017 election campaign. By pledging to respect the referendum and oppose a 'hard, ideological Tory Brexit', he skilfully diffused the divisive Brexit issue to defend Labour Leave areas from the Conservative advance and even managed to win Tory strongholds such as Canterbury and Kensington in Southern England. In return for a strong campaign and a moderate manifesto, Labour was rewarded with an impressive 40% vote share, the highest since Blair's second landslide in 2001.

Beneath the surface, though, cracks were beginning to show for Corbyn in 2017. Labour had lost its third general election in a row. Despite claiming he had won the election, Corbyn had fallen sixty seats short of a parliamentary majority and the Tory vote share had increased significantly too, in a brief return to two party politics. He had successfully constructed a broad coalition of metropolitan Remain voters and traditional Labour Leave voters in provincial England; however, holding such a broad coalition together as the government negotiated a withdrawal agreement would prove immensely challenging.

By 2019, as we have seen, Corbyn's popularity had sunk to unprecedented lows and his polling ratings were the lowest of any opposition leader in modern British history ahead of the election (negative 60). A large section of the Labour movement itself was either deeply sceptical or actively hostile to the idea of his premiership, and in the election dozens of former Labour MPs, including Ian Austin and Gisela Stuart, intervened to urge the public to vote Conservative.

It's the economy, stupid

The 2007-8 financial crisis fatally undermined Labour's hard-won reputation for economic competence and cast a distant shadow over the long decade and beyond. In the years following the crisis, the Labour Party struggled to move on from what the Conservatives labelled 'Labour's recession' and restore voters trust to manage public finances.

Figure 3 shows that the Conservatives maintained a consistent, and at times commanding, polling lead over Labour on the metric of economic competence even during the difficult early years of the Coalition government when economic growth flatlined. After March 2013, the macroeconomic environment improved drastically and a period of strong economic growth, falling unemployment and growing consumer confidence followed. Benign economic conditions contributed to the Conservatives' further widening the gap over Labour to 18% by September 2013.

An opposition leader's choice of Shadow Chancellor is also important in establishing a credible alternative to the government. Miliband's choice of Ed Balls between 2010 and 2015 presented difficulties given his closeness to Gordon Brown in the decade preceding the financial crisis. Under Corbyn's leadership and McDonnell's Shadow Chancellorship, the Conservatives extended their lead over Labour on economic competence and in April 2017 were 35% ahead.

Figure 3 Voters preference to manage the economy (2008-2020)
Source: IPSOS MORI, British Electoral Survey

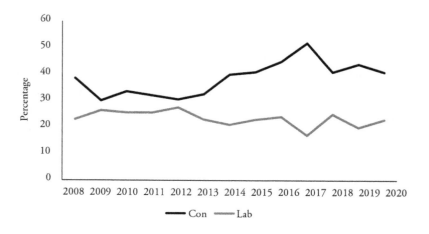

Between 2013 and 2020, the Conservatives presided over 28 consecutive quarters of economic growth. The unemployment rate also fell rapidly while the Conservatives were in office, from 9.5% in 2012 to just 3.8% by early 2020. This meant that the government entered consecutive general elections, in 2015, 2017 and 2019 with a benign economic backdrop.

Electoral trends (2007-2020)

Both the Conservative and Labour parties changed significantly over the long decade after 2007. During this time, the Conservatives expanded their voter coalition to incorporate a larger proportion of working-class and older voters, while at the same time managed to maintain the support of affluent Southern voters. As a result, and despite a decade in government, the Conservative vote share rose from 36% in 2010 to a commanding 44% in 2019.

In opposition, between 2010 and 2020, the Labour Party also won more voters and established a convincing lead among younger voters, minorities and metropolitan voters living in big cities. In a first-past-the-post system, this has led to consecutive Labour leaders stacking up large majorities in safe seats – such as in big metropolitan cities and university towns – but achieving limited national appeal.

Age profile

The Conservative Party has historically enjoyed an electoral advantage among older voters. There are several reasons for this. As voters grow older, they tend to become more socially conservative and therefore align more closely with the Conservative Party on certain social and cultural values. Given older voters are also more likely to pay taxes and own their own home, or multiple homes, they are less susceptible to the appeal of redistributive economic policies.

During the decade after 2010, the gap between support for Labour and the Conservatives among the over 65s widened considerably, as Figure 4 shows. This trend underpinned and was fundamental to Conservative electoral successes because older people are not just more likely than other demographic groups to turn out and vote, they are also well distributed across constituencies in the United Kingdom.

Figure 4 How over-65s voted in general elections (2010-2019)
Source: IPSOS MORI, British Electoral Survey

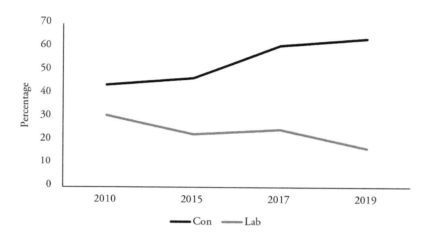

Older voters benefited in several ways from Conservative policies during the Coalition government between 2010 and 2015. As Prime Minister, Cameron made the controversial decision to protect the state pension portion of the welfare budget and chose to focus instead on reducing in- and out-of-work welfare payments. In the Coalition's first budget after the 2010 election, the Chancellor introduced a 'triple lock' on state pensions that guaranteed payments would rise by the highest of either inflation, average wages, or 2.5% at a time of public sector pay caps being introduced. The Conservatives contrasted his government's generosity in providing the elderly with security in old age with the derisory increases in the state pension between 1997 and 2010, when Labour was in power.

Elderly voters were also disproportionately advantaged by the mini boom in property prices between late-2012 through to the 2016 referendum. In 2013 alone, for instance, the average London property price increased by a staggering 17%. Older people, who are more likely to be asset rich, own their own home and to be landlords, stood to gain significantly from steeply rising property valuations in a housing market that was severely supply constrained. The economic growth model established after the financial crisis disproportionately benefited a constituency of Conservative voters, who reaped the benefits of higher asset prices and rental values.

Ahead of the 2015 election, the Conservatives made an explicit play for the grey vote. As well as the supportive policies he had introduced in government for the elderly, Cameron was also able to draw a sharp distinction between his own manifesto commitments and those set out by Miliband in the Labour manifesto. Combined, Labour's proposals to introduce a mansion tax on properties valued above £1 million and to replace universal pensioner benefits, such as the television licence, winter fuel payments and the Freedom Pass, with means tested support for over 65s would have made the average retiree significantly worse off compared with Cameron's plans.

In her report into the causes of Labour's 2015 election defeat, the Labour grandee Margaret Beckett identified the fact that the party 'went backwards among older voters' as being central to understanding what went wrong.[6]

The gap in support for Labour and the Conservatives among older voters widened further after 2015. While Corbyn's victory in the Labour leadership contest helped the party entrench support among students and millennial graduates, neither his leadership nor the policies he espoused had much appeal to older voters. Unlike young people, elderly voters better understood the significance of Corbyn's affiliation with dissident organisations, such as the IRA and were more likely to remember the Brighton bombing in 1982, in which an attempt was made by the IRA to take the life of an elected Prime Minister. The Labour leader's lack of patriotism and perceived willingness to side with Britain's enemies abroad repelled the post-war baby-boomer generation.

The EU referendum in June 2016 reflected deep intergenerational disparities in British politics: some 65% of over 65s were estimated to have voted Leave. A Conservative Party committed to respecting and delivering the referendum result was therefore well positioned to consolidate their already-dominant position among these voters. In the 2017 election, Conservative support among over 65s rose to over 60%.

The triple lock policy also remained in Conservative manifestos in 2017 and 2019, becoming a sacred cow for Prime Ministers who feared the repercussions of abolishing it. By the 2019 election, the Conservatives enjoyed a 47% lead over Labour among the over-65s and British Electoral Survey data shows that some 39% of Labour to Conservative switchers were retired. Johnson's promise to deliver Brexit and defeat Corbyn had an obvious appeal to older voters, especially in England and Wales.

Home ownership

Since 2010, the Conservative Party has established a formidable lead among homeowners, including those who owned a second property, as well as landlords. Support among this voter group reached 50% in the 2019 election, giving the Conservatives a lead over Labour of 23%. There is a significant overlap between older voters and homeowners, and therefore, as with the elderly, this group are also more likely to vote and are better distributed across constituencies nationally.

Ironically, the support of homeowners has been secured by the Conservatives against a backdrop of falling overall property ownership levels in the UK. There has been a failure overall of consecutive Conservative governments to construct enough housing units to meet the needs of a growing population and create a Property Owning Democracy. As the supply of housing failed to keep pace with demand following the financial crisis, homeowners saw the values of their properties rise significantly. Between 2010 and 2019, the average property value in the UK rose from £170,000 to £230,000 – an increase of 35%.[7] This helps explains how the Conservatives have established such a dominant electoral position among homeowners.

The Labour Party has been successful at attracting support from younger voters living in the private rented sector of the housing market. In 2010, the Conservatives enjoyed a small lead over Labour among this group, however, their support in subsequent elections fell and plateaued. Rising property prices under the Conservatives have priced many young professionals living in big cities like London out of the property market.

Figure 5 How homeowners voted in general elections (2010-2019)
Source: IPSOS MORI, British Electoral Survey

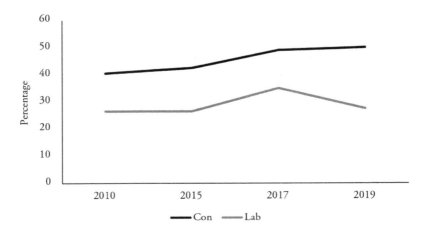

Labour's lead among private renters extended under Corbyn's leadership. Corbyn spoke of the need to take on exploitative landlords, including by introducing a charter of renters' rights and a national property MOT. Given that even right-of-centre think tanks acknowledge that the UK housing market is broken, it is unsurprising that many young people turned to more radical and interventionist solutions to address the problems of supply. Electorally, this has led to Labour stacking up large majorities in big, metropolitan cities where voters are more likely to live in crowded and over-priced rented accommodation. In the 2019 election, Labour won the support of 54% of private renters.

Social class

Working-class voters have been central to accounts of Labour's electoral difficulties in the decade after 2010. At the beginning of the decade, the Conservatives and Labour broadly split the working class vote evenly, with a 35% share each and the remainder split between smaller parties. In the 2015 election, the Conservatives lost support among the lowest income groups, suggesting that Miliband's cost of living agenda resonated with a precariat section of the labour market. Public spending cuts, and in particular reductions in welfare spending between 2010 and 2015, might also explain the decline in the Conservative share of low-income votes in this election.

After 2016, the Brexit vote offered the Conservative Party under the leadership of Theresa May an opportunity to reach working-class voters in Labour Leave areas. As well as promising to respect and deliver the referendum result, May signalled a change in the direction of government policy to tackle what she called the 'burning injustices' afflicting society. In the 2017 election, May increased the Conservative Party's support among working-class voters to 42%, although Labour's support also rose to 45%.

Figure 6 How the working classes voted in general elections (2010-2019)
Source: IPSOS MORI, British Electoral Survey

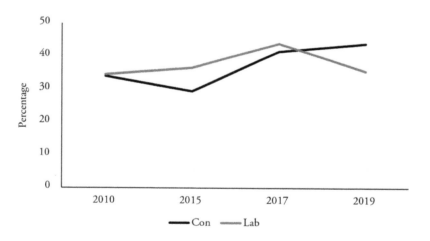

In the 2019 election, the Conservatives moved decisively ahead among working-class and low-income voters and their share of working voters rose to 44% while Labour's support collapsed.

Middle-class voters
As well as expanding their voter coalition to reach a growing number of working-class voters, the Conservatives managed to sustain the support of more affluent, middle-class voters. After 2015, Corbyn's leadership

197

helped prevent Conservative Remainers in southern England from tactically voting Liberal Democrat in opposition to Brexit. By 2019, the fear of a radical Corbyn government sweeping into Downing Street with the support of Sturgeon and the nationalists seemed to outweigh the discomfort some middle-class voters might have felt about Johnson and his Brexit policies.

In the 2019 election, the Conservatives led Labour across all social classes.

7

Smaller parties

Much of the analysis in the preceding chapters has focused on the two main political parties and the reasons for the relative success of the Conservatives compared with the Labour Party. In some ways, this is not surprising. British electoral politics tends to be examined through the prism of the governing and opposition parties – the principal actors who take centre stage – and smaller parties, who are marginalised as part of the 'side show'. The UK's winner-takes-all voting system has historically created formidable barriers to entry for smaller challenger parties, and as a result the 'Big Two' have dominated British politics since the First World War. Although the Liberal Democrats enjoyed a brief period in the sun between 2005 and 2015, their success was relatively short-lived, and the party failed to decisively break the stranglehold of the two parties over the levers of power. In the 2017 election, for instance, the two main parties won between them a commanding 85% of the national vote share as support for smaller parties collapsed.

Despite their limited representation in the House of Commons, smaller parties have nonetheless had an important impact on electoral events in the 21st century. General elections between 2005 and 2017 were characterised by relatively close results, with both parties coming close in terms of national vote share (as in the case of 2005) entering a formal coalition (2010) winning a relatively small working majority (2015) and forming a minority government (2017). As a result, the traditional power exercised by the executive in the British system was weakened considerably over this period.

The impact on smaller parties on electoral politics in the long decade has been considerable and ought not to be measured merely in terms of parliamentary representation. For instance, the rise of the Liberal Democrats and the phenomena of Cleggmania in the late 2000s constrained the Conservatives electorally and played an important role in depriving Cameron's party of a parliamentary majority in 2010. Equally, the failure of the Liberals to mount an electoral recovery after their time in Coalition government and to successfully mobilise the Remain vote after the 2016 EU referendum had important consequences, too.

In Scotland, the electoral hegemony enjoyed by the SNP has created an existential crisis for the Labour Party since 2014 and has created the conditions in which a revival of Conservative Unionism has been made possible. Over this period, Nicola Sturgeon has become an extremely important figure in both Scottish and British politics.

In England and Wales, the growing popularity of right-wing parties, most notably UKIP and the Brexit Party, presented difficulties for both the main parties after 2008. Arguably UKIP and the Brexit Party are the most successful single-issue parties in British political history because they achieved their stated aim(s) of securing a national referendum on membership of the EU and then helped to facilitate the UK's exit from the European Union.

The Liberal Democrats

The first two decades of the 21st century were a story of two halves for the Liberal Democrats. The first half was a story of political revival that culminated in a five-year stint in Coalition government with the Conservatives. The second half, after 2015, saw the Liberal Democrats significantly under-perform at consecutive general elections and fail to mobilise the Remain vote after 2016, which largely rallied to the Labour Party. The changing political fortunes of the Liberal Democrats has had a significant impact on the two main parties and the electoral dynamic of British electoral politics.

Revival: 1997-2015

The revival of the Liberals began in the late-1990s as the party grew closer to New Labour. In the run-up to the 1997 election, Tony Blair was even rumoured to have considered forming a formal Coalition with the Liberals, reviving a version of the Lib-Lab electoral pacts in the early 20th century. Blair might have hoped such an arrangement would help anchor Labour in the centre ground and support his ambitions to lock the Tories out of power for a generation.

Although a formal arrangement was never established, Blair's re-branding of New Labour drove tactical voting among Conservative voters across Southern England who felt empowered to vote Liberal Democrat. In the 1997 and 2001 general elections, the Liberal Democrats picked up Conservative seats in South-West England and suburban London. In these areas, the party offered voters a socially liberal and economically moderate alternative to the Tories, who had moved in a more Eurosceptic, rightward direction under the leadership of William Hague, Iain Duncan Smith and Michael Howard. The 2000s also ushered in a new generation of talented and ambitious Liberal Democrat MPs. In 2004, the *Orange Book: Reclaiming Liberalism* was published and contained contributions from future Coalition ministers including Nick Clegg, David Laws and Vince Cable. Emphasising the role of choice and competition in the market economy, the Orange Book provided the intellectual foundation for 21st century liberalism.

The success of the Liberal Democrats proved to be a significant electoral constraint on the Conservative Party over this period and the party had a symbiotic relationship with New Labour until 2003 when, under the leadership of Charles Kennedy, the party shifted leftward and reaped electoral benefits from opposing the Iraq War. In university towns, support for the Liberal Democrats rose among students as a result of their opposition to tuition fees, which Blair's government trebled in 2004, and to the Iraq War. In the 2005 election, the Liberals were rewarded with 62 seats (the highest count of any third party since 1923).

The 2010 General Election represented the peak of the Liberal Democrat Party's power and influence in British electoral politics. Clegg's impressive performance in televised leadership debates and the resulting phenomena of 'Cleggmania' contributed to Cameron's failure to win an outright majority for his party in 2010. The phenomena also illustrated that anti-establishment, 'populist' rhetoric can be harnessed by self-styled moderate, centrist leaders and Clegg enjoyed an outsider advantage by positioning himself against the two main parties. In the election, the Liberal Democrat national vote share rose to 23% (an increase of almost one million votes from 2005), underpinned by a broad voter coalition drawn from the affluent London suburbs and South-West England, university towns and seats in the Celtic fringes (especially Scotland). The UK's idiosyncratic electoral system reduced the Liberal Democrat seat count by five, despite the party's impressive national vote share.

Short of an overall majority, the Conservatives entered a formal coalition with the Liberal Democrats in 2010, the first time Liberals had served in government since the collapse of Lloyd George's administration in 1922. Clegg was given the title of Deputy Prime Minister and senior Liberal Democrats, such as David Laws and Vince Cable, were given big economic briefs at the Treasury and Department for Business.

Decline and disappointment: 2015-2020

Five years in Coalition government with the Conservatives badly damaged the Liberal Democrats' political standing and severely fractured the voter coalition the party had constructed in the preceding decade. Having served in government with the Conservatives, the Liberal Democrats no longer offered liberal-minded Conservative voters in suburban London and South-West England a potential protest vote. Likewise, by ordering his MPs to vote for a £6,000 rise in university tuition fees, Clegg made it impossible to mobilise student votes in Labour-facing university seats, such as Cambridge. The infamous Liberal 'U-turn' on tuition fees was worsened by the fact that Clegg had made an explicit play for student votes in the 2010 election campaign and had thereby staked his political authority on a policy of abolishing fees.

In the 2015 election, the Liberal Democrats were badly punished by voters for their time in the Coalition. Nationally, the party's vote share collapsed by 15% and no fewer than 49 seats were lost (mainly to the Tories who picked up 27 of them). Many senior 'Orange book' Liberal MPs, including Cable, Laws and Davey, lost their seats in the election. With just eight seats in the House of Commons, the vast majority having been lost to the Conservatives, the Liberals were also relegated to the fourth party in British politics behind Nicola Sturgeon's Scottish Nationalist Party.

Although the Tories were the prime beneficiaries of Liberal decline, Labour also picked up the university town of Cambridge in 2015, beginning a drift of student voters from the Liberal Democrats back to the Labour Party that would continue for the rest of the decade. Labour also tightened its grip over Central London and the veteran MP Simon Hughes was unseated in Bermondsey and Old Southwark.

After 2015, the failure of the Liberal Democrats under consecutive leaders to re-establish their electoral position continued to be to the overall advantage of the Conservatives. In several individual seats, the Labour Party benefited too.

The EU referendum result and resulting realignment in the electoral system around new Brexit loyalties had the potential to benefit the Liberal Democrats. At a time when the two main parties committed to respect the referendum result and take the UK out of the EU Single Market, the Liberals could present themselves as *the* opposition to a hard Brexit, thus reviving their role as a protest vote. In the end, this was not to be. In the 2017 election, the Liberals were made irrelevant by a brief return to two party politics and the party's leader, Tim Farron, became embroiled in a distracting debate about same-sex relationships. The Labour Party successfully united the Remain vote under a single banner and defeated Nick Clegg in the student-heavy constituency of Sheffield Hallam. In the South West, the Conservatives entrenched their electoral hegemony because many constituencies in this part of the country had voted by a majority for Brexit and tactical Liberal Democrat voting fell away under Corbyn's leadership of the Labour Party.

The Liberal Democrats enjoyed a brief renaissance in the early summer of 2019 under the temporary leadership of Vince Cable. The 'bollocks to Brexit' slogan, which clearly identified theirs as the party unambiguously opposed to Brexit, propelled the Liberal Democrats into second place in the European elections with 20% of the national vote. In opinion polling in the weeks and months that followed, the Liberal Democrat and Brexit parties were polling ahead of the two main parties. The party also benefited from the collapse of Change UK over this period. Many of the MPs who had defected to Change UK, including Chuka Umunna and Luciana Berger, transferred allegiance to the Liberal Democrats and in the summer several Conservative Remainer MPs, including former ministers Philip Lee and Sam Gyimah, crossed the House of Commons to sit on the Liberal Democrat benches.

Under the new leadership of the Scottish MP and former minister Jo Swinson, the Liberal Democrats discovered a new-found confidence. Emboldened by opinion polls, Swinson told party members in her first speech as leader that 'I stand before you today, not just as the leader of the Liberal Democrats, but as a candidate for Prime Minister.' Over the summer of 2019, the Liberal leader worked with other opposition parties, including Corbyn's Labour Party, to prevent a no-deal Brexit outcome. These efforts stepped up at the party conference in September when delegates agreed that should the Liberals win an outright majority in a general election, Swinson would have the authority to unilaterally 'revoke Article 50' and thus stop Brexit without the need for another referendum.

In retrospect, Swinson's bold claim to be standing in an election as a candidate for Prime Minister appears hubristic. Liberal Democrat success in the European elections, before Swinson had even become leader, was overwhelmingly driven by Conservative and Labour Remainers exercising a protest vote in a (relatively) inconsequential election. It might even have been the case that some Leave voters in the South West of England voted for the Liberals as a protest against the failure of the government to deliver Brexit too. How this would have translated in a Westminster election, under the conditions of a first-past-the-post system, was entirely unpredictable. In 2010, for instance, the Liberals had won a commanding 23% of the vote and returned just 57 MPs. Even in the politically febrile environment created by Brexit, the idea of the Liberal Democrats forming a majority government required a significant stretch of the imagination.

Given the way things turned out, the fact Swinson encouraged an early general election in December 2019 and helped make it possible, means the charge of hubris is particularly apposite. In Conservative-facing seats in Southern England, the fear of a Corbyn-led government prevented Tory Remainers from turning to the Liberal Democrats. Although the Liberal vote rose sharply in affluent seats, including Dominic Raab's Esher constituency, it was not enough to flip the seat. Voters in these areas might have been uncomfortable with how closely Swinson had worked with opposition party leaders, especially Corbyn, in the months preceding the election. If a condition of making a second referendum possible was Corbyn being made Prime Minister, that was not a price they were ultimately willing to pay.

For Labour voters in big cities and university seats, the Liberal Democrat brand continued to be associated with the policies of the Coalition government in which Swinson had served as a minister. In the campaign, she ended up in the uncomfortable position of having to defend Cameron-era spending cuts while Johnson, who had been mayor of London at the time, was able to distance himself from austerity policies earlier in the decade.

Despite increasing their vote share, Liberal Democrat representation in the Commons remained virtually unchanged after the 2019 election and Swinson's East Dunbartonshire seat fell to the SNP.

Change UK

For the duration of Jeremy Corbyn's leadership of the Labour Party from 2015, speculation raged about the possibility of a formal split to establish a new left-of-centre political force in British politics. Reminiscent of the 1980s, the Labour Party's sharp leftward shift had left moderate figures in the movement feeling disenfranchised and politically homeless. Moderates in the Parliamentary Labour Party grew impatient with many aspects of the Corbyn project, from their leader's style and presentation to the substance of his policies. Perhaps most importantly, after 2017, they became critical of Corbyn's handling of Brexit and refusal to adopt change official Labour policy in favour of a second EU referendum.

Liberal media publications expressed dismay at the choice voters faced, too. In June 2017, the *Economist* ran a leading article entitled 'The middle has fallen out of British politics', and *Metro* observed that 'the centre ground of politics has become the no man's land few dare to cross'. These publications grew wary of the Conservative Party under May's leadership, which they claimed was being held hostage by the European Research Group, and simultaneously lamented the absence of a credible opposition from Labour, which was seen as little more than a protest movement led by a man entirely unsuitable for the role of Prime Minister. Such disillusionment with the status quo inevitably fed calls for a shake-up through electoral reform and the formation of a new political start up to channel the views and frustrations of the disenfranchised masses of centrist voters.

In February 2019, the long-anticipated formal break away finally came. Chuka Umunna and Luciana Berger led five parliamentary colleagues to form a new political party, arguing that the Labour Party under Corbyn 'no longer exists'. The political start-up, Change UK, stood under the slogan 'Politics is broken… Let's fix it'; however, apart from a firm commitment to a second referendum on EU membership, the policy programme of the new party lacked substance. Reminiscent of the Blair years, Change UK distanced itself from the ideological extremes of the two main parties, arguing for an evidence-based approach to politics based on 'whatever works'.

Early opinion polling did not bode well for Change UK. Ahead of the European elections in the early summer of 2019, the *Financial Times* poll of polls gave the new party a 3% national vote share. More worrying still was the confusion some voters had about what the party actually stood for; just 38% of respondents to a YouGov poll believed that they were an anti-Brexit Party. Given that Change UK's only substantive policy position was a second EU referendum with the aim of overturning the 2016 Leave vote, this was a considerable problem. One explanation for the confusion is the incoherent way in which Change UK was branded.

The notion of 'Change' did not match up with the party's central policy position, which was to maintain Britain's existing relationship with the UK.

Change UK's communications and media operation was also extremely poor. As the *Economist* pointed out, 'One of the many ironies of the European election is that the supposedly backward-looking Brexit Party has exploited social media much more astutely than the self-consciously with-it Change UK.'[1] In the absence of a strong ground network of volunteers, Change UK required a sophisticated digital operation to compensate for its political infancy.

In pure electoral terms, the impact of Change UK on British politics was relatively marginal and arguably immaterial. After all, the party failed to achieve a decisive break-through in their first major test at the ballot box in the 2019 European elections, where they were eclipsed by the Liberal Democrats and received just 3% of the national vote. Furthermore, fears that dozens of moderate Labour MPs were on the verge of abandoning the party under Corbyn never materialised, and Change UK failed to attract big beasts from the Labour movement capable of seriously challenging the Labour leadership. If anything, Change UK's difficulties in establishing itself as a challenger party might have served mainly as a warning, discouraging further defections to others in the Parliamentary Labour Party who were contemplating leaving.

Change UK's fleeting existence in British politics was not inconsequential, though. By dramatically abandoning Labour and claiming that the party 'no longer existed' under Corbyn's leadership, the defectors further damaged the Labour brand in the eyes of the electorate. If his own moderate MPs could not feel at home, even safe, in the Labour Party, how then could voters possibly support Corbyn and make him Prime Minister? Perhaps Change UK's biggest impact then was the fact it needed to be created in the first place.

The Scottish Nationalist Party

Apart from the major realignment of voters away from Labour to the Conservatives in England and Wales, the other big story of the long decade has been the transformation of the political dynamic in Scotland. The Scottish National Party's electoral fortunes in Westminster elections were transformed following the 2014 independence referendum. The advance of the SNP came largely at the expense of Scottish Labour and provided the political space in which the Conservative (Unionist) Party could emerge as the official opposition in Holyrood.

Although Scotland voted decisively in favour of remaining part of the United Kingdom, the SNP enjoyed a meteoric rise in popularity north of the border in the years that followed. In the 2015 election, the SNP won a commanding 56 seats in Westminster (an increase of 50) with a 50% vote share. These gains came almost entirely at the expense of the Scottish Labour Party, which was reduced to holding just a single seat in Edinburgh South following the election. Given Labour's historical dominance in Scotland (as late as 2010 the party had won 41 seats north of the border) this was electorally devastating and posed enormous challenges for a party that had not won the popular vote in England since 2001. Several senior Labour MPs lost their seats, including the Shadow Foreign Secretary, Douglas Alexander, whose Paisley and Renfrewshire seat fell to the SNP on a 27% swing, depriving Scottish Labour of some of its most talented and capable politicians, who have since pursued careers outside of politics.

In the 2017 election, Labour mounted a minor recovery in Scotland and returned with 7 seats (an increase on 6 from the last election) as the SNP temporarily retreated from the impressive gains they had made two years earlier. Nonetheless, this was a relatively poor performance by Labour in a part of the United Kingdom that had once been a heartland. Corbyn's leadership also undermined Labour's credentials as a Unionist party given he, along with his Shadow Chancellor, had historically supported nationalist and Republican movements, such as the IRA.

In the 2019 election, Labour once again returned just a single MP, in Edinburgh South and the party's vote share collapsed catastrophically to its lowest level in a century.

The surging support for the nationalists north of the border has supported Conservative electoral successes. In the 2015 election, Cameron warned English voters that Miliband would only be able to enter Downing Street by forming a 'coalition of chaos' on the coat-tails of the SNP. The iconic image of Miliband peeking from out from Alex Salmond's shirt pocket captured the risks posed by a Labour-SNP coalition arrangement and the Labour leader's perceived impotence in such an arrangement.

Upsets in Scottish politics after 2014 also provided the Conservatives with the opportunity to present themselves as *the* Unionist opposition to the nationalists. In the 2017 election, the popular Scottish Conservative leader Ruth Davidson fought a campaign that was almost entirely detached from the party's Westminster operation and successfully united the Unionist vote behind the Conservative banner. The Conservatives won 13 Scottish seats, the party's best representation north of the border in a generation and had Davidson and the Scottish Conservatives not been so successful in that election, then May might not have had enough MPs to form a government.

Ahead of the 2019 election, the Scottish Conservatives once again fought a separate campaign from the operation in Westminster and instead focused on the constitutional question of whether there should be another independence referendum. Reviving the tactic Cameron had deployed in 2015, Johnson warned voters of the risks posed by a minority Corbyn government supported by the Scottish nationalists, claiming that 2020 could be the 'year of two referendums.' The Conservative vote held up well in Scotland at 25%, although the party lost several MPs to the SNP.

Overall, surging support for the nationalists in Scotland following the independence referendum in 2014 has supported Conservative electoral successes and undermined the Labour Party's prospects of winning a majority in Westminster. Sturgeon's party has robbed Labour of dozens of seats in what was once a political heartland and has allowed the Tories to position themselves as *the* official unionist alternative to the nationalists in Scotland. In England, the Conservatives have also successfully presented the spectre of a minority Labour government propped up the SNP as a risk to the economic security of the nation. This strategy helped the Conservatives win dozens of seats in South West England in the 2015 election.

UK Independence Party (UKIP)

The rise of right-wing political parties in the first two decades of the 21st century has been well documented in numerous accounts, such as Matthew Goodwin and Robert Ford's study *Revolt on the Right*. As the authors identify, the success of right-wing parties is a trend across continental Europe. In the Netherlands, the leader of Party for Freedom, Geert Wilders, has exerted significant influence on the Dutch government; in France, Marine Le Pen achieved a 35% vote share in the 2017 Presidential elections, and Matteo Salvini served as Deputy Prime Minister and Minister of the Interior in Italy. As Pippa Norris has shown, populist parties have won on an average 13.2% national vote share in national and European parliamentary elections, largely at the expense of centre (especially centre-left) parties.[2]

In the UK, the most obvious manifestation this trend has been the rise of UKIP since c.2008. Although the party was unable to achieve meaningful representation in parliament, UKIP has provided a certain constituency of voters with an outlet through which they could channel grievances about a range of cultural issues, including immigration. Indeed, the party's early success occurred at a time when both the main parties were fighting over swing voters in Middle England with the aim of occupying an economically moderate, socially liberal 'centre ground' position. This provided a political space on the right of British politics for a Eurosceptic party.

Both the major political parties made the mistake, at various points, of under-estimating the threat posed by UKIP. In 2006, Cameron infamously described the party as filled with 'a bunch of fruit cakes, loonies and closet racists'. At the time, distancing himself from UKIP might have made political sense as he focused on de-toxifying the Conservative brand. However, as it became clear that Farage was becoming a serious electoral threat in traditionally Conservative-voting areas, Cameron would be forced to adopt a more conciliatory tone and his party was pushed in a more Eurosceptic direction. Despite promising the British people a referendum on EU membership ion 2013, the Conservative MPs Douglas Carswell and Mark Reckless resigned the party whip to stand as UKIP MPs the following year.

Even greater complacency about the rise of UKIP can be seen in the Labour Party. It was for a long time assumed that Farage would pose a threat largely to the Conservatives in the South-East and East of England. In reality, working-class small-town Labour voters in the party's industrial and post-industrial heartlands were turning increasingly to Farage and UKIP too. As Nick Timothy has argued, what motivates working-class voters to support populists such as Farage is a sense 'that relative to others, they and their group had lost out, whether to more affluent middle-class citizens or to immigrants'.[3] Many in the Labour Party resisted efforts by various leaders, including Brown and Miliband, to respond to the threat posed by UKIP. Indeed, we saw in Chapter 3 how Brown's 'British jobs for British workers' speech and Miliband's pledges on immigration controls provoked fury from metropolitan MPs. As they saw it, the Labour Party should not pander to dangerous populists like Farage and in the Labour leadership contest in 2015, Corbyn suggested that support for UKIP was 'driven in many ways by racism'.

UKIP's voter coalition sewed together an alliance of affluent traditionally Conservative voters in Southern and Eastern England with working-class Labour voters in Northern England and Wales. Although superficially disparate groups, these voters shared an attachment to certain British 'values', resisted a liberal culture of political correctness and, importantly, embodied a certain English identity. They were also united in their Euroscepticism and a tendency to favour tighter immigration controls. Farage himself was central to efforts to pull together these constituencies and in particular reaching traditional Labour voters. He channelled their anxieties and concerns at a time when the institutional Labour Party was speaking increasingly to a narrow sub-set of voters in big, metropolitan cities.

The electoral impact of UKIP is easily underestimated. It could be argued that Farage's party represented little more than a protest vote for Labour and Conservative voters. By this account, UKIP enjoyed brief moments in the sun when European elections came around every five years or in some local and by-elections but were largely rendered irrelevant in general elections. In the 2015 election, for instance, in return for achieving their highest ever national vote share, in total no fewer than four million votes, UKIP were rewarded with just a single MP.

In practice, though, UKIP's contribution to electoral politics goes deeper than their ability to win parliamentary representation in the House of Commons. Farage and his party applied pressure on both the two main parties, especially the Conservatives, who were pushed in a more Eurosceptic direction than Cameron and Osborne felt comfortable with. Indeed, Cameron's decision in 2013 to call a referendum on EU membership was a response to the perceived threat posed by UKIP and the party ultimately succeeded in the aim of securing the UK's departure from the EU. In general elections, UKIP's impact at constituency level was more impactful. In the 2015 election, for instance, an increase in the UKIP vote share at the expense of Labour helped the Conservatives pick up several seats across Northern England and Wales, including Ed Ball's seat of Morley and Outwood.

Responding to Farage

The Conservatives were ultimately far more successful than Labour at responding to the threat of UKIP on their right flank. In 2013, David Cameron's decision to call a referendum on EU membership in the event of a majority Conservative government gave his party the initiative on the Europe question. Going into the 2015 election, Cameron was able to unite his party behind a compromise policy whereby his government should be allowed to negotiate a new agreement with the EU and then put it to a national referendum. After the surprise Brexit vote, the Conservatives neutered UKIP by pledging to respect and deliver the Leave result. Farage's departure as leader in September 2016 appeared to signal the final nail in the coffin for the party, something which was confirmed by the 2017 General Election, in which UKIP won less than 2% of the national vote.

The Brexit Party

The continued ability of Farage to shape and influence British politics, as well as respond to a political opportunity that presents itself at a given moment, was demonstrated in the early spring of 2019. His political start up, the Brexit Party, which had originally been formed to oppose

May's withdrawal agreement in November 2018, ruthlessly exploited the government's failure to deliver Brexit on schedule. With the support of wealthy backers, including the Eurosceptic multi-millionaire businessman Richard Tice, Farage quickly built a slick and effective political operation with the central demand for a 'clean Brexit'. A sophisticated social media operation and digital strategy allowed the Brexit Party to mobilise Leave voters furious at the failure of parliament to deliver the result of the referendum.

The Brexit Party was hugely successful in the European elections. Farage hoovered up discontented Labour voters across North, Midlands and Wales, as well as Tory voters in the South East and South West of England. In June 2019, the Brexit Party surged to 25% in the opinion polls – neck and neck with Labour and the Conservatives.

The return of Farage to frontline politics startled the Conservatives and paved the way for Johnson's premiership. Recognising the danger posed by the Brexit Party, dozens of Conservative MPs, many of whom might have had reservations about Johnson's suitability to lead the party, threw their weight behind his candidacy. As Prime Minister, Johnson's determination to deliver the Leave result, whatever the cost, was driven by, as much as anything else, the political threat posed by Farage.

A relatively small number of respect-the-referendum Labour MPs recognised the threat the Brexit Party posed. Following the European elections, MPs representing heavily Leave-voting constituencies in Northern England, including Caroline Flint, Lisa Nandy and Gareth Snell, argued forcefully against a second referendum position and in favour of a managed withdrawal from the EU with an agreement. These warnings fell on deaf ears and there was complacency in the Parliamentary Labour Party about the robustness of the Labour Leave vote right up to the 2019 election result itself.

Johnson eliminated the threat of the Brexit Party in 2019 by winning an 80 seat majority in the House of Commons, negotiating a Free Trade Agreement the following year and getting Brexit done.

Part III

Why do the Conservatives keep winning?

8

Key themes

(1900-2020)

As we have seen in Parts I and II, Labour's electoral record up to and including the recent past has been relatively poor and characterised by long stretches on the opposition benches. Historically, when the party has achieved political power, Labour governments have often been short-lived and prone to suffer major and destabilising crises. For much of its existence, the Labour Party has also been led by individuals who, for various reasons, have struggled to mobilise a broad coalition of voters and thus win general elections. Only three Labour leaders have become Prime Minister by winning an outright working majority in a general election.

Despite being historically associated with the political interests of the rich and propertied classes, the Conservatives have proved highly adept at winning general elections and have spent much of the 20th and 21st centuries in power. When the Conservatives have been consigned to the opposition benches, they have been quick to diagnose the reasons for the defeat and have often responded quickly, thus enabling them to return to power soon thereafter.

This Chapter reflects on the key themes that have characterised British electoral politics over the past 120 years to account for the contrasting performance of the two main parties at the ballot box. It is not for nothing that the British Conservative Party is the most successful political operation in Europe. Conservative electoral success has been achieved through tried and tested methods based on what works and their leaders have time and again reached for certain popular policies that cut across class, income and geography to appeal to a broad range of voters including, crucially, a section of aspirational working-class voters.

Constructing voter coalitions

To win power in the UK's first-past-the-post electoral system, political parties must reach beyond their core voter base and build broad coalitions to sustain working majorities in the House of Commons. Historically, the Conservative Party has proved more adept than Labour at achieving this. As we saw in Parts I and II, to win large parliamentary majorities, the Conservatives successfully sewed together a coalition of affluent middle-class voters in rural English shires with a section of upwardly socially mobile working-class voters across the rest of the UK.

Conservative leaders have been able to transcend the party's association with the interests of the privileged few and have spoken a political language that ordinary voters can understand by making the case for reduced state intervention and lower taxation; rewarding enterprise and hard work, and appealing to voters' aspirations, such as to own a home of their own. In the early 20th century, for instance, the Conservatives built a political alliance of business owners in consumer industries, such as brewing, and ordinary voters who wanted to enjoy the simple pleasure of a pint after a hard day's work. While the Liberal and Labour parties tended to regard alcohol and drunkenness as destructive to household finances, the Conservatives positioned themselves as the champions of the Englishman's basic freedoms. Socialist reformers also tended to see the interests of capital and labour as naturally antagonistic, rather than groups with mutually reinforcing interests.

Post-war Conservative electoral success was underpinned by a political appeal to win the support of a broad section of the electorate, especially aspirational Britons. Consecutive leaders from Churchill and Macmillan to Thatcher sought to identify the Conservatives as the true 'party of the people' by promising to deliver higher living standards, reducing personal tax rates and extending home ownership. Economic security at home was also supported by a robust national defence policy to protect British interests abroad. This combination of guaranteeing national and economic security offered a thread that sewed together a voter coalition of middle-class Southern voters with patriotic working-classes. That high defence spending might mean more British ships, airplanes and military equipment would be manufactured in Northern England or Wales also supported a regional growth policy to spread economic activity outside London and the South East.

To pull together a broad electoral coalition, it has long been possible for Conservative leaders to position themselves in opposition to socialism and the purported threat posed by a left-wing government to national and economic security. This appeal to the 'safety first' instincts of the British, and especially the English, electorate has been important in securing widespread support at the ballot box. For instance, the Labour Party's eighteen years in opposition after 1979 resulted, in large part, from a perception that their leaders could not be trusted on issues of national security and the economy.

In the long decade after 2007, the Conservatives proved equally adept at constructing sustainable voter coalitions to secure victory within a first-past-the-post system. During the Coalition years, Cameron and Osborne used the 'making work pay' agenda to unite the interests of traditional, fiscally hawkish Conservative voters with aspirational working-class households who supported measures to reduce a perceived culture of welfare dependency. After the EU referendum in 2016, May and Johnson recognised the potential to expand the Conservative voter coalition and incorporate an even larger proportion of working-class voters, some of whom might never have voted Tory before.

To cement the broad voter coalition he constructed in 2019, Johnson has thrown his weight behind the green industrial revolution.

Green policies intrinsically play well with affluent southern voters and if the wind turbines can be built in Northern England and Wales then the economic benefits via jobs and investment would appeal to working-class voters in the regions.

The Labour Party's voter coalition of middle-class metropolitan socialists and working-class voters in provincial England and Wales has proved comparably less durable in the face of changing social and economic conditions. As a result, this coalition has been liable to come apart at various points throughout the past 120 years, sometimes spectacularly.

Given its roots and early history, it might be assumed that the Labour Party has a natural claim over ordinary 'working-class' voters. In practice, as we have seen, any such claim appears entirely spurious. The British working class is not, and has never been, a political mass that exercised uniform voting behaviour. Rather, it consists of a geographically disparate and diverse constellation of voters, with different characteristics. Through the 20th century, the Labour Party lost touch with the aspirations of a section of these voters. In the post-war period, for instance, Labour's opposition to consumerism repelled aspirational households seeking a better standard of living. In the 1980s, the party's opposition to Thatcher's flagship 'Right to Buy' housing scheme suggested Labour was against ordinary people owning a home of their own. Likewise, the perceived weakness of Labour leaders on issues of foreign policy drove a wedge between Labour and a certain section of patriotic working-class voters.

In the 21st century the Labour Party has experienced a major rupture with working-class voters and one that has been more debilitating than ever before. Following the success of the Blair years, the Labour Party spoke increasingly to a socially and geographically smaller proportion of the British electorate. Under Corbyn's leadership, Labour retreated into being a sectional party, appealing to left-liberal voters in big cities and university towns, and few beyond. In a first-past-the-post system, the Labour Party will have to broaden its voter coalition, for instance by establishing a connection between the political interests of millennial graduates in metropolitan areas and small-town working-class voters in provincial England, to win power once again.

Unifying the nation

The success of their leaders in forging broad national voter coalitions has supported claims that the Conservative Party is a unifying force in British politics. At various points in the 20th century, Conservative leaders have adopted Benjamin Disraeli's language of 'One Nation' Conservatism to position themselves as a party that represents all parts of the United Kingdom and helps bind it together. While Labour has consistently been presented as a party that seeks to divide the country along class lines, the Conservatives have offered themselves as unifiers of different interest groups in society including the interests of industry and consumers, the constituent parts of the Union of the United Kingdom and working- and middle-class households. A Conservative appeal to national unity is supported by the party's patriotic credentials and reverence of certain British institutions, such as the Church of England and the Monarchy.

A broad appeal to the aspirations of the British electorate has underpinned the electoral success of the Conservative Party. Given most voters want to better themselves, their offspring and families, Conservative leaders consistently appeal to these instincts. As Adam Smith wrote in *The Wealth of Nations*, 'An augmentation of fortune is the means by which the greater part of men propose and wish to better their condition.'[1] To achieve this, Conservative governments have pursued popular policy programmes, including those aimed at widening property ownership, reducing personal taxation levels and encouraging personal responsibility. It is wrong to assume that low-income voters will automatically yearn for steep, redistributive fiscal policies, because the interests of working- and middle-class voters need not be antagonistic. In Smith's *Theory of Moral Sentiments* he suggests that far from envying the rich and powerful, the labouring classes encourage them to do even better.[2] As such, there is reason to believe that rather than envying the rich and powerful, the 'have nots' will applaud them for their achievements. They might also recognise that the success of wealthy entrepreneurs can create spill-over economic benefits, such as greater employment and investment, to the overall benefit of society.

Managing internal divides

As national parties of government, both Labour and the Conservatives are political coalitions. Consequently, both parties are internally divided on certain issues and different factions coexist within a broad political family underpinned by certain unifying beliefs. This explains how a politician like Tony Blair can exist in the same party as Jeremy Corbyn.

For much of its existence, competing ideological groups within the Labour Party have engaged in an ongoing struggle over how to bring about social and economic change. In the 1930s, divisions over how to respond to the economic crisis precipitated by the Great Depression caused the Labour Prime Minister Ramsay MacDonald to form a National Government which contained mainly Conservative MPs. In the post-war period, Hugh Gaitskell fought a losing battle with his party to amend the Labour Constitution and a section of the Parliamentary Labour Party – led by the so-called 'Gang of Four' – broke away to form the Social Democrat Party in 1982. Labour's difficulties in masking their internal divides compromised the party's ability to offer a credible alternative to Conservative governments throughout the 20th century and, as the adage goes, 'divided parties don't win elections'.

The period between 1994 and 2005 was an aberration in British electoral politics. During this period, the Conservatives and not Labour prioritised ideological beliefs – principally over Britain's relationship with Europe – over winning power. Tony Blair exploited Conservative weakness and attempted to establish a new electoral hegemony for his party under the branding of 'New Labour'. Having lost four consecutive elections, the Labour Party largely accepted Blair's argument that it would need to fundamentally change if it were to be politically competitive and win power again.

Despite being Labour's most electorally successful leader, Blair's legacy after leaving office in 2007 sharply divided opinion. Disciples of New Labour lamented the failure of Blair's successors – Brown and Miliband – to keep the project alive. It is common for moderates to identify Labour's choice of Ed Miliband in the 2010 leadership contest rather than the Blairite David Miliband as an important turning point, which badly compromised Labour's electoral competitiveness.

Other figures in the Labour movement developed a disdain for the Blair government and what they saw as a betrayal of socialism during his time as Prime Minister. A belief that it was necessary to put clear blue water between Labour and the Conservatives following New Labour's accommodationist approach helped pave the way for Corbyn's leadership.

The Conservatives historically proved better able to manage internal party divides and united to stop their opponents entering government. In the 1920s and 1930s, for instance, the Conservative Party attracted former Liberals, such as Winston Churchill, into a broad anti-socialist political coalition. In the post-war era Conservative Prime Ministers including Churchill and Macmillan shifted the party leftward on economic policy to accommodate the new Keynesian consensus, despite internal party resistance from those who favoured public spending restraint. In the 1980s there were those in the Parliamentary Conservative Party, known as the 'wets', who were uncomfortable with aspects of Thatcher's economic policy programme. These divides were manageable because Conservative MPs accepted the overall strategic course the government was charting and because Thatcher's authority within the parliamentary party was considerably enhanced by her electoral successes.

Since becoming leader in 2005, there were those in the Conservative Party opposed to Cameron's leadership and modernisation agenda. However, recognising the electoral demands of the time, Cameron was given considerable authority to mould the party in his image and thus win back middle-class voters that had been lost to Blair in the preceding decade. Similarly, in July 2019, Conservative MPs elected Johnson as leader despite reservations about his administrative competence and suitability to be Prime Minister because they believed he was the right person to lead the party out of its present predicament.

Electoral responsiveness

The British Conservative Party is not anchored by a written constitution and therefore lacks a discernible political ideology or fixed set of political beliefs. Such ideological flexibility helps explain both the party's long-standing electoral success and its durability as a political force in the face of economic and social change. If the end in electoral politics is to win and hold power, then the Conservative Party has been comfortable using whatever means is necessary to achieve this. The party's leaders have, above all else, focused on winning and holding power rather than the goal of achieving some political utopia.

Because the Conservative Party is light on ideological baggage, it has shown itself to be highly responsive to changing political circumstances. This has meant that when the Conservatives have been defeated in elections, they have recovered swiftly – identifying fertile political ground and moving quickly to occupy it. After the 1945 Labour landslide victory, for instance, Churchill quickly accommodated aspects of the Attlee government's economic policy, especially a commitment to full employment. Recognising that it would not be politically possible to allow a return to Great Depression-levels of unemployment of the 1930s, Conservative leaders adapted quickly and instead moved to challenge Labour on new frontiers, such as pledging rolling back state restrictions and boosting living standards. To tighten their grip on power in the 1950s, Tory Chancellors used budgets to fund large house-building programmes and cut taxes for ordinary working households.

Conservative ideology rests on a pragmatic assessment of contemporary political needs. Once the political ground shifts beneath them, the Tories adapt swiftly to remain electorally competitive. When, in the 1970s, the long post-war economic boom gave way to stagflation and large-scale industrial strife, Margaret Thatcher tore up the Keynesian economic orthodoxy her party had helped establish, in favour of monetarism. Thatcher's government prioritised containing high inflation levels and maintaining stable macroeconomic conditions over full employment. Her infamous conference speech in 1980 in which she insisted 'The lady's not for turning' represented a stark repudiation of the Heath government's failure to grapple with the structural problems afflicting the UK economy in the preceding decade.

As we have seen, the period between c.1992 and 2005 represented an aberration in the long history of the Conservative Party. For most of its existence the Conservatives have prioritised winning and holding power over ideological purity. However, for much of the 1990s and early 2000s, the Parliamentary Conservative Party allowed itself to become distracted and gripped by the contentious question of Britain's relationship with Europe. Resistance to further European integration from Conservative backbenchers following the Maastricht Treaty helped bring an end to Major's government and did serious and lasting damage to the Conservative brand, which historically had previously hinged on pragmatism, economic competence and a reputation for good government.

In 1997, Tony Blair swept Major's tired government aside and delivered for his party one of the largest parliamentary majorities in British political history. While Blair presented himself as the future, replete with a full-scale modernisation programme to transform Britain going into the new century, the Tory Party appeared divided and tired, ravaged by infighting over Europe and 18 years in office. Opposition to the minimum wage and the repeal of Section 28 seemed to confirm suspicions that the Conservative Party of the early 21st century had lost touch and in 2002 Theresa May pointed to members that 'some people call us the nasty party'. To regain power, the party would have to do what it had done so successfully for the preceding 100 years: respond and adapt to the electoral realities of the time.

In the long decade after 2007, the Conservative Party demonstrated characteristic flexibility in the face of changing circumstances. As leader, David Cameron de-toxified the Conservative brand to make it relevant in modern Britain, allowing his party to win back voters in Middle England that had been lost to New Labour in the preceding decade. After 2016, the Conservatives shifted rightward on certain cultural questions to win over the support of socially conservative Leave voters in provincial England and Wales. Similarly, having campaigned officially for the UK to remain in the EU, the Conservative government quickly pivoted under May's leadership to honour the result and deliver Brexit. This calculation, that the Conservatives should become the party to deliver Brexit, was based above all else on an understanding that the electoral geography favoured Leave.

On domestic policy, the Conservatives have successfully shaped and adapted to the public debate around public spending. Between 2010 and 2017, Conservative Prime Ministers contrasted their stewardship of public finances with the fiscal 'recklessness' of the last Labour government. However, following the 2017 election, May's government began increasing spending on public services and increased health spending by a record £6 billion in 2018. By 2019, Johnson had decisively turned a page on Cameron-era austerity and promised to deliver an ambitious regional growth policy aimed at 'levelling up'.

Leadership

The Conservative Party has also proved highly effective at producing leaders with widespread electoral appeal, who could build strong and lasting voter coalitions. Conservative leaders have tended to be assets to their party who could be used to widen its appeal and reach a broad section of the electorate. Importantly, the personalities of these leaders have allowed them to transcend their party's association with the rich. As we saw in Chapter 1, Conservative leaders have demonstrated an ability to reach beyond the core vote, converting a significant number of working-class voters to the Conservative column in the 20th century. Leaders such as Baldwin, Macmillan and Thatcher emerged at a time when their party needed a new direction. They also had the power and authority as leaders to shape the party in their own image – Thatcher set about undoing Heath's legacy after 1975 and Cameron de-toxified the Conservative brand by making it more middle class and Europhile.

Where necessary, the Conservatives have also prioritised the pursuit of political power over personal loyalty to individual leaders or Prime Ministers. If a leader is deemed to have passed their sell-by date, the Cabinet and Parliamentary Conservative Party have rarely hesitated in dispensing with them. The efficiency with which even admired leaders have been disposed of is testament to this. After the Suez Canal debacle in 1957, Anthony Eden was swiftly removed to make way for Harold Macmillan, who won a landslide electoral majority two years later. In 1975, Edward Heath was dispensed with by Margaret Thatcher, who went on to dominate British politics for over a decade thereafter. By the late 1980s, even the Iron Lady herself was judged to be dispensable.

The parliamentary party in conjunction with her Cabinet reached the conclusion that she had become an electoral liability by 1990 and was 'got rid of' to make way for John Major, who won for the Tories a historic fourth electoral victory in 1992. As William Hague once put it, the Conservative party is an 'absolute monarchy tempered by regicide'.

The Labour Party, on the other hand, has a long history of producing leaders that lack broad popular appeal. In the 20th century, only three Labour leaders – Attlee, Wilson and Blair – were able to win a majority in the House of Commons in a general election.

Labour leaders have tended to remain in post longer than Conservative leaders, despite their comparatively low success rate in general elections. Attlee, who won just one election of the five that he fought, remained Labour leader for a total of twenty years and Neil Kinnock led the party for a total of nine years despite never winning a general election. Tory leaders, whereas, have been moved on comparatively soon after electoral defeats.

Labour's electorally most successful leaders understood what had motivated voters to elect Conservative governments and adapted accordingly, as well as recognising the capabilities of their political opponents. Attlee described Churchill after the Second World War as 'the greatest leader in war this country has ever known' and someone who had 'the capacity for being a symbol, a figure that meant something to the fighting man.'[3] The Labour leader's decision in 1940 to enter a formal war time coalition with the Conservatives represented an act of national leadership at a time of crisis and the post-war Labour government's foreign policy was underpinned by a determination to maintain Britain as a great power, support the Americans against communism, develop the atomic bomb and slow the trend towards decolonisation.

Blair understood better than any figure in the Labour Party why voters had turned to the Conservatives in the 1980s and perhaps even sympathised with them for doing so. His modernisation of the Labour Party was both a response to and recognition of Thatcher's electoral successes in the 1980s. As Blair himself points out, it is unwise for Labour to demonise Conservative voters because these are precisely the people the party needs to win over to form a government.

Economic competence

The Conservative Party's electoral success has historically been predicated on a reputation for economic and governing competence. In the 20th century, Conservative leaders from Baldwin to Macmillan and Thatcher, appealed to the 'safety first' instincts of the British electorate by warning of the pernicious effects a Labour government might have on economic security. In the 1950s, the Conservatives presented themselves as the party of higher living standards and reduced taxes to stimulate the economy ahead of general elections. As leader, Thatcher frequently used the analogy of the frugal housewife to make the case for the careful stewardship of public finances and famously explained that 'the problem with socialism is that you eventually run out of other people's money.' That the Conservatives were the party of sound finance and good government while Labour governments pursued redistributive fiscal policies based on tax and spend became embedded in the public consciousness through the 20th century.

The perception that Conservative governments could be better trusted to manage the national economy was re-enforced by the tendency for Labour governments to preside over destabilising crises. The second Labour government formed in 1929, for instance, was knocked off course by the rapid deterioration in the British economy following the Wall Street Crash. Divisions over whether to pursue a deficit reduction programme and strategy of balanced budgets caused Labour to suffer historically large electoral defeats in subsequent elections in 1931 and 1935. Similarly, the sterling crisis of 1947 severely undermined the Attlee government's economic credibility and the Winter of Discontent, in which millions of working days were lost to strike action and inflation ran as high as 8% between 1978 and 1979, helped lock Labour out of power for almost two decades.

As part of their modernisation of Labour after 1994, Blair and Brown prioritised restoring the party's economic credibility. Ahead of the 1997 election, Brown pledged as Chancellor to maintain Conservative spending levels for three years, leave the headline income tax rates unchanged and accommodate many aspects of the economic architecture bequeathed by Thatcher and Major. A decade of uninterrupted economic growth, low unemployment and stable inflation helped make Blair's consecutive electoral successes possible.

As we have seen, the 2008 financial crisis severely damaged Labour's hard-won reputation for economic competence and contributed to consecutive electoral defeats thereafter. The Conservatives' commanding polling lead on the metric of economic competence in the long decade after 2007 helps explain their electoral successes.

The politics of the Union

Each of the constituent parts of the United Kingdom has a distinct political history and electoral dynamic.

For much of the 20th century, the Conservative Party was the dominant political force in England and the Conservative core vote has historically been concentrated in the southern shires. Given around 80% of seats in the House of Commons are English, electoral arithmetic suggests the Conservatives are advantaged by their hegemony in England.

Nonetheless, Conservative electoral victories throughout the 20th century were accompanied by a strong performance in Scotland and Wales. Indeed, winning support across the United Kingdom, and not just in England, underpinned the Conservative Party's credentials as *the* Unionist political party in Westminster. In the 1955 election, for instance, the Conservative and Unionist Party won a majority of seats in Scotland and as late as the 1992 election enjoyed solid representation in Scotland, with around 25% of the popular vote. Likewise, in Wales, Conservative representation remained strong up until 1992, in particular in rural constituencies and those bordering England.

The Labour Party's electoral support in England has historically been concentrated in the North-East and West Midlands, particularly in areas in which heavy manufacturing and coal mining loomed large in the local economy. Labour also performed well in the Celtic fringes in the 20th century. Indeed, the central Scottish industrial belt and mining-intensive constituencies in South Wales were Labour heartlands for much of the party's history.

In the 1997 landslide, the electoral dynamic shifted decisively in favour of New Labour across all parts of the United Kingdom. In Scotland, Blair won a commanding 56 of the 72 seats available and 34 seats in Wales out of a total of 40. After their worst election defeat in two centuries, the Conservatives were reduced to being an entirely English party having lost every single one of their seats in Scotland and Wales. Even within England, New Labour won a commanding 43% of the popular vote and reduced the Conservatives to their lowest share of English seats in two centuries.

Since 2010, the politics of the Union has become even more important to understanding the electoral dynamic in Westminster. In the 2015 election, as we have seen, the Labour Party lost all but one of its Scottish seats – a devastating loss of 40 constituencies. Labour emerged from the 2019 election more of an English party, in terms of representation in Westminster, than at any time in the party's history.

At the same time, the Conservatives expanded their representation outside their English heartlands and re-established a strong foothold in Wales and Scotland. Their credentials as *the* Unionist opposition to the nationalists in Scotland and swelling support base in Wales helps explain Conservative electoral victories after 2015.

Conclusion

A new politics

The 2019 General Election radically transformed Britain's political landscape and was a dramatic culmination of decades-long trends. The Conservatives, despite their long years in office, emerged in 2020 as a formidable national party of government, returning the highest number of MPs in a generation and enjoying strong representation across all parts of the United Kingdom. After the election, for every English seat held by Labour, the Conservatives held two, cementing the party's historically dominant position in England. In Wales, the Conservatives achieved their best result in three decades, picking up seven seats, including former mining communities in the South and 'Red Wall' constituencies in the North-East. Although they lost half their seats in Scotland in the election, the Conservatives have enjoyed a political renaissance north of the border by establishing themselves as *the* Unionist opposition to the Scottish Nationalists. The Scottish Conservative vote held up in the 2019 election at 25% even despite the unpopularity of Johnson and Brexit among Scots.

The Conservative Party of the 2020s is almost entirely unrecognisable from the one David Cameron led into the 2010 election just over a decade ago, a transformation that has manifested in several different ways.

The party's geographical representation has expanded across the whole United Kingdom. At the beginning of the decade, the Tories were still predominantly an English party and its representation was concentrated in Southern England and affluent rural shires. By 2019, the Conservatives enjoyed their best representation in Scotland and Wales in a generation and, with the exception of London, had advanced across all parts of England.

The style of Conservative leadership has shifted significantly too. While Cameron focused primarily on making the party more middle class and comfortable with modern Britain, his successors have consciously broadened the Tory voter base to incorporate a larger proportion of working-class voters. In 2019, the Conservatives led Labour across all social classes and enjoyed a 14% lead among low-income voters, something which is historically without precedent.

The change in the Conservative Party has also manifested in policy. Ahead of the 2010 election, the Conservatives under Cameron promised to restore fiscal discipline and sound public finances; adopted a more Europhile position and advocated establishing closer economic links with China. By the 2019 election, Johnson deliberately distanced himself from Cameron-era austerity, instead advocated an expansionist, levelling-up agenda; promised to facilitate the UK's exit from the EU and the Conservative Party turned far more hawkish on China.

Changes in leadership style and policy substance led to a shift in the demographic profile of the seats held by the Conservative Party in the decade after 2010. In the 2015 and 2017 general elections, the Tories lost a total of 42 seats to Labour and the Liberal Democrats. Of these, 18 (43%) were regained in the 2019 election, mainly in Leave voting parts of England and Wales. The remaining 24 seats (57%) were never regained (mostly located in metropolitan areas, such as London, or the commuter belt). As such, a significant majority (70%) of the seats that turned blue in 2019 – including Don Valley, Great Grimsby, and Darlington – were new gains that had not been held by the Conservatives in the preceding decade by either Cameron or May.

Having spent the best part of a decade on the opposition benches, Labour was reduced to a rump of just 209 seats in the 2019 election. Its votes were piled high in big cities such as London and university towns, but the party lacked broad national appeal. Across the rest of the UK, the party's representation was either diminished considerably (as in the case of Northern England, the Midlands and Wales) or eradicated almost entirely (in the case of Scotland). The Labour Party emerged from the election resembling more a sectional movement representing regional pockets in urban England and South Wales than a national political organisation capable of forming a government. As Tony Blair put it, 'the country didn't just decide not to elect us, they shut the door in our face'.[1]

Labour's relationship with small-town working-class voters deteriorated over the long decade after 2007 and the party's historic claim of being 'on your side' was compromised by a series of debilitating events, which began in government and continued in opposition. The financial crisis in 2007/08 required the Labour government to provide huge government bail outs for British banks (and by extension bankers) which, however necessary to protect the UK economy, contributed to a narrative that the Labour government had become divorced from the ordinary people it represented. It also suggested an incoherence in New Labour's economic policy given Blair and Brown had allowed national champions in the manufacturing sector such as MG Rover to collapse earlier in the decade. The Labour brand was further damaged by the unfolding expenses scandal in which senior Labour MPs, including Cabinet ministers, were found to have made risible claims for parliamentary expenses. At a time of rising unemployment and falling household incomes, the feeling that it is 'one rule for you and one rule for everyone else' did immense damage to the Labour brand. During a decade of opposition, the institutional Labour Party's relationship with working-class voters deteriorated further under Miliband and Corbyn's leadership and culminated with the party officially endorsing a second EU referendum in July 2019. By the 2019 election, Johnson's Conservatives were able to present themselves as on the side of ordinary voters and Labour suffered one of their worst electoral defeats in the party's history.

This book has considered the reasons for the Conservative Party's electoral success over the long decade and Labour's failure to regain the political initiative following the success of the Blair years. Understandably, attention has now rapidly shifted to the question of what this means for the future of British politics and what will happen next. The concluding remarks will address this important question, particularly focusing on Labour's electoral prospects going forward and what can be done to halt and then reverse the party's many years of decline.

9

Is Labour dying?

I began the Preface raising the question commentators were asking in the immediate aftermath of the 2019 election, namely, whether the Labour Party is dying, unable to re-invent itself in such a way that allows it to be politically competitive once again.

It is tempting to either be unduly optimistic (complacent even) about the British Labour Party's prospects and political future at one extreme, or deeply fatalistic at the other. The reality is more complicated. Labour begins the 2020s having suffered four consecutive electoral defeats and facing immense challenges. Equally though, as a party of opposition and under the new leadership of Keir Starmer, it is also being gifted opportunities to regroup and reform as Johnson's government grapples with the effects of the coronavirus crisis.

Inextricably linked to the question of Labour's electoral prospects is the question of whether the decades-long realignment of low-income and small-town voters away from the party is likely to continue and consolidate, or rapidly unwind as the Conservatives seek a fifth term in office. How voters in what was the Red Wall – what is now dubbed the 'Blue Barricade' – behave will have significant consequences for the outcome of future electoral events.

Optimists

Ironically, optimists in the Labour movement might be reassured about their prospects by reflecting on the recurring difficulties the party has faced throughout its 120 year history. Labour has been written off as a viable political competitor countless times in the past, only to be protected by the first-past-the-post system and returned to government relatively soon thereafter. In 1960, Abrams and Rose published a book that asked: *Must Labour Lose?*, after the Tories stormed to a third consecutive electoral victory a year earlier. In the following general election, Harold Wilson overturned Macmillan's three-digit landslide majority and formed a Labour government. Likewise, in 1994, Heath *et al.* wrote a book entitled *Labour's Last Chance?* following the party's fourth consecutive electoral defeat in the 1992 election. Five years later, Blair went on to win a historic landslide and locked the Conservatives out of power for thirteen years. Modern political history is littered with electoral events that appear to be fatal for a party at a particular moment, only for circumstances to quickly change and bring about an electoral recovery in spite of expectations.

On this basis, rather than spelling the end of Labour as a viable political competitor, the party's problems in the 21st century could merely be seen as part of the usual churn of British politics. Historically, it is not abnormal for the Labour Party to be electorally uncompetitive, abandoned by thousands of working-class voters and left to languish on the opposition benches for long periods of time. History suggests that eventually these voters will come back to Labour, and in the past the agony of opposition forced the party to fundamentally reform and respond to electoral realities. Some commentators have also pointed out that Labour's landslide defeat in 2019 was in some respects less devastating than previous electoral defeats. In the 1992 election, for instance, Labour endured a fourth consecutive defeat despite, they felt, having done everything necessary to give voters the reassurances they needed that they could be trusted to govern once again. The same cannot be said of the 2019 election. In 2019, Labour entered the election with a radical prospectus for government, led by an individual whose personal ratings were lower than any other opposition leader in modern political history and plagued by the unresolved Brexit issue. Perhaps reassuringly for Labour, the reasons for the defeat in 2019 were entirely explicable, not least to many moderate figures in the Labour movement itself who recognised Corbyn's limitations as a candidate for the office of Prime Minister.

Fatal crises that bring about the death of a major party occur relatively infrequently in Britain's first-past-the-post system. The last time such an event occurred was over a century ago, when the Liberals were replaced by Labour as the second major political party in the House of Commons. The causes of the death of the British Liberal Party are complex. However, the short-term trigger was the exceptional circumstances of the First World War and internal divisions over how the conflict was being prosecuted. At the time, the nascent Labour Party stood to be the obvious beneficiaries of Liberal decline; however, there is no obvious contender to replace the Labour Party in today's politics. By the time of the next election, the Conservatives will be asking for an unprecedented fifth term in office. Who else are voters going to turn to? The third largest political party in the House of Commons after 2019 was the SNP, hardly a future national party of government. Given that Labour held together through the twin crises brought about by Corbyn's victory in the 2015 leadership contest and the shock Leave vote a year later, it seems difficult to imagine the circumstances in which the party would come apart now.

Absent of the challenges that severely undermined the 2019 campaign, notably the divisive Brexit issue and Corbyn's controversial leadership, Labour's long path back to power could be cleared relatively quickly. Michael Ashcroft's polling in the immediate aftermath of Johnson's landslide found that Labour-to-Conservative switchers were driven to do so overwhelmingly with the combined idea of preventing Corbyn from becoming Prime Minister and a desire to see the Brexit vote delivered. In coming elections, the Labour Party will no longer be led by Corbyn, and given that negotiations with the EU over the UK's future trading relationship will have long been concluded, Brexit is unlikely to dominate future campaigns in the way it did in 2019.

Since becoming leader, Starmer has attempted to draw a line under the divisive Brexit issue and in December 2019 ordered his MPs to vote in favour of the free trade agreement the government had negotiated with the EU. Voters do not use elections to express gratitude to the governing party for its past achievements, something which potentially undermines the ability of Johnson or a future Conservative leader to mobilise the Leave coalition in coming elections.

Starmer has also conspicuously distanced himself from his predecessor and has repeatedly made the point that the Labour Party is under 'new management.' Given that so many voters were brought into, or kept in, the Conservative's 2019 voter coalition by a desire to prevent Corbyn from entering Downing Street and/or to see Brexit delivered, the government's support base might be broad and shallow. There could be a particular softness in the Conservative vote in former Red Wall seats, where much attention has been given to the phenomenon of former Labour supporters 'lending their vote' to help defeat Corbyn. A J.L. Partners poll in late 2020 showed a deterioration in support for the Conservatives in former Red Wall seats in the year following the general election. Although enthusiasm for Labour is still relatively low in these areas too, a suspicion that the Tories behave in the interest of the privileged few persists.

For optimists in the Labour movement, Starmer's leadership represents an important step on the path back to electability and to achieving power once again. As a former Director of Public Prosecutions, Starmer is a more conventional politician than his predecessor. He brings to the role a certain seriousness, level of organisation and competence that was judged to have been absent with Corbyn. Starmer's strengths – especially his forensic attention to detail and administrative abilities – have clearly exposed Johnson's administrative flaws during the pandemic.

Starmer's leadership might also lead to the return of tactical voting among Labour and Liberal Democrat voters, which would be to the overall disadvantage of the Conservatives. Southern voters, especially in more affluent Remain-leaning seats, might be willing to risk voting Liberal Democrat with a more moderate Labour leader of the opposition in place. Alternatively, Starmer himself might have greater appeal to

Remain-voting, affluent Southerners than traditional Northern Labour voters.

In the coming years, the Labour Party needs to establish a sustainable thread that connects a voter coalition of millennial graduates in big cities (Corbyn's voters) and low-income and working-class voters in provincial towns. An economic appeal to the precariat part of the labour force – both low-income graduates who are not entering graduate jobs and lower paid workers on flexible employment contracts – might be a profitable avenue to pursue. Voters need to be reminded what a Labour government can do for them and the party must prove that it is 'on the side' of ordinary, hardworking families, something which has been central to electoral successes in the past.

If Johnson's government fails to deliver for these voters in this parliament and their economic circumstances do not materially improve, there might be a rapid and sharp reaction against the Conservatives. Large-scale infrastructure projects, research and development investment and ultra-fast broadband will support the local economy in these areas. However, the actual impact of these policies for ordinary voters might not be felt for many years. As a result, short-term 'quick wins', such as tackling anti-social behaviour, offering support measures for struggling high streets and restoring regular bus services, will need to take priority if voters are to see a material improvement in the quality of their lives and communities before the next general election.

The precise economic consequences of the UK's departure from the EU have also yet to be fully realised. Two British Prime Ministers have spent much of the four years since the referendum either negotiating a withdrawal agreement to depart the bloc or in the formal transition period negating a Future Trade Agreement. If voters come to resent adverse economic disruption caused by Brexit and begin to experience 'buyer's remorse', it could damage Johnson and the Conservatives. Leave-voting former Red Wall seats are most exposed to the twin economic impact of Britain's exit from the EU and the coronavirus crisis. The government's ambitious plans to 'level up' and bring about a national economic renewal will thus require additional effort and resources if it is to succeed.

Pessimists

While optimistic interpretations of Labour's political position offer the party leadership hope for the future, the scale of the challenge the Labour Party currently faces is huge and should not be underestimated. Labour faces an uphill battle *just* to win back the seats they lost in opposition after 2010 and regain the trust of millions of voters who abandoned them for the Conservatives, the SNP, and, to a lesser extent, the Liberal Democrats. Even if they were able to do this in a single parliament, it would still not return them to anywhere near what is required to form a majority government, and as we have seen in recent elections, the Conservatives consistently benefit from the prospect of a minority Labour government supported by the nationalists in Scotland.

Worse still for Labour, the political re-alignment in the 21st century, which culminated in the 2019 election, might not be the end of the story, but rather represent the continuation of a decades-long shift of low-income voters away from Labour to the Conservatives. The bricks in the Red Wall that remain look precarious with dozens of seats across Northern England, the Midlands and Wales now marginal and held by Labour with three- and low four-digit majorities. If current trends continue and Labour does not address the 'cultural gap' with small-town working-class voters, then more seats behind the Red Wall, such as Ed Miliband's Doncaster constituency, could be lost too.

Given that millions of voters have shown a willingness to shed historic ties to political parties and support leaders whose message aligns closely with their own values, the Conservatives are well positioned to maintain the support of former Red Wall voters. In the current parliament, the Conservatives have an opportunity to entrench their electoral hegemony by delivering for 'left behind' communities and as Blair has argued, 'once they voted Tory for the first time... The first time was tough for them, the second time might be easier.'

Nationally, the Conservative Party is changing to reflect its new voter coalition. Following the referendum, under May and then Johnson's premiership, Conservative governments have been moving leftwards on economic policy by increasing central government spending on the NHS and education. Following the 2019 election, Johnson gave victory speeches with the words 'People's Government' emblazoned on the lectern in front of him, signifying his intention that, rather than simply being the beginning of a fourth Conservative term in office, this would be a new government with a distinct set of domestic economic priorities. In 2020, in response to the pandemic, the government has offered an unprecedented peacetime economic package to support businesses and maintain household incomes.

Having worked so hard to win support in these areas, the Conservatives will not willingly give them up. Many Northern constituencies now have Conservative MPs, some for the first time ever. These MPs can act as powerful local champions, lobbying the government for badly needed infrastructure investment. Given the government's commitment to a national levelling up agenda, they might find themselves pushing at an open door. The Chancellor's cheque book is open, and projects such as the £15 billion metro system in Birmingham, and Tees Valley Airport, illustrate the tangible benefits the levelling up agenda could deliver. Eye-catching initiatives such as these also serve to highlight the power of local personalities. the popular Tory mayor for the Tees Valley, Ben Houchen, is credited locally with attracting much needed investment into the area and the dynamic former John Lewis CEO and mayor for the West Midlands, Andy Street, has developed a strong local profile.

Strong local voices, who are close to the communities they serve and who understand the issues facing their constituents could help with the ongoing task of changing perceptions towards the Conservative Party in these areas. Mattinson's polling suggests that small-town working-class voters are proud of their local areas and communities, even if they have struggled with economic decline or social deprivation in recent decades. The former Labour MP for Stoke-on-Trent Central, Gareth Snell, pointed out after the 2019 defeat that Labour continuously said 'how bad everything is', indulging in miserabilism and showing little aspiration for these areas.[2] If the Tories can deliver an uplift through their levelling-up policies, then they have a huge opportunity to entrench support among these voters and demonstrate they are 'on their side'. They will also be well positioned to contrast the ambition they have for these areas with Labour's constant efforts to talk their communities down.

As we have seen in this book, the Labour brand has been damaged by a series of important events and crises in the 21st century – especially in the eyes of working-class voters. The Labour Party's eventual migration to an official second referendum position in July 2019 confirmed to these voters what they had long suspected, that Labour no longer took seriously their views and concerns.

While the divisive Brexit issue might now be settled, it has the potential to cast a long shadow on British politics in years to come. Focus groups and polling in former Red Wall seats reveal how real and deep the sense of betrayal in Labour communities goes. In fact, it is plausible that Labour's response to Brexit, especially the second referendum position, could have an even more devastating impact on their support base in parts of the North, the Midlands and Wales than Thatcher's macroeconomic policies had on the Tories in these areas after the 1980s. Although Thatcher's policies hurt the Conservative Party's standing in formerly industrialised areas, they were not interpreted in Northern England so much as a betrayal because the Conservatives did not exist primarily as a vehicle to represent and protect the interests of working-class voters in the manufacturing sector of the economy. Labour's neglect of traditional working-class voters in the 21st century, whereas, can more clearly be framed as betrayal because the party's founding purpose was to provide parliamentary representation for the working classes. It is not clear yet whether the electoral damage of the 2010s can be undone within a single five-year parliament, or even a single decade.

It is also the case that ancillary issues that overlap with the divides Brexit threw up will not easily be buried in the coming years. Although the debate over whether the UK remains part of or leaves the European Union might no longer be a live one, both Labour and the Conservatives must set out credible positions on the country's future immigration policy. While the Conservative Party might be comfortable arguing for a points-based immigration system to limit overall numbers, Labour's voter and internal party coalitions are far more divided on this question. Efforts by future leaders to move closer to traditional working-class voters on this issue are likely to be resisted by metropolitan Labour MPs, as they were when Brown and Miliband attempted to talk tough on immigration.

Similarly, Labour's experiment with Corbynism might now have ended but the impact and legacy of his time in the role could be lasting. During his time as leader, Corbyn damaged Labour's brand by allowing anti-Semitism to spread rampantly without recourse, appearing to side with Britain's enemies abroad and producing a policy programme that many, including within the Labour movement itself, regarded as fantastical. The politics of Corbynism will cast a long shadow and it will take time to rebuild from those foundations. Over a long period of time the Labour Party brand has increasingly become associated closely with the political interests of a relatively small, metropolitan subset of the electorate based in university towns and urban centres. Far from conveying a political message that appealed to the many and not the few, Corbyn entrenched Labour's support among a relatively narrow constituency of voters. As such, removing Corbyn from the leadership represented merely the first step in Labour's efforts to turn a page on its electoral malaise and begin the long road to recovery.

Regaining the trust of the electorate will take time. When Blair became Labour leader in 1994, his two predecessors had long before begun the important work of reforming and modernising the party to win power once again. Starmer, meanwhile, does not inherit such a legacy and does not have the luxury of building on strong foundations. Repairing the relationship with the Jewish community, for instance, represents only the most primitive of steps on the path to recovery because the damage should never have been done in the first place.

As well as internally professionalising his party, the new leadership must also construct an alternative vision for the United Kingdom under a Labour government. There are important reasons to believe this will not be a straightforward task. First, this vision will need to be articulated and forged in the context of Britain no longer being a member of the EU, something Starmer and many others in the Parliamentary Labour Party have little enthusiasm for. Johnson's government is arguably therefore better positioned to maximise the benefits of Britain's departure from the bloc. Second, Starmer's clear strengths as a politician, most notably a forensic attention to detail, are mitigated by an apparent weakness in pre-senting a compelling and coherent message about the direction in which he would take the country as Prime Minister. This has led some critics to ask if he is more of a technocrat, focused on the delivery of policy, than a strategic thinker. Third, the Conservatives have moved under Johnson to occupy a more interventionist position on economic policy, something which the global pandemic has accelerated. Therefore, the conventional attack lines, such as tactical opposition to 'Tory austerity', are not readily available against Johnson and his Chancellor Rishi Sunak.

The Labour Party's route back to power will also be contingent on its ability to connect with another political heartland, namely Scotland. Without a political revival north of the border, the Labour Party will struggle to establish itself once more as a national party capable of forming a majority government. The SNP leader, Nicola Sturgeon, is a formidable political operator and is extremely popular in Scotland, despite the difficulties that have engulfed her own administration. Scottish Labour is hardly able to offer a substantive assault on the SNP fortress. The party's decay north of the border goes back some years, having lost capable Scottish politicians in the 2015 electoral wipe-out, such as the former Shadow Foreign Secretary Douglas Alexander. With the constitutional question dominating Scottish politics, the Conservative Party has also successfully established itself both as the official opposition in Holyrood, and the main Unionist counterweight to Sturgeon's nationalism.

Finally, changes to electoral law in the coming years are likely to further entrench the Conservative Party's position in government, making a steep hill even steeper for Labour. The repeal of the Fixed Term Parliament Act will once again provide Johnson with the ability to determine the timing of the next general election. This executive power is a major advantage to an incumbent Prime Minister and means Johnson can allow the economy time to recover before voters next go to the polls. Additionally, the latest constituency boundary review will advantage the Conservative Party. While the overall number of constituencies in the United Kingdom is likely to remain at 650, it is thought that there will be a net increase in representation in South-East and East of England, while Wales and the North East will lose seats. Electoral Calculus estimates these changes will net the Conservatives an additional 15 seats.[3] Some estimates suggest that had every person voted in the same way during the 2019 election under the new boundaries, the Conservatives would have won an overall majority of 110 seats. Clearly these changes will have an impact on the outcome of major electoral events.

Changing, not dying

Writing the Labour Party's obituary might appear premature and alarmist; however, even if Labour isn't dying, it is certainly changing. The 202-strong Parliamentary Labour Party elected in 2019 was more left-wing, ethnically diverse and contained more female members than at any time in its history. In terms of representation, Labour is also now more of an English party than at any time before, left holding its lowest number of seats in a generation in Wales and reduced to just a single seat in Scotland. Even within England, Labour is now a much-diminished political force; the party has performed well in big cities and university towns since 2010 but has struggled to achieve broad national appeal.

There will no doubt be those in the Labour movement that welcome many of these changes to the character and composition of the party, despite the dire electoral consequences they have wrought. They might regard the loss of more socially conservative, nationalist working-class voters in the North as a necessary, even worthwhile, loss. Metropolitan Labour MPs have long resisted efforts by their leaders to address voter concerns over immigration, regarding them as nothing more than pandering to the nativist instincts of Farage and UKIP. Given that even after the 2019 election the Labour Party in 2020 still represented a majority of Leave seats (52%), any strategy that involves further neglecting small-town traditional Labour voters will be fraught with difficulty.

Without broad national support, including traditional voters in Northern England, it begs the question of what (or who) is the modern Labour Party for? In 2020, Labour seemed adrift, not only having forfeited the political initiative to the Conservatives but also appearing to have sacrificed its two core purposes as a party of equality and as a parliamentary vehicle for the working classes. On the former, Labour's moral authority was compromised by the spread of anti-Semitism, something that culminated in the humiliation of the Labour Party

247

being investigated by the Equality and Human Rights Commission. On the latter, a combination of Corbyn's perceived unwillingness to defend Britain's interests abroad as leader, and the migration to a second referendum position in July 2019, severely undermined any claim to be the party of the working class.

At the same time, the Conservative Party is changing rapidly too. Although it has never been a party merely of the rich and propertied classes, the Conservatives now represent more socially deprived parts of the United Kingdom to an extent that is historically unprecedented. Analysis by the think tank Onward found that the seats gained by the Conservatives in the 2019 election had average earnings that were 5% below the level of those held by Labour. As a result, of the lowest earning 25% of seats in the House of Commons, the majority are now held by the Conservatives (77) compared with Labour's 74.

This extraordinary fact will have important implications for the way Britain is governed in the future. The challenge of winning a large parliamentary majority, as Johnson is discovering, is that a strong and sustainable thread must be established to hold together a broad coalition of voters beyond successful slogans in an election campaign. In 2019, Johnson's pledge to defeat Corbyn and deliver Brexit united traditional Conservative voters in Southern England and rural shires with small-town provincial voters in the North. Now, his government must deliver for new, first time Conservative voters in the former Red Wall seats while simultaneously offering something for the traditional, affluent Tories in the South of England. During his time as Chief of Staff to the Prime Minister, Nick Timothy described managing the realignment following the Leave vote in 2016 as 'like riding a tiger' because it presented huge opportunities for the Conservatives but was also inherently risky.[4]

Johnson has already recognised the potential for certain government policies to help cement the Conservative Party coalition. Green industrial policies, for instance, play well with affluent southern voters and could gain traction in Northern England and Wales if wind turbines are manufactured in these areas, thus creating high-skilled well-paid jobs. Similarly, increased defence spending appeals to both parts of the Conservative voter coalition. Onshoring more domestic manufacturing of UK fighter jets, battleships and heavy equipment, would also create a further economic incentive for working-class voters to support spending on national defence.

To lock in political support across the whole United Kingdom, the Conservatives have swung decisively leftward on the economy under Boris Johnson's premiership. While aspects of the levelling-up agenda are lacking substance and detail, it represents a more radical and interventionist approach to the economy than anything Blair or Brown attempted in government. Given that Labour's appeal to working-class voters has historically relied on economic advancement, this presents a serious challenge for Starmer and offers his party little freedom for manoeuvre.

10

Future politics

The future direction of Britain's electoral politics must also be plotted within the context of rapid economic and social change – change that offers both opportunities and challenges for future governments. New technologies will transform Britain's labour markets, with profound implications for the way we live and interact in the future. Digitisation and automation of manual processes have the potential to drive national productivity and encourage a more efficient allocation of labour resources. They will also have an important impact on people's livelihoods; with more shopping online or on smart-phone devices, what is the future of bricks and mortar retail and how can this change be managed given that many communities depend on their local high street for social interaction? Retailers themselves will need to be more creative in the use of physical space to entice shoppers and offer an exceptional instore customer service. In the 21st century, business rates appear an increasingly anachronistic and damaging levy on physical retailers, and further tilt the playing field in favour of nimble online and digital suppliers.

The economic and social crisis precipitated by the spread of coronavirus has accelerated trends towards a 'digital future' that may completely transform the way we live, work and interact. In 2020 and 2021, global business travel collapsed, commuter traffic fell precipitously and a host of leisure activities temporarily ceased. Although many of these economic activities will return, there is a strong likelihood that the pandemic will have a permanent and lasting effect on human behaviour. Given that the UK's large service economy has tended to rely upon people's mobility and the economic activity such movement supports, these behavioural changes – such as fewer people commuting to work each day or business travellers conducting meetings remotely – will adversely affect the hospitality sector of the economy.

If the economic recovery from the 2008 financial crisis was driven by a precipitous fall in unemployment and underpinned by relatively slow productivity growth, the recovery in the 2020s is likely to be very different. For the government, this presents an opportunity to support sustainably higher wages and living standards for working households. Equally, though, a return to levels of unemployment not seen since the 1980s presents clear and profound political risks for any government, especially a Conservative government keen to emphasise its 'One Nation' credentials.

The other feature of the post-2008 recovery was the steep rise in asset prices, which disproportionately advantaged older people. This has been especially acute in the housing market, where supply failed to keep pace with demand, in turning pushing property valuations in London and other big cities out of reach for many young people. Politically, this has not damaged the Conservatives nationally, despite their failure to create a Property Owning Democracy. However, in big cities such as London, the Tories have been going backwards electorally and the party's voters have been getting older. This has led some Conservatives to argue for more ambitious housing policies to re-engage disillusioned young voters who have abandoned it for Labour.

Future governments will also need to manage the opportunities and challenges presented by Britain's departure from the European Union. Formally leaving the EU on 31st January 2020 was not an end in of itself, but rather the beginning of the UK's future relationship with important economic and security partners in Europe. This relationship will not merely be defined by the precise legal contents of a negotiated Free Trade Agreement but must be configured by governments to come. With Britain formally outside the transition period, it will be possible to maximise the opportunities of leaving the EU, not least to reinvigorate domestic politics and bring about national renewal. This opportunity requires proactive ministers in Westminster to seize on the opportunities offered to improve access to educational opportunities and better align the skills provision provided by formal educational institutions with the needs of the wider economy.

Britain's future outside of the EU is being configured as the government deliver on their domestic priorities, such as addressing regional inequalities. Some important questions about the government's foreign and domestic policies remain unanswered. How, for instance, does the domestic levelling-up agenda fit with the UK's external orientation with the rest of the world via free trade agreements? It is not clear if greater infrastructure spending outside London and the South is designed to safeguard against the potentially pernicious economic effects of leaving the European Union or if it is an end in itself. Ahead of the next election, 'levelling up' will have to be more than just a slogan.

Constitutionally, Britain's future as a multinational state is threatened by renewed nationalism in Scotland. The United Kingdom must be held together to maintain the Conservatives' credentials as a Unionist party. However, polling suggests that Johnson's premiership has been a significant driver of the drift towards independence. Similarly, in Northern Ireland, polling is not that encouraging and in England support for the Union has deteriorated in recent years, driven by the challenges of delivering the 2016 Leave result. During the Brexit years, there was a frustration among English voters that Northern Ireland appeared to be holding up the process of the UK leaving the EU, leading to greater enthusiasm for a united Irish solution. Only in Wales is the Union of the United Kingdom genuinely popular in the current political climate.

The short-term impact of Brexit seemed to be to increase the likelihood of Scottish independence. After all, Scotland voted 65%

Remain in the EU referendum and therefore only left the EU because a majority of English and Welsh voters supported Brexit. As has been mentioned, Johnson himself is also very unpopular north of the border and the Tory vote share has held up in Scotland despite and not because of the Prime Minister. In the medium term, though, the consequences of the UK leaving the EU Single Market and customs union have had a profound impact on the economics and politics of Scottish independence. An independent Scotland would no longer be able to be part of both the EU and UK single markets, raising the prospect of considerable economic dislocation in the event of a vote for independence. Defenders of the Union will continue to make the economic case for the Union; however, this alone will not be enough. As the 2016 EU referendum campaign demonstrated, questions of belonging and national identity are important in shaping the dynamics of British politics too.

Killing nationalism with kindness (the policy of post-war British governments) also presents risks for the Union as a whole. If future devolution settlements continue a path towards a more federalised United Kingdom, the Union could become more and not less stable because of the lingering resentment felt among English voters at the tendency for their political interests to be subordinated to those of the Scots.

The increased relevance of cultural issues of identity and belonging has had a profound impact on British electoral politics over a relatively short space of time. In Scotland, the main beneficiaries of this trend have been the nationalists (since 2015) and, to a lesser extent, the Conservative Unionists (since 2017). In England and Wales, the Conservatives have undoubtedly been the winners from the 'cultural shift', and they have reached millions of new voters over the course of the 21st century who felt overlooked by Labour in government and then abandoned during their time in opposition under Corbyn. Thus, Labour has been squeezed and left representing a relatively narrow and limited section of the electorate, largely residing in big English cities. The twin challenges of mounting a recovery in Scotland on the one hand and regaining millions of lost votes in England and Wales are formidable.

The identity politics of the 21st century has led some political commentators to theorise that the 'centre ground' might no longer be a relevant analytical framework within which to understand the dynamics of modern British electoral politics. Perhaps the politics of Corbynism and the Brexit vote have fundamentally changed the rules of the game and elections are now more about assembling coalitions of interest groups rather than staking a claim to an economically moderate, socially liberal 'centre ground' position.

It is true that conventional left-right cleavages have become less relevant; however, the 'centre ground' of British politics is a constantly shifting space and is not predefined or set in time. In the immediate aftermath of the Second World War, for instance, the centre ground shifted leftwards as both Labour and the Conservatives accommodated a new post-war settlement of managed demand and lower unemployment. Then, in the hyperinflation of the 1970s, the centre shifted towards consensus around the need for trade union reform and the liberalisation of the domestic economy. Under Blair's leadership, New Labour accepted that the world had moved on and accommodated much of the economic architecture they inherited. After the EU referendum, some moderates argued that the centre had fallen out of British politics as the Conservatives committed to a 'hard Brexit', in which the UK would leave the EU Single Market and customs union, while Labour experimented with Corbynism. However, it is not clear this was the case. One could argue that the moderate position was respecting the referendum result, negotiating a phased and managed withdrawal from the bloc and maintaining cordial relations with the UK's allies in Europe – something May and Johnson delivered in office, and Corbyn supported in principle for much of his time as leader of the opposition. It is not clear how respecting a national referendum result and delivering it in government was extreme and, as critics pointed out at the time, it was arguably the Liberal Democrat policy to Revoke Article 50 unilaterally which was the truly extreme Brexit position.

The centre ground is not a fixed point on the political spectrum or a proxy for Blairism. Rather it is where political parties locate to make themselves electorally relevant at any given time. In practice, the centre ground can mean any number of things at once: it could mean delivering the Leave referendum result, favouring immigration controls, increasing NHS spending or being tough on law and order all at the same time. It is

254

also possible for a Prime Minister to shape and influence the parameters of the centre ground at any given time. Thatcher's government established a new centre ground in the 1980s based on a market economy, while Blair created an economically moderate, socially liberal centre ground which Cameron went on to occupy for the duration of his premiership too. The overwhelming tendency through British political history has been for the Conservative Party to identify and shape the 'centre ground' space where the majority of voters are and quickly occupy it, which helps to explain why it has been so successful electorally.

Endnotes

Preface

1   D. Mattinson 'Five things Labour should do to win back the red wall' (The Times, September 21, 2021)

Introduction

1   P. Surridge in D. Mattinson *Beyond the Red Wall: Why Labour Lost, How the Conservatives Won and What Will Happen Next?* (Biteback, September 2020)

2   M. Ashcroft 'Diagnosis of defeat: Labour's turn to smell the coffee' (February 2020)

Chapter 1

1   J. Callaghan, S. Fielding, S. Ludlam *Interpreting the Labour Party: Approaches to Labour Politics and History* (Manchester University Press, 2003)

2   M Pugh *Speak for Britain!: A New History of the Labour Party* (Vintage, April 2011)

3   Ibid.

4   Ibid.

5   In Ibid.

6   David Sassoon *One hundred years of socialism: The West European Left in the Twentieth Century* (I B Tauris Co Ltd, August 2010)

7   Labour General Secretary Report (June 1983)

Chapter 2

1   Labour Together Election Review 2019 (June 2020)

2   D. Mattinson 'Five things Labour should do to win back the red wall' (The Times, September 21, 2021)

3   K. Hoey Interview for Labour Tube (May 2018)

4   R. Ford and M. Sobolewska *Brexitland: Identity, Diversity and the Reshaping of British Politics* (Cambridge University Press, October 2020)

5   'Migration: An Economic and Social Analysis' (Policy and Innovation Unit, November 2000)

6   T. Blair, speech to Confederation of British Industry (April 2004)

7   Office for National Statistics (Accessed 17th March 2021)

8   R. Rowthorn 'The Costs and Benefits of Large-scale Immigration: Exploring the economic and demographic consequences for the UK (Civitas, December 2015)

9   M Kitson and J. Michie 'The Deindustrial Revolution: the Rise and Fall of UK Manufacturing, 1870-2010' (Centre for Business Research, University of Cambridge, 2014)

10 T. O'Grady 'Careerists Versus Coal-Miners: Welfare Reforms and the Substantive Representation of Social Groups in the British Labour Party' (Comparative Political Studies, July 2018)

11 I. Lavery and J. Trickett 'Northern Discomfort' (Tribune Magazine, March 2020)

12 In S. Rayson *The Fall of the Red Wall: 'The Labour Party no longer represents people like us'* (July 2020)

13 T. Blair *A Journey* (Arrow, June 2011)

14 C. Ainsley *The New Working Class: How to Win Hearts, Minds and Votes* (Policy Press, May 2018)

Chapter 3

1 Dispatches 'Gordon Brown: Where did it all go wrong?' (Channel 4, 2008)

2 B. Obama *A promised land* (Viking, November 2020)

3 G. Brown Speech to Labour Conference (September 2007)

4 M. Goodwin and R. Ford *Revolt on the right: Explaining support for the radical right in Britain* (Routledge, March 2014)

5 https://www.theguardian.com/politics/2009/jan/02/immigration-working-class

6 https://www.theguardian.com/politics/2019/nov/15/how-immigration-became-britains-most-toxic-political-issue

7 The Office for National Statistics (Accessed 17th March 2021)

8 Vince Cable *After the storm: The World Economy and Britain's Economic Future* (Atlantic Books, September 2015)

9 'Living standards 2017: the past, present and possible futures of UK incomes' (Resolution Foundation, January 2017)

10 https://www.theguardian.com/politics/2014/nov/20/emily-thornberry-resigns-rochester-tweet-labour-shadow-cabinet

11 M. Goodwin and R. Ford *Revolt on the right: Explaining support for the radical right in Britain* (Routledge, March 2014)

12 D. Skelton (ed.) 'Access All Areas: Building a Majority' (Renewal, 2014)

13 BBC Newsnight Interview (August 2015)

14 T. Blair Speech to Labour Progress group (July 2015)

15 BBC Interview (July 2015)

16 BBC Interview (November 2015)

17 BBC Radio Ulster Interview (May 2017)

18 J. Woodcock 'We can't go on like this' (Daily Mirror, March 2016)

Chapter 4

1 The Cameron Years (BBC, September 2019)

2 C. Ainsley *The New Working Class: How to win Hearts, Minds and Votes* (Policy Press, 2018)

3 https://www.theguardian.com/commentisfree/2016/dec/10/brexit-must-be-fair-to-working-people-ed-miliband

4 https://www.bbc.co.uk/news/uk-scotland-scotland-politics-40249433

5 'Labour contemplates life after Corbyn' (The Economist, September 2019)

6 P. Maguire and Pogrund *Left Out: The Inside Story of Labour Under Corbyn* (Vintage, September 2020)

7 'Barnsley MP resigns from frontbench' (The Star, March 2019)

8 BBC Interview (April 2019)

9 A. Seldon *May at 10* (Biteback, November 2019)

10 Ibid.

11 https://www.standard.co.uk/news/politics/miliband-public-vote-could-be-last-resort-to-end-eu-deadlock-a4130161.html

12 T. Blair speech '120 years of the Labour Party: In conversation with Tony Blair'

Chapter 5

1 R. Sunak, O. Dowden and R. Jenrick 'The Tories are in deep peril. Only Boris Johnson can save us' (June 2019)

2 Daily Politics (August 2019)

3 ITV Acting Prime Minister (September 2019)

4 https://www.theguardian.com/commentisfree/2019/oct/18/we-as-mps-need-to-come-together-to-get-brexit-done-and-move-on

5 S. Rayson *The Fall of the Red Wall: 'The Labour Party no longer represents people like us'* (July 2020)

6 P. Maguire and Pogrund *Left Out: The Inside Story of Labour Under Corbyn* (Vintage, September 2020)

7 M. Goodwin and O. Heath 'The UK 2017 General Election examined: income, poverty and Brexit' (Joseph Rowntree Foundation, September 2017)

8 T. Blair speech '120 years of the Labour Party: In conversation with Tony Blair'

9 Labour Together Election Review 2019 (June 2020)

10 In S. Rayson *The Fall of the Red Wall: 'The Labour Party no longer represents people like us'* (July 2020)

11 In Ibid.

12 In Ibid.

Chapter 6

1 IPSOS MORI Political Monitor poll (September 2019)

2 The Cameron Years (BBC, September 2019)

3 BBC Interview (December 2020)

4 Labour Together Election Review 2019 (June 2020)

5 YouGov; IPSOS MORI

6 M. Beckett Learning the lessons from defeat taskforce report (January 2016)

7 The Office for National Statistics (Accessed 7th March 2021)

Chapter 7

1 Bagehot Column (The Economist, May 2019)

2 P. Norris, R. Inglehart 'Trump, Brexit and the Rise of Populism: Economic Have-nots and cultural backlash' (Harvard Kennedy School Research Paper, August 2016)

3 N Timothy *Remaking One Nation: The Future of Conservatism* (Polity, March 2020)

Chapter 8

1 A Smith *An inquiry into the nature and causes of the wealth of nations* (Library of Economics and Liberty)

2 A Smith *The Theory of Moral Sentiments* (Library of Economics and Liberty)

3 L. McKinstry *Atlee and Churchill: Allies in War, Adversaries in Peace* (Atlantic Books, October 2019)

Conclusion

1 T. Blair speech '120 years of the Labour Party: In conversation with Tony Blair'

2 In S. Rayson *The Fall of the Red Wall: 'The Labour Party no longer represents people like us'* (July 2020)

3 https://www.electoralcalculus.co.uk/bdy2023_ec_auto.html

4 Talking Politics Podcast 'Is Boris Back?' (February 2021)

Lightning Source UK Ltd.
Milton Keynes UK
UKHW010743180821
389043UK00001B/59